THE RIGHT THING
TO DO

THE HERITAGE SERIES IN PHILOSOPHY
CLASSIC AND CONTEMPORARY READINGS

Tom Regan

North Carolina State University
General Editor

THE RIGHT THING TO DO

Basic Readings in Moral Philosophy

EDITED BY

JAMES RACHELS

University of Alabama at Birmingham

McGraw-Hill, Inc.
New York   St. Louis   San Francisco   Auckland   Bogotá
Caracas   Lisbon   London   Madrid   Mexico City   Milan
Montreal   New Delhi   San Juan   Singapore
Sydney   Tokyo   Toronto

THE RIGHT THING TO DO

BASIC READINGS IN MORAL PHILOSOPHY

This book is printed on acid-free paper.

First Edition

11 12 13 14 15 16 17 DOC/DOC 9 9 8 7 6

Library of Congress Cataloging in Publication Data
The Right thing to do: basic readings in moral philosophy/edited by
    James Rachels.—1st ed.
        p. cm.—(The Heritage series in philosophy)
    Includes bibliographies and index.
    ISBN 0-07-557002-5
    1. Ethics. I. Rachels, James, 1941- . II. Series.
BJ21.R54 1989   88-28142
170—dc 19   CIP

Reproduced on the cover:
Alexander Rodchenko.
Non-Objective Painting: Black on Black. 1918.
Oil on canvas, 32¼ × 31¼".
Collection, The Museum of Modern Art, New York. Gift of the
artist,
through Jay Leyda.
Photograph © 1989 The Museum of Modern Art, New York.

Text design: Susan Phillips

*P*reface

Moral philosophy is the attempt to achieve a systematic understanding of what morality is and what it requires of us—of how we ought to live, and why. This anthology is an introduction to moral philosophy, conceived in this broad sense. The readings spotlight some of the main theories developed by moral philosophers in the Western tradition and illustrate how these theories help us (or, one might sometimes think, hinder us) in dealing with practical moral issues.

This anthology is a companion volume to my book *The Elements of Moral Philosophy*, also published by McGraw-Hill, Inc. The two books complement one another and may profitably be read together. However, they are independent works, and nothing in either book presupposes acquaintance with the other.

Contents

PART I

Introductory Essays

1 Morality and Moral Philosophy

James Rachels

An ancient legend tells the story of Gyges, a poor shepherd who found a magic ring in a fissure opened by an earthquake. The ring would make its wearer invisible, so that he could go anywhere and do anything undetected. Gyges was an unscrupulous fellow, and he quickly realized that the ring could be put to good advantage. We are told that he used its power to gain entry to the royal palace, where he seduced the queen, murdered the king, and seized the throne. (It is not explained how invisibility helped him to seduce the queen—but let that pass.) In no time at all, he went from being a poor shepherd to being king of all the land.

This story is recounted in Book II of Plato's *Republic*. Like all of Plato's works, the *Republic* is written in the form of a dialogue between Socrates and his companions. Glaucon, who is having an argument with Socrates, uses the story of Gyges's magic ring to make a point.

Glaucon asks us to imagine two such rings, one given to a man of virtue and the other given to a rogue. How might we expect them to behave? The rogue, of course, will do anything necessary to increase his own wealth and power. Since the cloak of invisibility will protect him from discovery, he can do anything he pleases without fear of being caught. Therefore, he will recognize no moral constraints on his conduct, and there will be no end to the mischief he will do.

But how will the so-called virtuous man behave? Glaucon suggests that he will do no better than the rogue:

> No one, it is commonly believed, would have such iron strength of mind as to stand fast in doing right or keep his hands off other men's goods, when he could go to the market-place and fearlessly help himself to anything he wanted, enter houses and sleep with any woman he chose, set prisoners free and kill men

at his pleasure, and in a word go about among men with the powers of a god. He would behave no better than the other; both would take the same course.

Moreover, Glaucon asks, why shouldn't he? Once he is freed from the fear of reprisal, why shouldn't a person simply do what he pleases, or what he thinks is best for himself? Why should he care at all about "morality"?

The *Republic,* written over 2300 years ago, was one of the first great works of moral philosophy in Western history. Since then, many philosophers have formulated theories to explain what morality is, why it is important, and why it has the peculiar hold on us that it does. One of the awkward problems encountered by students of moral philosophy is that there is no general agreement about which of these theories, if any, is correct. Philosophers continue to disagree, and each theory has its advocates as well as its detractors. In this book we focus on eight of the most important moral theories.

Cultural Relativism

Perhaps the oldest philosophical theory about morality is that right and wrong are relative to the customs of one's society. Herodotus, the first of the great Greek historians, lived in the fifth and fourth centuries B.C. His *History* is full of wonderful anecdotes that illustrate his belief that "right" and "wrong" are little more than names for social conventions. Of the Massagetae, for example, he writes:

> The following are some of their customs—Each man has but one wife, yet all the wives are held in common. . . . Human life does not come to its natural close with these people; but when a man grows very old, all his kinsfolk collect together and offer him up in sacrifice; offering at the same time some cattle also. After the sacrifice they boil the flesh and feast on it; and those who thus end their days are reckoned the happiest. If a man dies of disease they do not eat him, but bury him in the ground, bewailing his ill-fortune that he did not come to be sacrificed. They sow no grain, but live on their herds, and on fish, of which there is great plenty in the Araxes. Milk is what they chiefly drink. The only god they worship is the sun, and to him they offer the horse in sacrifice; under the notion of giving the swiftest of the gods the swiftest of all mortal creatures.

Herodotus did not think the Massagetae were to be criticized for such practices. Their customs were neither better nor worse than those of other peoples: they were merely different. The Greeks, who considered themselves more "civilized," may have thought that their customs were superior, but, Herodotus says, that is only because everyone believes the customs of his own society to be the best. The "truth" depends on one's point of view—that is, on the society in which one happens to have been raised.

This basic idea has been repeated by many thinkers down through the centuries. Social scientists tell us that whenever we study cultures other than our own, we almost always find practices that seem "wrong" when judged by the standards of our society— but, they emphasize, our customs would seem equally "wrong" to people in those other cultures. Herodotus concluded that "custom is the king o'er all," and other observers have frequently agreed. The Theory of Cultural Relativism, therefore, asserts that:

> Different cultures have different moral codes;
>
> There is no objective standard that can be used to judge one societal code better than another;
>
> The moral code of our own society has no special status; it is merely one among many;
>
> There is no "universal truth" in ethics—that is, no moral truths hold for all peoples at all times; and, finally,
>
> The moral code of a society determines what is right within that society—that is, if the moral code of a society says that a certain action is right, then that action *is* right, at least within that society.

Cultural Relativists tend to think that all this is obviously true, and that those who believe in "objective" right and wrong are merely naive. Critics, however, object to the theory on a number of grounds. First, it is exceedingly conservative in that the theory endorses whatever moral views happen to be current in a society. Consider our own society. Many people believe that our society's moral code is mistaken, at least on some points—for example, they may disagree with the dominant social view regarding capital punishment, or homosexuality, or the treatment of nonhuman animals. Must we conclude that these would-be reformers are wrong, merely because they oppose the majority view? Why must the majority always be right?

Ethical Subjectivism

Cultural Relativism denies that there is any such thing as objective moral truth, and so does Ethical Subjectivism, but in a different way. Ethical Subjectivism is the view that right and wrong are relative, not to the standards of culture, but to the attitudes of each individual person. Roughly put, the Subjectivists say that anyone who pronounces something to be right or wrong is only expressing a *personal* attitude, and nothing more.

Ethical Subjectivism begins with the observation that values are very different from facts. A factual statement (such as "Leonardo da Vinci was a homosexual") is a statement that is objectively true or false. Where facts are concerned, if people disagree, someone must be mistaken. Moral judgments, on the other hand (such as "Prejudice against homosexuals is wrong"), are neither true nor false. They are matters of opinion, not knowledge, about which people can disagree without anyone being "mistaken."

The outstanding philosophical defender of Ethical Subjectivism was the great Scottish thinker David Hume (1711–1776). For Hume, the crucial question about ethics was whether our moral judgments are based on reason or sentiment. Hume thought it was impossible to account for the nature of ethics as a matter of reason. Reason, he said, only informs us of the nature and consequences of our actions. For example, reason may tell you that if you give someone poison, he will die. After your reason has told you this, it is necessary for your sentiments to come into play—do you *want* the person to die, or not?—in order for you to decide what you are going to do. If you want the person to die, then you should give him the poison; if you do not want him to die, you should not poison him. All decisions about what to do are like this: they depend on one's passions, and not merely on one's reason. Hume concludes that "Reason is, and ought to be, the slave of the passions." But he did not simply assert this; he tried to prove it by advancing a number of arguments:

1. Hume's first argument concerned the motivational power of moral judgments. "Morals," he said, "move men to act. Reason alone is utterly impotent in this particular." Suppose you think that

you *ought* to perform a certain action. It follows that you will feel at least some impulse to do that action. (If someone claimed to believe that he should not drink, yet showed absolutely no hesitation when drink was offered, we would conclude that he does not *really* believe drinking is wrong.) However, our beliefs about what *is* the case, which are the products of our reason, do not have this motivational content. Thus our moral judgments cannot be the products of our reason.

On the other hand, our sentiments do prompt us to act. If we *want* to remain sober or to avoid injury to our livers, then we will be motivated not to drink. Thus it is our sentiments, not our reason, that must supply the impetus for moral behavior.

2. Suppose, Hume said, we examine a case of wicked behavior: willful murder, for example. We look at it very carefully, to discover all the facts. What do we see? We can see one man giving poison to another; we see the victim dying; and so on. But can we see the wickedness? No. "You can never find it," Hume says, "till you turn your reflexion into your own breast, and find a sentiment of disapprobation, which arises in you, toward this action." *That* is the origin of your judgment that the action is wicked.

3. Ethical judgments are concerned with what we ought to do. Reason informs us of what is the case. But there is a deep logical gap between *is* and *ought:* we can never validly deduce any conclusions about what ought to be done from premises that concern only what is the case. Therefore, ethics cannot be a deduction from reason alone. This is one of Hume's most famous doctrines: we cannot derive "ought" from "is."

These arguments, and others like them, have convinced many people that morality must be primarily a matter of how we feel about things, rather than a matter of how things are. Again, however, critics have objected on a number of grounds. For example, if Ethical Subjectivism is correct, it is difficult to understand how anyone could ever be *mistaken* in her moral views, so long as she is truly reporting how she feels. Are we all infallible? Moreover, if Ethical Subjectivism is correct, it is difficult to see how it is possible for people ever to disagree about right and wrong. If I say that something is right, I am only saying that I have certain feelings, and if you say it is wrong, you are only saying that you have different feelings. I agree that you have your feelings, and you should agree that I have mine. What, then, do we disagree about? These are both longstanding arguments against Ethical Subjectivism.

Morality and Religion: The Divine Command Theory

In the minds of many people, religion and ethics are inseparable. Thus, when these people begin to think about the theoretical foundations of morality, they find it natural to turn to religion for an explanation.

All the great world religions contain ethical teachings. The religions most influential in our society, Judaism and Christianity, are no exception. In both the Jewish and Christian traditions, God is conceived of as a lawgiver who created us and the world we live in for a purpose. That purpose is not completely understood, but much has been revealed through the prophets, Holy Scripture, and the church. These sources teach that, to guide us in righteous living, God promulgated rules which we are to obey.

The most famous of the divinely given rules are the Ten Commandments, as recorded in Exodus:

You shall have no other gods before me;

You shall make no graven images to worship;

You shall not take the name of God in vain;

You shall keep the sabbath day holy;

You shall honor your father and mother;

You shall not kill;

You shall not commit adultery;

You shall not steal;

You shall not bear false witness against your neighbor;

You shall not covet your neighbor's house, wife, servants, or property.

The Ten Commandments, however, are only the tip of a very large iceberg. Over the centuries the rabbis developed a complex body of ethical doctrine that specified in great detail how the Jewish people were expected to live. Some of this law can be found in the Old Testament scriptures, especially in the first five books.

During the early days of Christianity, whether Christians should be required to adhere to the Jewish law was hotly debated. St. Paul, who was eager to see the new faith spread to the gentiles, argued that the teachings of Jesus were, in effect, a replacement for the old law. Jesus had said that the first rule of action was "do unto others as you would have them do unto you." This was an attractive precept, which could be acknowledged by everyone; it would not offend potential converts. Paul was opposed by other early Christians, who wanted to retain the traditional Jewish rules. Paul's point of view eventually won out, and so Christianity was able to emerge as something more than just another Jewish sect.

Christian theologians then went on to develop their own moral conceptions, which sometimes agreed with Jewish teachings and sometimes did not. But the Christians and Jews always had this in common: they believed that moral living meant living in accordance with God's plan. Morality and religion were inseparable. However, this vague statement does not tell us precisely *how* morality and religion are connected. Exactly what is the relation between them supposed to be?

The Divine Command Theory provides the most obvious way of connecting morality with religion. It is a theory about the nature of right and wrong which says that "morally right" means "commanded by God," whereas "morally wrong" means "forbidden by God." Therefore, according to this theory, a moral statement such as "adultery is morally wrong" should be understood to mean, simply, "God forbids adultery."

A great many theologians, however, have rejected the Divine Command Theory. The problem is that the theory has consequences that seem offensive to religious faith. For one thing, it seems to make God's commands arbitrary: if nothing was wrong with adultery prior to God's command, then he could have no reason to forbid it; and if something was wrong with it, then its wrongness is not dependent on God's command. Moreover, the theory makes it quite difficult to account for the goodness of God: if things are good only because God approves of them, does God's goodness consist in his approving of himself? Such considerations have led many theologians to look for an alternative way of understanding the relation between morality and religion.

Morality and Religion: The Theory of Natural Law

If the Divine Command Theory is untenable, it does not follow that there is no connection between morality and religion. After all, the Divine Command Theory is only one way of explaining what the connection is supposed to be. Perhaps there is another, better way of explaining the connection.

The Theory of Natural Law offers another possibility. This theory was formulated by Saint Thomas Aquinas (1225–1274), who is commonly regarded as the greatest of all the Christian thinkers (after, perhaps, Saint Paul).

According to the Theory of Natural Law, God, who is perfectly rational, has created the world as a rational order and us, in his image, as rational agents. Just as nature operates in conformity with natural laws—"laws of nature"—so there are natural laws that govern how we should behave. These natural laws are laws of reason, which we are able to grasp because God has made us rational. But it is all people, not merely believers whom he has made rational—rationality is the essence of human nature; it is the "divine spark" in us.

Moral judgments, then, are "dictates of reason." The best thing to do, in any circumstance, is whatever course of conduct has the best reasons on its side. Thus the believer and the nonbeliever are in similar positions when it comes to making moral judgments. Both are endowed with powers of conscience and reason. For both, making a responsible moral judgment is a matter of listening to reason and being true to one's conscience. That is why moral precepts are binding on everyone, and not merely on believers. A person's reason, or conscience, is the "voice of God," whether the "hearer" realizes it or not.

But the emphasis on reason is only one aspect of the Theory of Natural Law; the theory also emphasizes the idea that some types of behavior are *natural*, whereas others are unnatural, and the theory's advocates condemn "unnatural" conduct. Homosexuality is an example of "unnatural" behavior.

As in so many matters, Western attitudes toward homosexuality have been shaped largely by Christianity; and within the Christian tradition, homosexuality has been condemned time and again. Saint Paul declared that "idolators, thieves, homosexuals, drunkards, and robbers" cannot inherit the Kingdom of God. Clearly, he regarded homosexuals as "immoral men." Aquinas, following Paul's lead, cited "unisexual lust" as a "sin against nature."

The idea that homosexual acts are "against nature" is connected with the idea that sex has a natural purpose—namely, procreation. Sexual acts are the means by which women become pregnant. When sex is separated from this basic purpose, it becomes "unnatural." That is one reason the Catholic Church condemns the use of contraceptives: the use of birth control devices separates sex from its natural purpose of procreation. (Similarly, oral sex, whether practiced by heterosexuals or homosexuals, is "unnatural" because it is a form of sexual activity that cannot result in pregnancy.)

These principles have been reaffirmed by the Church on numerous occasions, most recently in the "Vatican Declaration on Some Questions of Sexual Ethics" in 1976. This document describes the Church's position on a variety of sexual matters, including homosexuality. The Declaration takes note of the fact that many people today regard the condemnation of homosexuality as an outdated prejudice. Psychologists no longer regard homosexuality as a "sickness," but instead recognize that for many people it is a permanent, unchosen condition, as "natural" for them as heterosexuality is for others. For such people, homosexuality is an unavoidable part of their lives. Moreover, being gay is not associated with any other "undesirable" characteristics: homosexuals are as decent and "normal" as heterosexuals in every respect save sexual preference. Thus many people, including many Christians, have concluded that heterosexual majority should stop condemning gays. The Vatican Declaration notes:

> Contrary to the perennial teaching of the Church and the moral
> sense of the Christian people, some individuals today have, on
> psychological grounds, begun to judge indulgently or even
> simply to excuse homosexual relations for certain people.

However, this modern trend of thought is quickly rejected. It is permissible for Christians to be charitable toward homosexuals, but it must not be forgotten that they are perverts in need of correction. The Vatican Declaration continues:

> As far as pastoral care is concerned, such homosexuals
> are certainly to be treated with understanding and encouraged

to hope that they can some day overcome their difficulties and their inability to fit into society in a normal fashion. Prudence, too, must be exercised in judging their guilt. However, no pastoral approach may be taken which would consider these individuals morally justified on the grounds that such acts are in accordance with their nature. For, according to the objective moral order homosexual relations are acts deprived of the essential ordination they ought to have.

In Sacred Scripture such acts are condemned as serious deviations and are even considered to be the lamentable effect of rejecting God. This judgment on the part of the divinely inspired Scriptures does not justify us in saying that all who suffer from this anomaly are guilty of personal sin but it does show that homosexual acts are disordered by their very nature and can never be approved.

Critics have often argued that the two themes of Natural Law Theory are at odds with one another here: if we emphasize that moral judgments must be backed by good reasons, we reach the conclusion that there is nothing immoral about homosexual conduct, for there is no objectively good reason for condemning it. Homosexuals, say these critics, do no harm, either to themselves or to others—bigotry toward gays is simply that, bigotry. Moreover, critics argue that "unnaturalness" is an unreliable guide. It does not follow, from the fact that something is unnatural, that it is wrong: writing left-handed is, for many people, unnatural, yet there is nothing immoral about it. Other examples are easy to find.

Ethical Egoism

Ethical Egoism is very different from the theories we have mentioned so far. It is a secular theory, in that it appeals to no theological considerations, and yet it proposes an objective foundation for determining how one ought to behave. That foundation is self-interest. According to this theory, each person ought always to do whatever is in his or her own self-interest.

This theory is easily misunderstood, and so we should be careful to state clearly what it says and what it does not say. Ethical Egoism does not say that one should promote one's own interests *as well as* the interests of others. That would be an ordinary, unexceptional view. Ethical Egoism is the radical view that one's *only* duty is to promote one's own interests. According to Ethical Egoism, there is only one ultimate principle of conduct, the principle of self-interest, and this principle sums up *all* of one's natural duties and obligations.

However, Ethical Egoism does not say that you should *avoid* actions that help others, either. It may very well be that, in many instances, your interests coincide with the interests of others, so that in helping yourself you will be aiding others willynilly. Or it may happen that aiding others is an effective *means* for creating some benefit for yourself. Ethical Egoism does not forbid such actions; in fact, it may demand them. The theory only insists that, in such cases, the benefit to others is not what makes the act right. What makes the act right is, rather, the fact that it is to one's own advantage.

Finally, in pursuing one's interests, Ethical Egoism does not imply that one ought always to do what one wants to do, or what gives one the most pleasure in the short run. People may want to do things that are not good for themselves, or that will eventually cause them more grief than pleasure—drink a lot, or smoke cigarettes, or take drugs, or waste their best years at the racetrack. Ethical Egoism would frown on all this, regardless of the momentary pleasure it affords. It says that a person ought to do what *really is* to his or her own best advantage, over the long run. It endorses selfishness, but it doesn't endorse foolishness.

What are the practical implications of this view? In many ways, Ethical Egoism agrees with our ordinary moral opinions. As we grow up, each of us learns a large number of rules of conduct: we learn that we should tell the truth; that we should keep our promises; that we should work hard and try to earn our own way; that we should not steal; that we should avoid harming one another; and so on. Such precepts form the core of our understanding of morality, and Ethical Egoism agrees with all this. The theory simply adds that *the reason why* we should behave in these ways is that it is in our own interests to do so. Generally speaking, we will prosper if we obey such rules, and we will not prosper if we habitually violate them.

On some other matters, however, Ethical Egoism may lead to conclusions that contradict our usual moral opinions. Therefore, the question of whether to adopt an egoistic approach to ethics is not merely a matter of theory. It makes a difference to one's conduct. Do we, for example, have a duty to contribute money for famine relief? If Ethical Egoism is correct, the answer is no—or at least, not unless there is some advantage to be gained for *us*. For according to Ethical Egoism, the mere fact that we would be helping *others* is not a reason for doing anything at all. On the other hand, if we reject Egoism, we open ourselves to obligations that might be quite demanding. Do we, in fact, have an obligation to aid the starving?

Although we do not know exactly how many people die each year of malnutrition and related health problems, the number is very high, in the millions. The most common pattern among children in poor countries is death from dehydration caused by diarrhea brought on by malnutrition. In 1983, not a particularly bad year, James Grant, executive director of the United Nations Children's Fund (UNICEF), estimated that 15,000 children were dying in this way every day. That comes to 5,475,000 children annually. Even if Grant's estimate was high by a factor of three, it would still be a staggering number of deaths—and this estimate includes only one way of death, among only one class of victims.

People do, in fact, feel an obligation to respond, although not enough money is ever contributed to really solve the problem. But people feel this obligation only intermittently. Generally speaking, in a "crisis"—when many starving people are concentrated in one area, as in Ethiopia in 1984—the problem of starvation gets a lot of publicity and people in the affluent countries feel that they must do something. But when there is no "crisis," people tend to ignore the problem. The problem, however, is still there. It is just that starving people who are scattered are easier to ignore. A little thought-experiment might help to make the point. We noted that, according to the director of UNICEF, 5,475,000 children die from malnutrition-related problems annually. Only three cities in the United States have larger populations than that. Suppose all these children were dying in one huge city; it would be a front-page emergency. But in fact they are scattered, and so we don't seem to mind as much.

This, surely, is irrational—it makes no difference to the starving child whether it is surrounded by millions of other dying children, or only thousands. If we have an obligation in one case, surely we have the same obligation in the other case. But do we have an obligation to help *at all?* The Ethical Egoist says no, not unless something is in it for us; other philosophers think this is an immoral attitude and say that Ethical Egoism should be rejected.

Utilitarianism

Ethical Egoism might seem to be an unjustifiably narrow doctrine, because it says that each of us should be concerned only with our own welfare. Why should the moral circle be drawn so narrowly? Why shouldn't we be concerned with the welfare of *all* people? Such thoughts lead naturally to Utilitarianism, the view that we should seek to promote "the greatest happiness for the greatest number." The classical version of Utilitarianism, which was developed by such thinkers as Jeremy Bentham (1748–1832) and John Stuart Mill (1806–1873), is a combination of three distinct points.

First, actions are to be judged right or wrong solely by virtue of their consequences. Nothing else matters. Right actions are, simply, those that have the best consequences.

Second, in assessing consequences, the only thing that matters is the amount of happiness or unhappiness that is caused. Everything else is irrelevant. Thus right actions are those that produce the greatest balance of happiness over unhappiness.

Third, in calculating the happiness or unhappiness that will be caused, no one's happiness is to be counted as more important than anyone else's. Each person's welfare is equally important. This is what separates Utilitarianism from narrower doctrines such as Ethical Egoism. Thus right actions are those that produce the greatest possible balance of happiness over unhappiness, *with each person's happiness counted as equally important.*

Today, Utilitarianism strikes some people as the merest common sense. But when it was first championed in the nineteenth century it was a radical doctrine. Bentham's new conception of morality was remarkable as much for what it left out as for what it included. The typical citizen of the nineteenth century would have said that morality consists in following the will of God, or perhaps adhering to a set of inviolable rules. Bentham would have none of this. Morality, he urged, is nothing more than the attempt to bring about as much happiness as possible in this world. Bentham argued that if God is beneficent, as Christians say he is, then he would command us to follow the Principle of Utility, for the Principle of Utility is nothing other than the supreme principle of beneficence. And as for the traditional "moral rules," they are not "inviolable." On the contrary, they are valid only to the extent that they would lead us to do what utility requires. Utility alone is the ultimate measure of right and wrong. It is the standard that determines which actions should be done, which laws should be enacted, and which rules should be accepted.

Utilitarianism is a radical view because it is a *revisionist* moral philosophy. Its aim is not simply to describe our moral views, but to change them. As our society has evolved over the centuries, it has incorporated into its moral code various elements of prejudice, superstition, and false religion. Therefore, although traditional morality contains some sensible components, it also contains much that could be improved. The improvements can be made, according to Bentham and Mill, by applying the Principle of Utility. Whatever parts of traditional morality are consistent with the principle should be retained; whatever is inconsistent with it should be discarded.

Let us consider three ways in which Utilitarianism might require changes in our moral outlook.

Euthanasia Consider, first, the moral rule against killing. Obviously, killing people is wrong—it is contrary to their most basic interests—and any adequate moral system must condemn murder. However, as Western culture has evolved, the rule against killing has been given a peculiar interpretation. It has been interpreted as an absolute prohibition that can be violated only in the special cases of self-defense, wartime killing, and capital punishment. Western moralists, from Saint Augustine to the present day, have summarized this interpretation by saying that *the intentional killing of the innocent is always wrong.*

This means, for one thing, that mercy killing is forbidden. Suppose someone is suffering from an agonizing terminal illness, and wishes to be given a lethal injection, to bring about a quick, painless death, rather than to die slowly in pain. Traditional Western morals would not permit this; the killing would be regarded as plain murder. The law in our society reflects this attitude. Although juries often choose to go easy on mercy killers, under our law such killing is technically murder in the first degree.

The prohibition of mercy killing (or "euthanasia," as it is called) has also found its way into official statements of medical ethics, such as the 1973 policy statement of the American Medical Association (A.M.A.) on "The Physician and the Dying Patient." That statement said, in its entirety:

The intentional termination of the life of one human being by another—mercy killing—is contrary to that for which the medical profession stands and is contrary to the policy of the American Medical Association.

The cessation of the employment of extraordinary means to prolong the life of the body when there is irrefutable evidence that biological death is imminent is the decision of the patient and/or his immediate family. The advice and judgment of the physician should be freely available to the patient and/or his immediate family.

Several moral judgments are expressed here. Mercy killing is clearly condemned; it is "contrary to that for which the medical profession stands." But at the same time, allowing patients to die (by ceasing treatment) is condoned, at least in some circumstances. This is an important point. As medical technology has advanced, it has become possible to keep patients alive almost indefinitely, even when they have become little more than human vegetables. The A.M.A. statement acknowledges the pointlessness of this by saying that a physician may not kill patients but may nevertheless sometimes allow death by omitting treatment that would prolong life.

In 1982 the A.M.A. issued a more general set of guidelines with the title "Principles of Medical Ethics." Unlike the 1973 statement, this one included comment on a variety of matters, and went into some detail in discussing them. Four paragraphs were devoted to the treatment of hopeless or terminal cases:

QUALITY OF LIFE. In the making of decisions for the treatment of seriously deformed newborns or persons who are severely deteriorated victims of injury, illness or advanced age, the primary consideration should be what is best for the individual patient and not the avoidance of a burden to the family or to society. Quality of life is a factor to be considered in determining what is best for the individual. Life should be cherished despite disabilities and handicaps, except when prolongation would be inhumane and unconscionable. Under these circumstances, withholding or removing life supporting means is ethical provided that the normal care given an individual who is ill is not discontinued.

. . . .

TERMINAL ILLNESS. The social commitment of the physician is to prolong life and relieve suffering. Where the observance of one conflicts with the other, the physician, patient, and/or family of the patient have discretion to resolve the conflict.

For humane reasons, with informed consent a physician may do what is medically indicated to alleviate severe pain, or cease or omit treatment to let a terminally ill patient die, but he should not intentionally cause death. In determining whether the administration of potentially life-prolonging medical treatment is in the best interest of the patient, the physician should consider what the possibility is for extending life under humane and comfortable conditions and what are the wishes and attitudes of the family or those who have responsibility for the custody of the patient.

Where a terminally ill patient's coma is beyond doubt irreversible, and there are adequate safeguards to confirm the accuracy of the diagnosis, all means of life support may be discontinued. If death does not occur when life support systems are discontinued, the comfort and dignity of the patient should be maintained.

We can see, in these paragraphs, a kind of struggle between conflicting ethical ideas. On the one hand, the quality of a person's life is explicitly made relevant to the decision of whether the life should be prolonged, and it is implied that the relief of suffering is as important as the prolongation of life. Moreover, the pointlessness of life-support systems for people in irreversible comas is explicitly acknowledged. At the same time, the sterner ideas of the 1973 statement are unchanged: it is still forbidden to cause death intentionally, and it is still forbidden to omit ordinary means of treatment. (The terminology "extraordinary means" has been eliminated, but the distinction between ordinary and extraordinary means is still being assumed—it is now said to be the difference between "life supporting means" and "the normal care given an individual who is ill.")

Utilitarians would applaud certain parts of the 1982 A.M.A. statement. In particular, they would agree that "quality of life is a factor to be considered in determining what is best for the individual," and that the prolongation of life can sometimes be "inhumane and unconscionable." But they would then argue that, for this very reason, mercy killing is not *always* wrong. In the tragic circumstances in which prolonging of life has become "inhumane and unconscionable," euthanasia, rather than being morally unacceptable, might actually be morally required, as the best available means of minimizing suffering.

Nonhuman Animals By the time Mill published his book *Utilitarianism* in 1861, the ethical ideas of Bentham and his followers were widely known and had attracted much critical comment. One of the most popular complaints was that Utilitarianism made no distinction between man and the lower animals. According to Utilitarianism, the crucial fact about human beings is that they are capable of enjoying pleasure and suffering pain, and our duty toward them is simply to increase their enjoyment and decrease their suffering. But, the objection went, other animals are also capable of experiencing pleasure and pain—and so it seems that, according to Utilitarianism, man has no special status. But man is exalted above the other animals, intellectually and spiritually. Mustn't our moral theory take some account of this? Some wags summarized this complaint by remarking that "Utilitarianism is a philosophy fit for pigs, not men."

Mill's reply was that mankind's greater intellectual and spiritual gifts are relevant to ethics, but only because they make it possible for people to enjoy special kinds of pleasures, and suffer special kinds of pains, that other animals are not able to suffer or enjoy. Human beings are able to appreciate music; therefore they can take pleasure in a Mozart sonata. They have emotional lives rich enough to include friendships; therefore they can suffer the special pains of betrayal. Other animals, who lack human capacities, may not be capable of experiencing these pleasures and pains. Therefore, we have duties to people—the duty to teach our children about music, or the duty not to betray friendship, for example—that we could not have to some other animals. (We could have no duty to teach music to a rabbit, or to be loyal to a shrimp.) This Mill considered to be a complete and sufficient answer to the critics' objection.

Nevertheless, the critics were on to something. Utilitarianism's view of our moral relation with nonhuman animals is very much at odds with traditional Western ethics. The dominant view of our tradition is that humans and nonhumans are in separate moral categories. Human life is precious and must be protected at all cost. The other animals, however, were placed on earth for the benefit of the humans, who may use them in any way they please. And of course we do use the other animals in a great variety of ways. We eat them;

we use them as experimental subjects in our laboratories; we use their skins for clothing and their heads as wall ornaments; we make them the objects of our amusement in zoos, circuses, and rodeos; and, indeed, one popular sport consists in tracking them down and killing them just for the fun of it. According to traditional ethics, there is nothing wrong with any of this.

The utilitarians, however, found a lot wrong with it. Bentham emphasized that humans are not the only animals who suffer: non-human animals suffer also. Therefore, he argued, it is inconsistent to object to causing pain to a human, and yet to raise no objection when the same pain is inflicted on a nonhuman. Because both can suffer, we have the *same* reason for not mistreating both. If a human is tormented, why is it wrong? Because he or she suffers. Similarly, if a nonhuman is tormented, he also suffers, and so it is equally wrong for the same reason. To Bentham and Mill, this line of reasoning was conclusive. Humans and nonhumans are in exactly the same moral category. Insofar as the welfare of other animals is affected by our conduct, we have a strict moral duty to take that into account, and their suffering counts equally with any similar suffering experienced by a human.

If this reasoning were taken seriously, it would lead to a radical restructuring of our relations with the nonhuman world. For one thing, it would require us to become vegetarians. The production of meat for our tables involves great suffering for the animals; therefore, Utilitarianism would insist that we ask what justification there is for it. What answer can we give? Since we can nourish ourselves very well without eating meat, the only reason for preferring to eat the animals is apparently our enjoyment of the way they taste—and that seems too feeble a reason to justify causing so much pain. From a philosophical point of view, it is fascinating that such a simple and conservative moral principle—"It is wrong to cause pain, unless there is a good reason to justify it"—can lead to such an apparently radical conclusion.

Punishment Bentham said that "All punishment is mischief: all punishment in itself is evil." By this he meant that punishment always involves treating someone badly, whether by taking away their freedom (imprisonment), their property (fines), or even their life (capital punishment). Since these things are all evils, they require justification. *Why* is it right to treat people like this?

One traditional answer is that punishment is justified as a way of "paying back" the offender for an evil deed. Those who have committed crimes, such as theft or assault, deserve to be treated badly in return. It is essentially a matter of justice: justice requires that someone who harms other people be harmed also. As the ancient saying has it, "An eye for an eye, a tooth for a tooth."

This view is known as *Retributivism.* Retributivism is, according to Utilitarianism, a wholly unsatisfactory idea, because it advocates the infliction of suffering without any compensating gain in happiness. Retributivism would have us increase, not decrease, the amount of suffering in the world.

Utilitarianism takes a very different approach. According to Utilitarianism, our duty is to do whatever will increase the amount of happiness in the world. Punishment is, on its face, an "evil" because it makes someone—the person who is punished—*unhappy.* Thus Bentham says, "If it ought at all to be admitted, it ought to be admitted in as far as it promises to exclude some greater evil." In other words, it can be justified only if it will have good results that, on balance, outweigh the evil done.

So, for the utilitarian, the question is: does punishment have such good results? Is there a *good purpose* served by punishing criminals, other than simply making them suffer? Utilitarians have traditionally answered in the affirmative. The practice of punishing lawbreakers benefits society in two ways.

First, punishing criminals helps to prevent crime, or at least to reduce the level of criminal activity in a society. People who are tempted to misbehave can be deterred from doing so if they know they will be punished. Of course, the threat of punishment will not always be efficacious. Sometimes people will break the law anyway. But they will misbehave less if punishments are threatened.

Second, a well-designed system of punishment might have the effect of rehabilitating wrongdoers. Without trying to excuse them, it must be admitted that criminals are often people with emotional problems, who find it difficult to function well in society. They are often ill educated and lack marketable skills. Considering this, why should we not respond to crime by attacking the problems that give rise to it? A person who is breaking society's rules is a danger to society and may first be imprisoned to remove the danger. But while he is there, his problems should be addressed with psychological therapy, educational opportunities, or job training, as appropriate.

If this person can eventually be returned to society as a productive citizen, rather than as a criminal, both the individual and society will benefit.

These utilitarian ideas have dominated Anglo-American law for the past century; today the utilitarian theory of punishment is the reigning orthodoxy. Prisons, once mere places of confinement, have been redesigned (in theory, at least) as centers for rehabilitation, complete with psychologists, libraries, educational programs, and vocational training. The shift in thinking has been so great that the term "prison" is no longer in favor; in many places the preferred nomenclature is "correctional facility." Notice the implications of the new term—inmates are there not to be "punished" but to be "corrected." Of course, in many instances the programs of rehabilitation have been dismally unsuccessful. Nevertheless, the programs are *designed* as rehabilitation. The victory of the utilitarian ideology has been virtually complete.

Kant's Theory

The major alternative to Utilitarianism, in the view of many commentators, is the system of ethical ideas devised by the great German philosopher Immanuel Kant (1724–1804). Like the Ethical Egoists and the Utilitarians, Kant believed that morality can be summed up in one ultimate principle, from which all our duties and obligations are derived. But his version of the "ultimate moral principle" was very different from those others, because Kant did not emphasize the *outcomes* of actions. What was important for him was doing one's duty, and he held that a person's duty is not determined by calculating consequences.

Kant called the ultimate moral principle the *Categorical Imperative.* But he gave this principle two very different formulations. The first version of the categorical imperative, as expressed in his *Fundamental Principles of the Metaphysics of Morals* (1785), goes like this:

> Act only on that maxim whereby thou canst at the same time
> will that it should become a universal law.

Stated in this way, Kant's principle summarizes a procedure for deciding whether an act is morally permissible. When you are contemplating doing a particular action, you are to ask what rule you would be following if you were to do that action. (This will be the "maxim" of the act.) Then you are to ask whether you would be willing for that rule to be followed by everyone all the time. (That would make it a "universal law" in the relevant sense.) If so, the rule may be followed, and the act is permissible. However, if you would *not* be willing for everyone to follow the rule, then you may not follow it, and the act is morally impermissible.

An example might help make this clearer. Suppose you have a neighbor who works at the same place as you. One day your neighbor's car breaks down and he asks you for a ride to work. Should you give him the ride? Applying the Categorical Imperative, you might reason as follows:

(1) If you refused, you would be following the rule: Don't give rides to people whose cars have broken down. (That would be "the maxim of your act.")

(2) Would you want everyone to act on that rule, all the time? Suppose, for example, that your car broke down one morning, and you desperately needed a ride to work. Would you want your neighbor to adopt the policy of not giving rides? No, you wouldn't.

(3) Therefore, if you refused your neighbor's request, you could not will that the maxim of your act be made into a universal law.

(4) Therefore, you should not refuse your neighbor's request.

This example makes it clear that Kant's Categorical Imperative is closely related to the ancient principle of the Golden Rule—the Categorical Imperative would permit us to treat others only in ways that we would be willing to be treated ourselves.

However, Kant also gave another formulation of the Categorical Imperative. Later in the same book, he said that the ultimate moral principle may be understood as saying:

> So act as to treat humanity, whether in thine own person or in that of any other, in every case as an end withal, never as means only.

What does it mean to say that persons are to be treated as "ends" and never as "means"? Kant gives the following example. Suppose you need money, and so you want a "loan," but you know you could not repay it. In desperation, you consider making a false promise (to repay) in order to trick a friend into giving you the money. May you do this? Perhaps you need the money for a good purpose—so good, in fact, that you might convince yourself the lie would be justified. Nevertheless, if you lied to your friend, you would merely be manipulating him, and using him "as a means."

On the other hand, what would it be like to treat your friend "as an end"? Suppose you told the truth, that you need the money for a certain purpose, but could not repay it. Then your friend could make up his own mind about whether to let you have it. He could exercise his own powers of reason, consulting his own values and wishes, and make a free, autonomous choice. If he did decide to give the money for this purpose, he would be choosing to make that purpose his own. Thus you would not merely be using him as a means to achieving your goal. This is what Kant meant when he said, "Rational beings . . . ought always be esteemed also as ends, that is, as beings who must be capable of containing in themselves the end of the very same action."

Kant believed that his theory had very different practical implications from Utilitarianism. To illustrate this, let us return to the examples we considered earlier.

Euthanasia In Kant's view, human beings have "an intrinsic worth, i.e., *dignity,*" which makes their lives valuable "above all price." This thought led him, in his general theory of ethics, to hold that human persons are "ends in themselves," never to be used as mere "means." It also led him to draw traditional, conservative conclusions about the termination of life. Kant did not discuss euthanasia directly, but he did discuss the related issue of suicide at some length.

Murder is forbidden, obviously, because it is the destruction of a human life, which is "valuable above all price." But what of suicide? One might think that, since the suicide takes only his *own* life, the prohibition upon it would not be so strict as the prohibition upon killing others. Prior to the coming of Christianity, the philosophers of Greece and Rome took this attitude. Although they condemned cowardly suicides, they thought suicide could be permissible in special circumstances. The Christians took a sterner view. Saint Augustine, whose thought shaped much of our tradition, argued, "Christians have no authority for committing suicide in any circumstances whatever." His argument was based mainly on an appeal to authority. The sixth commandment says "Thou shalt not kill." Augustine pointed out that the commandment does not say "Thou shalt not kill *thy neighbor*"; it says "Thou shalt not *kill,*" period. Thus, he argued, the rule applies with equal force to killing oneself.

Like Aristotle, Augustine held that man's reason is "the essence of his soul," and in this he laid the foundation for later thought on the subject. A rational being, later thinkers would insist, can never justify doing away with himself, for he must realize his own value is too great to be destroyed. Thus Saint Thomas Aquinas, who made man's rationality central to his nature, argued that suicide is absolutely opposed to that nature. Suicide, he said, is "contrary to that charity whereby every man should love himself."

If human life has such extraordinary worth, then it is only to be expected that one can never justify killing oneself. Kant draws this conclusion. Like Augustine and Aquinas, he believed that suicide is never morally permissible. His argument relies heavily on comparisons of human life with animal life. People may offer various reasons to justify self-murder, he says, but these attempted justifications overlook the crucial point that "humanity is worthy of esteem." To kill oneself, in his view, is to regard one's life as something of so little value that it can be obliterated simply to escape troubles. In the case of mere animals, this might be true. We kill animals to put them out of misery, and that is all right, because animals are not worth much to begin with. However, we should not think that the same may be done for a man, because the value of a man's life is so much greater: "If [a man] disposes over himself," Kant says, "he treats his value as that of a beast." Again, "The rule of morality does not admit of [suicide] under any condition because it degrades human nature below the level of animal nature and so destroys it."

All this follows, Kant thought, from taking seriously the idea of man as a rational being (and therefore as an exalted being). Thus far he invokes no religious notions. One might think, then, that the secular version of man's specialness is supposed to do the job alone, unaided by religious conceptions. However, Kant saw the secular argument and the religious story as working hand in hand. To secure his conclusion, he added:

But as soon as we examine suicide from the standpoint of religion we immediately see it in its true light. We have been placed in this world under certain conditions and for specific purposes. But a suicide opposes the purpose of his Creator; he arrives in the other world as one who has deserted his post; he must be looked upon as a rebel against God.

Nonhuman Animals On this subject, too, Kant's view follows traditional thought and avoids the revisionist extremes of Utilitarianism. From ancient times, humans have considered themselves to be essentially different from all other creatures—and not just different, but *better*. In fact, humans have traditionally thought themselves to be quite fabulous. According to the ancient myth, man was made in the image of God, "just a little lower than the angels," and the earth was made by God to provide a home for him. The other animals, by contrast, were made for man's use.

The doctrine of man's exalted status has been elaborated, in one way or another, by virtually every important thinker in the Western tradition. Aristotle's defense of human superiority was cast in nontheological terms: he argued that man is the *rational* animal, and is superior to all other animals for that reason. This idea has dominated Western thought. For centuries it has been used to explain why human life is morally precious, while the lives of other creatures are unimportant. Saint Thomas Aquinas, for example, argued that mere animals have no moral importance because "other creatures are for the sake of the intellectual creatures." Therefore, he said, "It is no wrong for man to make use of them, either by killing or any any other way whatever."

In this way of looking at things, animals have no moral standing whatever. Should we even be kind to them out of simple charity? No, Aquinas says, and once again the reason is that they are not rational:

> The love of charity extends to none but God and our neighbour. But the word neighbour cannot be extended to irrational creatures, since they have no fellowship with man in the rational life. Therefore charity does not extend to irrational creatures.

Kant, who defends traditional morality at almost every point, says much the same thing. Lacking the all-important quality of rationality, nonhuman animals are entirely excluded from the sphere of moral concern. It is man who is an "end in himself." Other entities have value only as means, to serve that end. Thus for Kant animals have the status of mere things, and we have no duties to them whatsoever: "But so far as animals are concerned," he says, "we have no direct duties. Animals . . . are there merely as means to an end. That end is man."

By a "direct duty" Kant meant a duty based on a concern for the animal's own welfare. We may indeed have duties that *involve* animals, but the reason behind these duties will always refer to a human interest, rather than to the animal's own interests. Kant admits that we should not torture animals pointlessly, but the reason, he insists, is only that "he who is cruel to animals becomes hard also in his dealings with men." Thus, while the Utilitarians viewed the welfare of animals as something that is morally important for its own sake, Kant saw it as having no intrinsic importance at all.

Punishment Like all orthodoxies, the utilitarian theory of punishment has generated opposition. Much of the opposition is practical in nature; programs of rehabilitation, despite all the efforts that have been put into them, have not worked very well. In California, for example, more has been done to "rehabilitate" criminals than anywhere else; yet the rate of recidivism is higher there than in most other states. But some of the opposition is also based on purely theoretical considerations that go back at least to Kant.

Kant abjured "the serpent-windings of Utilitarianism" because, he said, the theory is incompatible with human dignity. In the first place, it has us calculating how to use people as means to an end, and this (he says) is morally impermissible. If we imprison the criminal in order to secure the well-being of society, we are merely *using* him for the benefit of others. This violates the fundamental rule that "one man ought never to be dealt with merely as a means subservient to the purpose of another."

Moreover, the aim of "rehabilitation," although it sounds noble enough, is actually no more than the attempt to mold people into what *we* think they should be. As such, it is a violation of their rights as autonomous beings who are entitled to decide for themselves what sort of people they will be. We do have the right to respond to their wickedness by "paying them back" for it, but we do *not* have the right to violate their integrity by trying to manipulate their personalities.

Thus Kant would have no part of utilitarian justifications of punishment. What, then, is the justification of inflicting such harms on people? Here, as before, Kant defends traditional ideas: he was a retributivist. Punishment, he argued, is justified simply as a way of paying back wrongdoers for their wicked deeds. It doesn't matter if no utilitarian purpose is served; such punishment is good in itself. In Part I of *The Metaphysics of Morals* (1797) he wrote:

> When someone who delights in annoying and vexing peace-loving folk receives at last a right good beating, it is certainly an ill, but everyone approves of it and considers it as good in itself *even if nothing further results from it.*

Thus punishing people may increase the amount of misery in the world, but according to Kant that is all right, for the extra suffering is borne by the criminal, who, after all, deserves it.

Retributivist punishment, Kant argued, should be governed by two principles. First, people should be punished simply because they have committed crimes, and for no other reason. And second, it is important to punish the criminal proportionately to the seriousness of the crime. Small punishments may suffice for small crimes, but big punishments are necessary in response to big crimes. This second principle leads Kant inevitably to endorse capital punishment, for in response to murder, only death is a sufficiently stern penalty.

It is worth noting that Utilitarianism has been faulted for violating both of Kant's principles. Nothing in the basic idea of Utilitarianism, say the critics, limits punishment to the guilty or limits the amount of punishment to the amount deserved. If the purpose of punishment is to secure the general welfare, as Utilitarianism says, it could sometimes happen that the general welfare will be served by "punishing" someone who has *not* committed a crime—an innocent person. Similarly, it might happen that the general welfare is promoted by punishing people excessively—a greater punishment might have a greater deterrent effect. But both of these are, on their face, violations of justice, which Kantian Retributivism would never allow.

The Social Contract Theory

The Social Contract Theory is a secular theory that offers an approach to understanding morality strikingly different from the other theories discussed in this book. It is appealing because it is based on some straightforward reasoning about human nature and the conditions under which human society is possible. The basic idea is that moral rules are rules that human beings must accept if they are to live together in societies. The essentials of the theory can be stated quite simply:

1. Human beings are not naturally hermits. We live together in social groups, wanting and needing one another's company.
2. Moreover, we are much better off in social groups than we would be if each of us tried to make it "on his own." Social living makes possible incalculable benefits; isolated living would be miserable. (The benefits of living in organized societies include the existence of science and technology, agriculture, medicine, education, and the arts, plus personal goods such as friendship, and much more.)
3. But social living would not be possible unless we all agreed to follow certain rules. We must keep our agreements with one another, act honestly, avoid harming one another, and so on. If we did not keep our agreements with one another, all cooperative endeavors such as large-scale agriculture and the building trades would collapse, and all the advantages gained by division of labor would be lost. If we did not agree to refrain from harming one another, we would all have to guard our backs constantly. Countless other examples of the same kind could be given.
4. Therefore, in order to secure the advantages of social living, it is reasonable for each of us to agree to abide by such rules, on the condition that others will obey them as well. This agreement, in which every citizen participates, is called the *social contract*. The social contract makes society possible.

Therefore, we can summarize the social contract conception of morality like this: morality consists in the set of rules, governing how people are to treat one another, that rational people will agree to accept for their mutual benefit, on the condition that others follow those rules as well. The most important advocates of the Social Contract Theory were Thomas Hobbes (1588–1679), John Locke (1632–1704), and Jean Jacques Rousseau (1712–1778). In our own time John Rawls, a professor of philosophy at Harvard, has formulated an important contemporary version of the theory.

The Social Contract Theory offers an objective, secular foundation for morality that seems to answer the old questions about the "subjectivity" of morals very satisfactorily. It can account for such duties as promise-keeping and respecting the rights of others in a plausible way. And, because it is based on an important insight about the nature of society and its institutions, it is especially well suited to helping us deal with issues involving those institutions. Take, for example, the question of civil disobedience. As a result of the social contract, we have an obligation to obey the law. But are we ever justified in defying the law? And if so, when?

The classic modern examples of civil disobedience are, of course, the actions taken in connection with the Indian independence movement led by Mohandas K. Gandhi and the American civil rights movement led by Martin Luther King, Jr. Both movements were characterized by public, conscientious, nonviolent refusal to comply with the law. But the goals of the movements were importantly different. Gandhi and his followers did not recognize the right of the British to govern India; they wanted to replace British rule with an entirely different system. So they were only defying a "law" that they did not recognize as legitimate in the first place. King and his followers, on the other hand, did not question the legitimacy of the basic institutions of American government. They objected only to particular laws and social policies that they regarded as unjust.

The problem was that racial segregation, with all its attendant evils, was enforced not merely by social custom, but by law as well, a law that black citizens were denied a voice in formulating. When urged to rely on ordinary democratic processes to redress his grievances, King first pointed out that there had been many attempts at negotiation, but these efforts had met little success. And as for "democracy," the word had little meaning to southern blacks, who, by and large, were not permitted to register to vote.

Thus a question was raised: are people justified in refusing to obey the law when they consider it to be blatantly unjust? The Social Contract Theory provides a particularly interesting answer. But first we have to ask another question: why do we have an obligation to obey the law in the first place? According to the Social Contract Theory, it is because each of us participates in a complicated arrangement whereby we gain certain benefits in return for accepting certain burdens. The benefits are the benefits of social living: we escape the "state of nature" and live in a society in which we are secure and enjoy basic rights under the law. To gain these benefits, we agree that we will do our part to uphold the institutions that make them possible. This means that we must obey the law, pay our taxes, and so forth—these are "burdens" we accept in return.

But what if things are arranged so that one group of people within the society is not accorded the rights enjoyed by others? What if, instead of protecting them, the police become the agents of a repressive system? What if people are denied rights to equal housing, employment, and education? If the denial of these rights is sufficiently widespread and sufficiently systematic, we are forced to conclude that the terms of the social contract are not being honored. Thus, if we continue to demand that the disadvantaged group obey the law and otherwise respect society's institutions, we are demanding that they accept the burdens imposed by the social arrangement, even though they are denied its benefits.

This line of reasoning suggests that, rather than civil disobedience being an undesirable "last resort" for socially disenfranchised groups, it is in fact the most natural and reasonable means of expressing protest. For when they are denied a fair share of the benefits of social living, the disenfranchised are in effect released from the contract that otherwise would require them to support the arrangements that make those benefits possible. This is the deepest reason that justifies civil disobedience, and it is to the credit of the Social Contract Theory that it exposes this point so clearly.

When confronted with certain other moral issues, however, the Social Contract Theory has greater difficulty. In particular, the theory has trouble accounting for our duties to creatures who lack the capacity to participate in the agreements of mutual benefit on which the whole setup depends—namely, nonhuman animals and mentally retarded humans. Animals are not participants in the social contract, and so we can have no moral duties to them. This outcome will not bother people who agree with the traditional view that mere animals don't matter anyway. But the status of mentally defective humans is bound to be troublesome. Mentally retarded people might also lack the capacity for reciprocal concern which the contract requires; and so it is hard to see why, according to this theory, they would not have the same status as animals. Few people would be willing to accept this result, and so the Social Contract Theory seems to be missing something important.

Conclusion

Philosophical ideas are often very abstract, and it is difficult to see what sort of evidence counts for or against them. It is easy enough to appreciate, intuitively, the ideas behind each of these theories, but how do we determine whether they are *correct?* It is a daunting question. Faced with this problem, people are tempted to accept or reject philosophical ideas on the basis of their intuitive appeal: if an idea sounds good, one may embrace it; or if it rubs one the wrong way, one may discard it. But this is hardly a satisfactory way to proceed if we want to discover the truth. How an idea strikes us is not a reliable guide, for our "intuitions" may be mistaken.

Happily, we have an alternative. An idea is no better than the arguments that support it. So to evaluate a philosophical idea, we may examine the reasoning behind it. The great philosophers knew this very well: they did not simply announce their philosophical opinions; instead, they presented arguments in support of their views. The leading idea, from the time of Socrates to the present, has been that truth is discovered by considering the reasons for and against the various alternatives—the "correct" theory is, simply, the one that has the best arguments on its side.

Thus philosophical thinking consists, to a large extent, in formulating and assessing arguments. This is not the whole of philosophy, but it is a big part of it. It is what makes philosophy a rational enterprise, rather than an empty exercise in theory-mongering. Therefore, the second introductory essay in this book is a brief introduction to the evaluation of arguments.

2 *Some Basic Points about Arguments*

James Rachels

Philosophy without argument would be a lifeless exercise. What good would it be to produce a theory without reasons for thinking it correct? And of what interest is the rejection of a theory without good reasons for thinking it incorrect? A philosophical theory is exactly as good as the arguments that support it.

Therefore, if we want to think clearly about philosophical matters, we have to learn something about the evaluation of arguments. We have to learn to distinguish the sound ones from the unsound ones. This can be a tedious business, but it is indispensable if we want to come within shouting distance of the truth.

In ordinary English the word *argument* often means a quarrel, and the word has a hint of acrimony. That is not the way the word is used here. In the logician's sense, an argument is a chain of reasoning designed to prove something. It consists of one or more *premises,* and a *conclusion,* together with the claim that the conclusion *follows from* the premises. Here is a simple argument. This example is not particularly interesting in itself, but it is short and clear, and it will help us grasp the main points we need to understand about the nature of arguments.

(1) All men are mortal.
     Socrates is a man.
     Therefore, Socrates is mortal.

The first two statements are the premises; the third statement is the conclusion; and it is claimed that the conclusion follows from the premises.

What does it mean to say that the conclusion "follows from" the premises? It means that a certain logical relation exists between the premises and the conclusion: *if* the premises are true, then the conclusion must be true also. (Another way to put the same point is: the conclusion follows from the premises if and only if it is *impossible* for the premises to be true, and the conclusion false, at the same time.) In example (1), we can see that the conclusion does follow from the premises. If it is true that all men are mortal, and Socrates is a man, then it must be true that Socrates is mortal. (Or: it is impossible for it to be true that all men are mortal, and for Socrates to be a man, and yet be false that Socrates is mortal.)

In example (1), the conclusion follows from the premises, *and* the premises are in fact true. However, the conclusion of an argument may follow from the premises even if the premises are not actually true. Consider this argument:

(2) All people from Georgia are famous.
Jimmy Carter is from Georgia.
Therefore, Jimmy Carter is famous.

Clearly, the conclusion of this argument does follow from the premises: *if* it were true that all Georgians are famous, and Jimmy Carter was from Georgia, then it follows that Jimmy Carter would be famous. This logical relation holds between the premises and conclusion even though one of the premises is in fact false.

It will help to introduce a bit of terminology. Let us say that an argument is *valid* just in case its conclusion follows from its premises. Both the examples given above are valid arguments, in this sense.

In order for an argument to be *sound,* however, two things are necessary: the argument must be valid, *and* its premises must be true. Thus the argument about Socrates is a sound argument, but the argument about Jimmy Carter is not sound, because even though it is valid, the premises are not all true.

It is important to notice that an argument may be unsound even though its premises and conclusion are all true. Consider the following silly example:

(3) The earth has one moon.
John F. Kennedy was assassinated.
Therefore, snow is white.

The premises of this "argument" are both true, and the conclusion is true as well. Yet it is obviously a bad argument, because it is not valid—the conclusion does not follow from the premises. The important point is that *when we ask whether an argument is valid, we are not asking whether the premises actually are true, or whether the conclusion actually is true. We are asking only whether, if the premises were true, the conclusion really would follow from them.*

Our examples so far have all been trivial. I used these trivial examples because they permit us to make the essential logical points clearly and uncontroversially. But these points are applicable to the analysis of any argument, trivial or not. To illustrate, let us consider how these points can be used in analyzing a more important and controversial issue. We will look at the arguments for Moral Skepticism in some detail.

Moral Skepticism

Let us consider the idea that *there is no such thing as objective moral truth.* We may call this idea Moral Skepticism. It is not merely the idea that we cannot *know* the truth about right and wrong. It is the more radical idea that such "truth" does not *exist.* The essential point may be put in several different ways. At one time or another, you have probably heard these remarks, or remarks like them:

> Morality is subjective; it is a matter of how we feel about things, not a matter of how things *are.*

> Morality is only a matter of opinion, and one person's opinion is just as good as another's.

> Values exist only in our minds, not in the world outside us.

However the point is put, the underlying thought is the same: the idea of "objective moral truth" is only a fiction; in reality, no such thing exists.

Is Moral Skepticism *correct?* Is the idea of moral "truth" only an illusion? What arguments can be given in favor of this idea? To determine whether it is correct, we need to ask what arguments can be given for it, and whether those arguments are sound.

The Cultural Differences Argument One argument for Moral Skepticism can be based on the observation that in different cultures people have different ideas concerning right and wrong. For example, in traditional Eskimo society, infanticide is thought to be morally acceptable: if a family already has too many children, a new baby might be placed in the snow and allowed to die. (This is more likely to happen to girl than to boy babies.) In our own society, however, this would be considered wrong. There are many other examples of the same kind; different cultures have different moral codes.

Reflecting on such facts, many people have concluded that there is no such thing as objective right and wrong. Thus they advance the following argument:

> (4) In some societies, such as among the Eskimos, infanticide is thought to be morally acceptable.
>
> In other societies, such as our own, infanticide is thought to be morally odious.
>
> Therefore, infanticide is neither objectively right nor objectively wrong. It is merely a matter of opinion, which varies from culture to culture.

We may call this the "Cultural Differences Argument." This kind of argument has been tremendously influential; it has persuaded many people to be skeptical of the whole idea of moral "truth." (This argument is the primary thought behind Cultural Relativism, discussed in the first introductory essay in this book.) But is it a sound argument? We can ask two questions about it: first, Are the premises true? and second, Does the conclusion really follow from them? If the answer to either question is "No," then the argument must be rejected as unsound. In this case, the premises seem to be correct—there have been many cultures in which infanticide was accepted. Therefore, our attention must focus on the second question, Is the argument valid?

In examples (1) and (2) given above, it is clear that the conclusion does follow from the premises. In example (3) it is obvious that the conclusion does not follow. In the Cultural Differences Argument, however, it is not obvious whether the conclusion follows from the premises, and some thought is required to decide the matter.

To figure this out, we begin by noting that the premises concern *what people believe.* In some societies, people think infanticide is all right. In others, people believe it is immoral. The conclusion, however, concerns not what people believe, but whether infanticide *really is* immoral. Now the problem is that this sort of conclusion does not follow from this sort of premise. It does not follow, from the mere fact that people have different beliefs about something, that there is no "truth" in the matter. Therefore, the Cultural Differences Argument is not valid.

To make the point clearer, consider this parallel argument:

(5) In some societies, the world is thought to be flat.
In other societies, the world is thought to be round.
Therefore, objectively speaking, the world is neither flat nor round. It is merely a matter of opinion, which varies from culture to culture.

Clearly *this* argument is not valid. We cannot conclude that the world is shapeless simply because not everyone agrees what shape it has. But exactly the same can be said about the Cultural Differences Argument: we cannot validly move from premises about what people *believe* to be the case to a conclusion about what *is* the case, because people—even whole societies—can be wrong. The world has a definite shape, and those who think it is flat are mistaken. Similarly, infanticide might be objectively wrong (or not wrong), and those who think differently might be mistaken. Therefore, the Cultural Differences Argument is not valid, and so it provides no legitimate support for the idea that moral "truth" is only an illusion. There are two common reactions to this analysis. These reactions illustrate traps that people often fall into.

The first misguided reaction goes like this. Many people find the conclusion of the Cultural Differences Argument very appealing. This makes it hard for them to believe that the argument is invalid; when it is pointed out that the argument is fallacious, they tend to respond: "But right and wrong really *are* only matters of opinion!" They make the mistake of thinking that if we reject an argument, we are somehow impugning the truth of its conclusion. But that, as we have seen, is not so. An argument can have a true conclusion and still be a bad argument. [Remember example (3) above.] If an argument is unsound, then it fails to provide any reason for thinking the conclusion is true. The conclusion may still be true—that remains an open question—the point is just that the unsound argument gives it no support.

Second, some might object that it is unfair to compare morality with an obviously objective matter like the shape of the earth. We *know* what shape the earth has—it is provable by scientific methods—and so we know that the flat-earthers are simply wrong. But, this objection continues, morality is different: there is no way to prove a moral opinion true or false. Thus morality might be a subjective matter even though the shape of the earth is perfectly objective.

This objection misses the point. The Cultural Differences Argument tries to derive the skeptical conclusion about morality *from a certain set of facts,* namely, the facts about cultural disagreements. The objection suggests that the conclusion might be validly derived from a *different* set of facts, namely, facts about what is and what is not provable. It suggests, in effect, a different argument, which might be formulated like this:

> **(6)** If infanticide (or anything else, for that matter) is objectively right or wrong, then it should be possible to *prove* it right or wrong.
> But it is not possible to prove infanticide right or wrong. Therefore, infanticide is neither objectively right nor objectively wrong. It is merely a matter of opinion, which varies from culture to culture.

This argument is fundamentally different from the Cultural Differences Argument, even though the two arguments have the same conclusion. They are different because they appeal to entirely different considerations in trying to prove that conclusion—in other words, they have different premises. Therefore, the question of whether argument (6) is sound is separate from the question of whether the Cultural Differences Argument is sound. The Cultural Differences Argument is not valid, for the reason given previously.

We should emphasize the importance of *keeping arguments separate.* It is easy to slide from one argument to another without realizing what one is doing. It is easy to think that if moral judgments are "unprovable," then the Cultural Differences Argument is strengthened. But it is not. Argument (6) merely introduces a different set of issues. It is important to pin down an argument, and evaluate *it* as carefully as possible, before moving on to different considerations.

The Provability Argument Let us now consider in more detail the question of whether it is possible to prove a moral judgment true or false. The following argument, which we might call the *Provability Argument,* is a more general form of argument (6):

(7) If there were any such thing as objective truth in ethics, we should be able to *prove* that some moral opinions are true and others false.
But in fact we cannot prove which moral opinions are true and which are false.
Therefore, there is no such thing as objective truth in ethics.

Once again, we have an argument with a certain superficial appeal. But are the premises true? And does the conclusion really follow from them? It seems that the conclusion does follow. Therefore, the crucial question will be whether the premises are in fact true.

The general claim that moral judgments cannot be proven *sounds* right: anyone who has ever argued about a matter like abortion knows how frustrating it can be to try to "prove" that one's point of view is correct. However, if we inspect this claim more closely, it turns out to be dubious.

Let's begin with a matter that is simpler than abortion. Suppose a student says that a test given by a teacher was unfair. This is clearly a moral judgment—fairness is a basic moral value. Can this judgment be proven? The student might point out that the test was so long that not even the best students could complete it in the time allowed (and the test was to be graded on the assumption that it *should* be completed). Moreover, the test covered in detail matters that were quite trivial, while ignoring matters the teacher had stressed as very important. Finally, the test included questions about some matters that were not covered in either the assigned readings or the class discussions.

Suppose all this is true. And further suppose that the teacher, when asked to explain, has no defense to offer. (In fact, the teacher, who is rather inexperienced, seems muddled about the whole thing and doesn't seem to have had any very clear idea of what he was doing.) Now, hasn't the student proved the test was unfair? What more in the way of proof could we possibly want?

It is easy to think of other examples that make the same point:

Jones is a bad man. To prove this, one might point out that Jones is a habitual liar; he manipulates people; he cheats when he thinks he can get away with it; he is cruel to other people; and so on.

Dr. Smith is irresponsible. She bases her diagnoses on superficial considerations; she drinks before performing delicate surgery; she refuses to listen to other doctors' advice; and so on.

A certain used-car salesman is unethical. He conceals defects in his cars; he takes advantage of poor people by high-pressuring them into paying exorbitant prices for cars he knows to be defective; he runs false advertisements in any newspaper that will carry them; and so on.

The point is that we can, and often do, back up our ethical judgments with good reasons. Thus it does not seem right to say that they are all unprovable, as though they were nothing more than "mere opinions." If a person has good reasons for his judgments, then he is not *merely* giving "his opinion." On the contrary, he may be making a judgment with which any reasonable person would have to agree.

If we can sometimes give good reasons for our moral judgments, what accounts for the persistent impression that they are "unprovable"? Why is the Provability Argument so persuasive? There are two reasons why the argument appears to be more potent than it actually is.

First, there is a tendency to focus attention only on the most difficult moral issues. The question of abortion, for example, is an enormously complicated and troublesome matter. No one, to my knowledge, has yet produced a perfectly convincing analysis that would show once and for all where the truth lies. If we think of questions like *this,* it is easy to believe that "proof" in ethics is impossible. The same could be said of the sciences. There are many complicated matters that physicists cannot agree on; and if we focused our attention entirely on *them* we might conclude that there is no "proof" in physics. But of course, many simpler matters in physics *can* be proven, and about those all competent physicists agree. Similarly, in ethics there are many matters far simpler than abortion, about which all reasonable people must agree. The examples given above are examples of this type.

Second, it is easy to confuse the following two matters, which are really very different:

1. Proving an opinion to be correct.
2. Persuading someone to accept your proof.

Suppose you are having an argument with someone about some moral issue, and you have perfectly cogent reasons in support of your position, while they have no good reasons on their side—or, if they do have some reasons, you can refute them convincingly. Still, they refuse to accept your logic and continue to insist they are right. This is a common, if frustrating, experience. You may be tempted to conclude that it is impossible to prove you are right. But this would be a mistake. Your proof may be impeccable; the trouble may be that the other person is being bull-headed. (Of course, that is not the *only* possible explanation of what is going on; but it is one possible explanation that cannot be dismissed out of hand.) The same thing can happen in any sort of discussion. You may be arguing about creationism versus evolution, and the other person may be unreasonable. But that does not necessarily mean something is wrong with your arguments. Something may be wrong with him.

The Psychological Argument Now we turn to a third argument that has often been advanced in support of Moral Skepticism. This argument undermines confidence in the objectivity of ethics by making us aware of the nonrational ways in which moral beliefs are formed in the individual. Among psychologists, there is considerable agreement about how this happens; the picture remains remarkably constant, even when we consider radically different psychological theories.

Sigmund Freud (1856–1939) was, of course, the "father of psychoanalysis" and was one of the most influential figures in the history of psychology. Among other things, Freud formulated an account of how we acquire our moral beliefs. Young children, he said, have no conception of right and wrong. However, they *are* capable of experiencing pleasure and pain, and they naturally strive to maximize one and minimize the other. The child therefore adapts its behavior in whatever ways are necessary to increase pleasure and avoid suffering.

Freud emphasized that children are almost totally dependent on their parents; without the parents' constant attention and help the child cannot satisfy its most basic needs (the need for food, for example). Thus retaining the parents' love becomes the most important thing in the child's life; without it, the child cannot survive. For their part, parents have definite ideas about how children should behave. They are ready to reward children when they behave in desired ways and to punish them when they behave in unwanted ways. The rewards and punishments may be very subtle; they may consist of nothing more than smiles, frowns, and harsh words. This is enough because, as Freud notes, the parent's disapproval is the thing the child fears most.

This little drama is played out over and over again as children grow up. As a result, children learn to behave in "accepted" ways. Children also learn how to *talk* about their behavior: they learn to call the approved ways "right" and the disapproved ways "wrong." This is the origin of our moral concepts. "Moral" and "immoral" are simply names for approved and disapproved conduct.

To this, Freud adds one other distinctively "Freudian" idea. He says that there exists within us a psychic mechanism for internalizing the role of the parent. After a while, we no longer need parents to punish us for acting "badly"—we come to punish ourselves, through feelings of guilt. This mechanism he calls the "superego." It is, Freud says, the same thing that is commonly called the conscience. But in reality it is nothing more than the internalized voice of the parent.

Other psychologists tell much the same story. The behaviorists regard psychology as the study of human *behavior,* and have little patience with Freudian speculations. Nevertheless, their fundamental ideas concerning moral development are quite similar. Where Freud speaks of "the pleasure principle" and of parental approval, the behaviorists speak of "positive reinforcements." Children are positively reinforced (rewarded) when they behave in certain ways; and so they tend to repeat those behaviors. They are negatively reinforced (punished) for other actions, which they subsequently tend not to repeat. Thus patterns of behavior are established: some types of conduct come to be accepted, others come to be rejected. A child whose vocabulary has become sufficiently rich learns to speak of the former behavior as right and the latter as wrong. Indeed, the leading theorist of behaviorism, B. F. Skinner, goes so far as to suggest that the word "good" may be *defined* as "positively reinforcing."

All this suggests a certain conclusion. Our values are simply the result of our having been conditioned to behave in a certain way. We may feel that certain actions are good and others are evil, but that is only because we have been trained to have those feelings, starting when we were babies. If we had been trained differently, we would have different values, and we would feel just as strongly about them. The obvious conclusion is that the belief that one's values are anything more than the result of this conditioning is simply naive.

We may, therefore, call this the "Psychological Argument":

(8) We acquire our moral beliefs by a process of psychological conditioning. If we had been conditioned differently, we would have different moral beliefs.

Therefore, our moral beliefs are neither true nor false; there is no such thing as objective truth in ethics.

The Psychological Argument is, without doubt, impressive. And if it is sound, it provides powerful evidence that Moral Skepticism is true. However, it contains a serious flaw. The argument begins with a premise concerning *how we acquire* our moral beliefs, and ends with a conclusion about the *status* of those beliefs. Now, for our purposes at least, we may grant that the premise is true—as far as we know, we do acquire our moral beliefs by a process like the one the psychologists describe. But, even granting the truth of the premise, we may still ask: *does the conclusion follow logically from it?*

Consider this. Virtually every kind of belief is acquired, in the beginning, through a process of rewards and punishments (or, as the behaviorists would say, through a system of positive and negative reinforcements). The facts of American history are certainly learned in this way. A teacher asks a first-grade student "Who was the first president of the United States?" If the student responds "George Washington," the teacher smiles approval. If some other answer is given, the teacher frowns and the student is upset. In this way the student is conditioned to believe that Washington was the first president.

Now suppose the following argument were proposed:

(9) Our beliefs about American history are the result of our having been conditioned to have certain beliefs rather than others.

We may be very confident of our beliefs—we may feel

strongly that George Washington *really was* the first president.

However, if we had been conditioned differently, we would have different beliefs, and we would feel just as confident about *them.* (For example, if our teachers had smiled approval when we answered "Abraham Lincoln," we might now firmly believe that Lincoln was the first president.) Therefore, it is naive to think there are any "objective facts" in American history. There are no facts. No one was "really" the first president.

This argument, of course, is transparently fallacious. But why? It is not because the premises are false. The premises are true: we do acquire many of our early beliefs about American history through a system of positive and negative reinforcements. The argument is fallacious because, *even if the premises are true, the skeptical conclusion does not follow from them.* The question of how we acquire our beliefs is logically independent of, and separate from, the question of whether there are any objective facts to which those beliefs correspond.

But exactly the same thing can be said of the Psychological Argument. The Psychological Argument commits the same mistake—it tries to reach a conclusion about the status of our beliefs ("There is no objective truth in ethics") from a premise about how we acquire those beliefs ("We acquire them through a process of conditioning"). The conclusion simply does not follow.

Now you may feel uneasy about this, because you think learning American history is not comparable to learning about right and wrong. Nevertheless, the logical point is the same in both cases: the conclusion of the argument does not follow from the premises. In fact, the analogy is instructive in other ways as well. Let us take it one step further.

Why do we think that the facts of American history are objectively true? Consider this. A student goes through two stages of development. In the first stage, he learns by rote. He learns to say things like "George Washington was the first president" even though he has no idea *why* we think this is so. He has no conception of historical evidence, no understanding of records or the methods historians use to verify such things. Later, however, he may learn about evidence, records, and historical method. Then he not only believes Washington was the first president; he has *good reasons* for that belief. Thus he can be confident that this belief is not "merely a matter of opinion."

Something very much like this is true of a child's instruction in how to behave. When a child is very young, he will respond to the parent's instructions even though he has no idea *why* the parent gives those instructions. The mother may say "Don't play in the street" and the child may obey, even though he does not understand why playing in the street is undesirable. He may obey simply because he fears a spanking. Later, however, he will become capable of understanding the reason: he will see that if he plays in the street, he may be seriously hurt or even killed.

Again, when the child is very young, the mother may say "Don't kick your brother" and the child may obey because she will be spanked. But later, when the child is older and more mature, the mother may say something very different. She may say "When you kick your brother, it *hurts* him," or "How would you like it if someone went around kicking *you?*" In saying these things, and others like them, the mother is bringing the child to understand the most elementary reasons why little brother should not be abused.

At one stage of development, children learn to behave in certain ways simply because they will be rewarded if they do and punished if they don't. At a later, more mature stage they learn that there are good reasons for behaving in those ways. At which stage is a child learning morality? In one sense, of course, children are learning to behave morally even at the earliest stage: they are learning to do things that it is morally good to do. But in a deeper sense, real moral instruction begins only at the later stage. There is a difference between *being made to do what's right* and *acting as a moral agent.* Only at the later stage do children begin to learn how to reason and act as moral agents. Spanking children just keeps them in line until they are old enough to understand reasons.

This suggests that the Psychological Argument makes another subtle mistake. It represents the process of acquiring moral beliefs as though it were only a matter of being conditioned to behave in certain ways. But morality is more than that. Functioning as a moral agent means making choices based on reasons; it means deliberating, weighing alternatives, and deciding for oneself what is best. It may very well be that we learn all this by being taught by our parents, and rewards and punishments may fit somewhere into the picture even at this level of learning. But it is important, if we are going to speculate about the sources of morality, first to be clear about what morality *is*.

Conclusion

We have examined three of the most important arguments in support of Moral Skepticism, and seen that these arguments are no good. Moral Skepticism might still turn out to be true, but if so, then other and better arguments will have to be found. Provisionally, at least, we have to conclude that Moral Skepticism is not nearly as plausible as we might have thought.

The purpose of this exercise, however, was to illustrate the process of evaluating philosophical arguments. We may summarize what we have learned about evaluating arguments like this:

1. Arguments are offered to provide support for a theory or idea; a philosophical theory may be regarded as acceptable only if there are sound arguments in its favor.
2. An argument is sound only if its premises are true and the conclusion follows logically from them.
   a. A conclusion "follows from" the premises just in case the following is so: *if* the premises were true, then the conclusion would have to be true also. (An alternative way of saying the same thing: a conclusion "follows from" the premises just in case it is impossible for the premises to be true, and the conclusion false, at the same time.)
   b. A conclusion can "follow from" premises even if those premises are in fact false.
   c. A conclusion can be true and yet not follow from a given set of premises.
3. Therefore, in evaluating an argument, we ask two *separate* questions. Are the premises true? And does the conclusion follow from them?
4. It is important to avoid two common mistakes. We should be careful to keep arguments separate and not slide from one to the other, confusing different issues.

And we should not think an argument stronger than it is simply because we happen to agree with its conclusion. Moreover, we should remember that if an argument is unsound, that does not mean the conclusion must be false—it only means that *this* argument does nothing to show it is true.

PART II

The Main Philosophical Theories about the Nature of Morality

3 Cultural Relativism

William Graham Sumner

William Graham Sumner (1840–1910) was one of the founders of modern sociology. A native of New Jersey, he entered Yale in 1859, just before the outbreak of the Civil War, and just as Darwin's *The Origin of Species* was being published in England. Later he became Yale's most popular professor and America's leading defender of Social Darwinism. The study of society, he thought, must be divorced from superstitious assumptions about "right" and "wrong." There are no natural rights; there is only the struggle for survival. "Millionaires," he wrote, "are a product of natural selection."

The following selection, from Sumner's book *Folkways*, is one of the classic defenses of Cultural Relativism. Sumner contends that moral codes grow out of the "folkways" of a culture. And, he argues, there is no standard of right and wrong other than that provided by the cultural standard— thus we can never say that any society's code is morally superior to any other's.

How "true" and "right" are found. If a savage puts his hand too near the fire, he suffers pain and draws it back. He knows nothing of the laws of the radiation of heat, but his instinctive action conforms to that law as if he did know it. If he wants to catch an animal for food, he must study its habits and prepare a device adjusted to those habits. If it fails, he must try again, until his observation is "true" and his device is "right." All the practical and direct element in the folkways seems to be due to common sense, natural reason, intuition, or some other original mental endowment. It seems rational (or rationalistic) and utilitarian. Often

From William Graham Sumner, *Folkways* (New York: Ginn and Company, 1907).

in the mythologies this ultimate rational element was ascribed to the teaching of a god or a culture hero. In modern mythology it is accounted for as "natural."

Although the ways adopted must always be really "true" and "right" in relation to facts, for otherwise they could not answer their purpose, such is not the primitive notion of true and right.

The folkways are "right." Rights. Morals. The folkways are the "right" ways to satisfy all interests, because they are traditional, and exist in fact. They extend over the whole of life. There is a right way to catch game, to win a wife, to make one's self appear, to cure disease, to honor ghosts, to treat comrades or strangers, to behave when a child is born, on the warpath, in council, and so on in all cases which can arise. The ways are defined on the negative side, that is, by taboos. The "right" way is the way which the ancestors used and which has been handed down. The tradition is its own warrant. It is not held subject to verification by experience. The notion of right is in the folkways. It is not outside of them, of independent origin, and brought to them to test them. In the folkways, whatever is, is right. This is because they are traditional, and therefore contain in themselves the authority of the ancestral ghosts. When we come to the folkways we are at the end of our analysis. The notion of right and ought is the same in regard to all the folkways, but the degree of it varies with the importance of the interest at stake. The obligation of conformable and coöperative action is far greater under ghost fear and war than in other matters, and the social sanctions are severer, because group interests are supposed to be at stake. Some usages contain only a slight element of right and ought. It may well be believed that notions of right and duty, and of social welfare, were first developed in connection with ghost fear and other-worldliness, and therefore that, in that field also, folkways were first raised to mores. "Rights" are the rules of mutual give and take in the competition of life which are imposed on comrades in the in-group, in order that the peace may prevail there which is essential to the group strength. Therefore rights can never be "natural" or "God-given," or absolute in any sense. The morality of a group at a time is the sum of the taboos and prescriptions in the folkways by which right conduct is defined. Therefore morals can never be intuitive. They are historical, institutional, and empirical.

World philosophy, life policy, right, rights, and morality are all products of the folkways. They are reflections on, and generalizations from, the experience of pleasure and pain which is won in efforts to carry on the struggle for existence under actual life conditions. The generalizations are very crude and vague in their germinal forms. They are all embodied in folklore, and all our philosophy and science have been developed out of them.

. . . .

Ethnocentrism is the technical name for this view of things in which one's own group is the center of everything, and all others are scaled and rated with reference to it. Folkways correspond to it to cover both the inner and the outer relation. Each group nourishes its own pride and vanity, boasts itself superior, exalts its own divinities, and looks with contempt on outsiders. Each group thinks its own folkways the only right ones, and if it observes that other groups have other folkways, these excite its scorn. Opprobrious epithets are derived from these differences. "Pig-eater," "cow-eater," "uncircumcised," "jabberers," are epithets of contempt and abomination. The Tupis called the Portuguese by a derisive epithet descriptive of birds which have feathers around their feet, on account of trousers. For our present purpose the most important fact is that ethnocentrism leads a people to exaggerate and intensify everything in their own folkways which is peculiar and which differentiates them from others. It therefore strengthens the folkways.

Illustrations of ethnocentrism. The Papuans on New Guinea are broken up into village units which are kept separate by hostility, cannibalism, head hunting, and divergences of language and religion. Each village is integrated by its own language, religion, and interests. A group of villages is sometimes united into a limited unity by connubium. A wife taken inside of this group unit has full status; one taken outside of it has not. The petty group units are peace groups within and are hostile to all outsiders. The Mbayas of South America believed that their deity had bidden them live by making war on others, taking their wives and property, and killing their men.

When Caribs were asked whence they came, they answered, "We alone are people." The meaning of the name Kiowa is "real or principal people." The Lapps call themselves "men," or "human beings." The Greenland Eskimo think that Europeans have been sent to Greenland to learn virtue and good manners from the Greenlanders. Their highest form of praise for a European is that he is, or soon will be, as good as a Greenlander. The Tunguses call themselves "men." As a rule it is found that nature peoples call themselves "men." Others are something else—perhaps not defined—but not real men. In myths the origin of their own tribe is that of the real human race. They do not account for the others. The Ainos derive their name from that of the first man, whom they worship as a god. Evidently the name of the god is derived from the tribe name. When the tribal name has another sense, it is always boastful or proud. The Ovambo name is a corruption of the name of the tribe for themselves, which means "the wealthy." Amongst the most remarkable people in the world for ethnocentrism are the Seri of Lower California. They observe an attitude of suspicion and hostility to all outsiders, and strictly forbid marriage with outsiders.

The Jews divided all mankind into themselves and Gentiles. They were the "chosen people." The Greeks and Romans called all outsiders "barbarians." In Euripides' tragedy of *Iphigenia in Aulis* Iphigenia says that it is fitting that Greeks should rule over barbarians, but not contrariwise, because Greeks are free, and barbarians are slaves. The Arabs regarded themselves as the noblest nation and all others as more or less barbarous. In 1896, the Chinese minister of education and his counselors edited a manual in which this statement occurs: "How grand and glorious is the Empire of China, the middle kingdom! She is the largest and richest in the world. The grandest men in the world have all come from the middle empire." In all the literature of all the states equivalent statements occur, although they are not so naïvely expressed. In Russian books and newspapers the civilizing mission of Russia is talked about, just as, in the books and journals of France, Germany, and the United States, the civilizing mission of those countries is assumed and referred to as well understood. Each state now regards itself as the leader of civilization, the best, the freest, and the wisest, and all others as inferior. Within a few years our own man-on-the-curbstone has learned to class all foreigners of the Latin peoples as "dagos," and "dago" has become an epithet of contempt. These are all cases of ethnocentrism.

. . . .

Definition of the mores. When the elements of truth and right are developed into doctrines of welfare, the folkways are raised to another plane. They then become capable of producing inferences, developing into new forms, and extending their constructive influence over men and society. Then we call them the mores. The mores are the folkways, including the philosophical and ethical generalizations as to societal welfare which are suggested by them, and inherent in them, as they grow.

. . . .

Mores and morals; social code. For every one the mores give the notion of what ought to be. This includes the notion of what ought to be done, for all should coöperate to bring to pass, in the order of life, what ought to be. All notions of propriety, decency, chastity, politeness, order, duty, right, rights, discipline, respect, reverence, coöperation, and fellowship, especially all things in regard to which good and ill depend entirely on the point at which the line is drawn, are in the mores. The mores can make things seem right and good to one group or one age which to another seem antagonistic to every instinct of human nature. The thirteenth century bred in every heart such a sentiment in regard to heretics that inquisitors had no more misgivings in their proceedings than men would have now if they should attempt to exterminate rattlesnakes. The sixteenth century gave to all such notions about witches that witch persecutors thought they were waging war on enemies of God and man. Of course the inquisitors and witch persecutors constantly developed the notions of heretics and witches. They exaggerated the notions and then gave them back again to the mores, in their expanded form, to inflame the hearts of men with terror and hate and to become, in the next stage, so much more fantastic and ferocious motives. Such is the reaction between the mores and the acts of the living generation. The world philosophy of the age is never anything but the reflection on the mental horizon, which is formed out of the mores, of the ruling ideas which are in the mores themselves. It is from a failure to recognize the to and fro in this reaction that the current notion arises that mores are produced by doctrines. The "morals" of an age are never anything but the consonance between what is done and what the mores of the age require. The whole revolves on itself, in the relation of the specific to the general, within the horizon formed by the mores. Every attempt to win an outside standpoint from which to reduce the whole to an absolute philosophy of truth and right, based on an unalterable principle, is a delusion. New elements are brought in only by new conquests of nature through science and art. The new conquests change the conditions of life and the interests of the members of the society. Then the mores change by adaptation to new conditions and interests. The philosophy and ethics then follow to account for and justify the changes in the mores; often, also, to claim that they have caused the changes. They never do anything but draw new lines of bearing between the parts of the mores and the horizon of thought within which they are inclosed, and which is a deduction from the mores. The horizon is widened by more knowledge, but for one age it is just as much a generalization from the mores as for another. It is always unreal. It is only a product of thought. The ethical philosophers select points on this horizon from which to take their bearings, and they think that they have won some authority for their systems when they travel back again from the generalization to the specific custom out of which it was deduced. The cases of the inquisitors and witch persecutors who toiled arduously and continually for their chosen ends, for little or no reward, show us the relation between mores on the one side and philosophy, ethics, and religion on the other.

. . . .

Meaning of "immoral." When, therefore, the ethnographers apply condemnatory or depreciatory adjectives to the people whom they study, they beg the most important question which we want to investigate; that is, What are standards, codes, and ideas of chastity, decency, propriety, modesty, etc., and whence do they arise? The ethnographical facts contain the answer to this question. . . . "Immoral" never means anything but contrary to the mores of the time and place. Therefore the mores and the morality may move together, and there is no permanent or universal standard by which right and truth in regard to these matters can be established and different folkways compared and criticised.

Suggestions for Further Reading

An interesting discussion of William Graham Sumner may be found in Richard Hofstadter, *Social Darwinism in American Thought* (Philadelphia: University of Pennsylvania Press, 1944), ch. 3.

In addition to Sumner, another classic defense of Cultural Relativism by a social scientist is Ruth Benedict, *Patterns of Culture* (New York: Pelican, 1946).

Kai Nielsen's essay "Ethical Relativism and the Facts of Cultural Relativity," *Social Research* 33 (1966): 531–551, is an excellent philosophical discussion of the significance, or lack of it, of anthropological data.

John Ladd, ed., *Ethical Relativism* (Belmont, Calif.: Wadsworth, 1973) is a good collection of articles on Cultural Relativism.

Jack W. Meiland and Michael Krausz, eds., *Relativism: Cognitive and Moral* (Notre Dame, Ind.: University of Notre Dame Press, 1982) is another useful anthology.

Also see James Rachels, *The Elements of Moral Philosophy* (New York: Random House, 1986), ch. 2.

4 Morality As Based on Sentiment

David Hume

The most influential advocate of Ethical Subjectivism was David Hume, the great Scottish philosopher of the eighteenth century. Born in Edinburgh in 1711, Hume was a precocious youth. He wrote his greatest work, *A Treatise of Human Nature*, before he was 24 years old, and went on to write many other important books on history, philosophy, religion, and politics. He held a variety of jobs, including librarian at Edinburgh University and first secretary of the British Embassy in Paris, where he was a favorite of the French intellectuals. But when he applied for the post of professor of moral philosophy at Edinburgh, influential clergymen saw to it that his application was rejected.

The clergymen were scandalized by Hume's ethical views. One of them, the bishop of Gloucester, wrote to Hume's publisher to complain about another of his books, the *Enquiry Concerning the Principle of Morals:* "You have often told me of this man's moral virtues," the bishop wrote. "He may have many, for aught I know; but let me observe to you, there are vices of the mind as well as of the body: and I think a wickeder mind, and more obstinately bent on public mischief, I never knew."

Apparently the bishop believed that Ethical Subjectivism leads to a breakdown in public morals. This is a common complaint—it is argued that without objective standards of right and wrong, then "anything goes" and all manner of mischief is permitted. But, as Hume knew, this does not follow. Ethical Subjectivism is a theory about the *nature* of morality—it says that a person's moral judgments are an expression of his feelings—and it implies nothing at all about what moral beliefs should be accepted or rejected. Hume believed that our conduct should be directed by a general sentiment of beneficence toward all mankind, and so he favored an enlightened morality of universal altruism. But he did not think this could be a matter of reason. Instead, the possibility of such a morality depends on whether, in fact, human beings have beneficent sentiments.

Those who affirm that virtue is nothing but a conformity to reason; that there are eternal fitnesses and unfitnesses of things, which are the same to every rational being that considers them; that the immutable measures of right and wrong impose an obligation, not only on human creatures, but also on the Deity himself: All these systems concur in the opinion, that morality, like truth, is discern'd merely by ideas, and by their juxta-position and comparison. In order, therefore, to judge of these systems, we need only consider, whether it be possible, from reason alone, to distinguish betwixt moral good and evil, or whether there must concur some other principles to enable us to make that distinction.

If morality had naturally no influence on human passions and actions, 'twere in vain to take such pains to inculcate it; and nothing wou'd be more fruitless than that multitude of rules and precepts, with which all moralists abound. Philosophy is commonly divided into *speculative* and *practical;* and as morality is always comprehended under the latter division, 'tis supposed to influence our passions and actions, and to go beyond the calm and indolent judgments of the

---

From David Hume, *A Treatise of Human Nature* (1740), Book III, Part I, Section 1; and *An Inquiry Concerning the Principles of Morals* (1751), Appendix I.

understanding. And this is confirm'd by common experience, which informs us, that men are often govern'd by their duties, and are deter'd from some actions by the opinion of injustice, and impell'd to others by that of obligation.

Since morals, therefore, have an influence on the actions and affections, it follows, that they cannot be deriv'd from reason; and that because reason alone, as we have already prov'd, can never have any such influence. Morals excite passions, and produce or prevent actions. Reason of itself is utterly impotent in this particular. The rules of morality, therefore, are not conclusions of our reason.

. . . Take any action allow'd to be vicious: Wilful murder, for instance. Examine it in all lights, and see if you can find that matter of fact, or real existence, which you call *vice*. In whichever way you take it, you find only certain passions, motives, volitions and thoughts. There is no other matter of fact in the case. The vice entirely escapes you, as long as you consider the object. You never can find it, till you turn your reflexion into your own breast, and find a sentiment of disapprobation, which arises in you, towards this action. Here is a matter of fact; but 'tis the object of feeling, not of reason. It lies in yourself, not in the object. So that when you pronounce any action or character to be vicious, you mean nothing, but that from the constitution of your nature you have a feeling or sentiment of blame from the contemplation of it.

. . . I cannot forbear adding to these reasonings an observation, which may, perhaps, be found of some importance. In every system of morality, which I have hitherto met with, I have always remark'd, that the author proceeds for some time in the ordinary way of reasoning, and establishes the being of a God, or makes observations concerning human affairs; when of a sudden I am surpriz'd to find, that instead of the usual copulations of propositions, *is,* and *is not,* I meet with no proposition that is not connected with an *ought,* or an *ought not.* This change is imperceptible; but is, however, of the last consequence. For as this *ought,* or *ought not,* expresses some new relation or affirmation, 'tis necessary that it shou'd be observ'd and explain'd; and at the same time that a reason should be given, for what seems altogether inconceivable, how this new relation can be a deduction from others, which are entirely different from it. But as authors do not commonly use this precaution, I shall presume to recommend it to the readers; and am persuaded, that this small attention wou'd subvert all the vulgar systems of morality, and let us see, that the distinction of vice and virtue is not founded merely on the relations of objects, nor is perceiv'd by reason.

. . . .

Examine the crime of *ingratitude,* for instance, which has place wherever we observe good-will expressed and known, together with good-offices performed, on the one side, and a return of ill-will or indifference with ill-offices or neglect on the other: anatomize all these circumstances and examine, by your reason alone, in what consists the demerit or blame. You never will come to any issue or conclusion.

Reason judges either of *matter of fact* or of *relations.* Enquire then, *first,* where is that matter of fact which we here call *crime;* point it out, determine the time of its existence, describe its essence or nature, explain the sense or faculty to which it discovers itself. It resides in the mind of the person who is ungrateful. He must, therefore, feel it and be conscious of it. But nothing is there, except the passion of ill-will or absolute indifference. You cannot say that these, of themselves, always and in all circumstances are crimes. No, they are only crimes when directed towards persons who have before expressed and displayed good-will towards us. Consequently, we may infer that the crime of ingratitude is not any particular individual *fact,* but arises from a complication of circumstances which, being presented to the spectator, excites the *sentiment* of blame by the particular structure and fabric of his mind.

This representation, you say, is false. Crime, indeed, consists not in a particular *fact,* of whose reality we are assured by *reason,* but it consists in certain *moral relations,* discovered by reason, in the same manner as we discover by reason the truths of geometry or algebra. But what are the relations, I ask, of which you here talk? In the case stated above, I see first good-will and good-offices in one person, then ill-will and ill-offices in the other. Between these, there is a relation of *contrariety.* Does the crime consist in that relation? But suppose a person bore me ill-will or did me ill-offices, and I, in return, were indifferent towards him, or did him good offices. Here is the same relation of *contrariety,* and yet my conduct is often highly laudable. Twist and turn this matter as much as you will, you can never rest the morality on relation, but must have recourse to the decisions of sentiment.

When it is affirmed that two and three are equal to the half of ten, this relation of equality I understand perfectly. I conceive that, if ten be divided into two parts, of which one has as many units as the other, and if any of these parts be compared to two added to three, it will contain as many units as that compound number. But when you draw thence a comparison to moral relations, I own that I am altogether at a loss to understand you. A moral action, a crime, such as ingratitude, is a complicated object. Does the morality consist in the relation of its parts to each other? How? After what manner? Specify the relation: be more particular and explicit in your propositions, and you will easily see their falsehood.

No, say you, the morality consists in the relation of actions to the rule of right; and they are denominated good or ill, according as they agree or disagree with it. What then is this rule of right? In what does it consist? How is it determined? By reason, you say, which examines the moral relations of actions. So that moral relations are determined by the comparison of action to a rule. And that rule is determined by considering the moral relations of objects. Is not this fine reasoning?

All this is metaphysics, you cry. That is enough; there needs nothing more to give a strong presumption of falsehood. Yes, reply I, here are metaphysics surely; but they are all on your side, who advance an abstruse hypothesis which can never be made intelligible, nor quadrate with any particular instance or illustration. The hypothesis which we embrace is plain. It maintains that morality is determined by sentiment. It defines virtue to be *whatever mental action or quality gives to a spectator the pleasing sentiment of approbation;* and vice the contrary. We then proceed to examine a plain matter of fact, to wit, what actions have this influence. We consider all the circumstances in which these actions agree, and thence endeavour to extract some general observations with regard to these sentiments. If you call this metaphysics and find anything abstruse here, you need only conclude that your turn of mind is not suited to the moral sciences.

Suggestions for Further Reading

A great deal has been written about Hume's ethical theory. J. L. Mackie, *Hume's Moral Theory* (London: Routledge and Kegan Paul, 1980), is a good book, as is Rachel Kydd, *Reason and Conduct in Hume's Treatise* (New York: Russell and Russell, 1964).

In Chapter III of his little book *Ethics* (London: Oxford University Press, 1912), G. E. Moore gives the classic critique of Simple Subjectivism. C. L. Stevenson discusses Moore's arguments in "Moore's Arguments Against Certain Forms of Ethical Naturalism," which is included in a volume of Stevenson's collected essays, *Facts and Values* (New Haven: Yale University Press, 1963).

Stevenson is the chief exponent of a subtler form of subjectivist ethical theory known as Emotivism. His primary defense of Emotivism is found in his great work *Ethics and Language* (New Haven: Yale University Press, 1944). The beginner, however, should start with Stevenson's essays in *Facts and Values,* which are much easier to read.

The literature on Emotivism is immense; one accessible critical work is J. O. Urmson, *The Emotive Theory of Ethics* (London: Hutchinson, 1968). Chapter III of G. J. Warnock's *Contemporary Moral Philosophy* (London: Macmillan, 1967) is also recommended.

Also see James Rachels, *The Elements of Moral Philosophy* (New York: Random House, 1986), ch. 3.

5 *The Divine Imperative*

Emil Brunner

Emil Brunner (1889–1966) was one of the most influential Protestant theologians of the twentieth century. Brunner was professor of theology at the University of Zurich, in Switzerland, from 1924 until his retirement in 1953. *The Divine Imperative* (1932), from which the following selection is taken, is one of his many works on theological ethics. Brunner argues that the essence of morality is to follow the will of God. At the same time, he rejects the idea that God's will is revealed in absolute rules. The Christian, he says, must obey God's *specific* commands for each distinctive situation.

The Christian conception of the Good differs from every other conception of the Good at this very point: that it cannot be defined in terms of principle at all.

Whatever can be defined in accordance with a principle—whether it be the principle of pleasure or the principle of duty—is legalistic. This means that it is possible—by the use of this principle—to pre-determine "the right" down to the smallest detail of conduct. . . . This legalistic spirit corrupts the true conception of the Good from its very roots. The Christian moralist and the extreme individualist are at one in their emphatic rejection of legalistic conduct; they join hands, as it were, in face of the whole host of legalistic moralists; they are convinced that conduct which is regulated by abstract principles can never be good. But equally sternly the Christian moralist rejects the individualistic doctrine of freedom, according to which there is no longer any difference between "right" and "wrong." Rather, in the Christian view, that alone is "good" which is free from all caprice, which takes place in unconditional obedience. There is no Good save obedient behaviour, save the obedient will. But this obedience is rendered not to a law or a principle which can be known beforehand, but only to the free, sovereign will of God. The Good consists in always doing what God wills at any particular moment.

This statement makes it clear that for us the will of God cannot be summed up under any principle, that it is not at our disposal, but that so far as we are concerned the will of God is absolutely free. The Christian is therefore "a free lord over all things," because he stands directly under the personal orders of the free Sovereign God. This is why genuine "Christian conduct"—if we may use this idea as an illustration—is so unaccountable, so unwelcome to the moral rigorist and to the hedonist alike. The moral rigorist regards the Christian as a hedonist, and the hedonist regards him as a rigorist. In reality, the Christian is neither, yet he is also something of both, since he is indeed absolutely *bound* and obedient, but, since he is bound to the *free* loving will of God, he is himself free from all transparent bondage to principles or to legalism. Above all it is important to recognize that even love is not a principle of this kind,

Reprinted from *The Divine Imperative,* by Emil Brunner; translated by Olive Wyon. Copyright © MCMXLVII, by W. L. Jenkins. Used by permission of The Westminster Press, Philadelphia, PA.

neither the love which God Himself *has,* nor the love which He *requires.* Only God Himself defines love in His action. We, for our part, do not know what God is, nor do we know what *love* is, unless we learn to know God in His action, in faith. To be in this His Love, is the commandment. Every attempt to conceive love as a principle leads to this result: it becomes distorted, either in the rigoristic, legalistic sense, or in the hedonistic sense. Man only knows what the love of God is when he sees the way in which God acts, and he only knows how he himself ought to love by allowing himself to be drawn by faith into this activity of God. . . .

But this does not mean that the Christian ethic makes no claim to universal validity. Whatever God demands *can* only be universal, that is, valid for all men, even if those who do not hear this demand do not admit this validity and indeed do not even understand the claim to universal validity. The believer alone clearly perceives that the Good, as it is recognized in faith, is the sole Good, and that all that is otherwise called good cannot lay claim to this title, at least not in the ultimate sense of the word. It is precisely faith and faith alone which knows this: that alone is good which God does; and, indeed, faith really consists in the fact that man knows this—and that he knows it in such a way as it alone can be known, namely, in the recognition of faith. But once man does know this he also knows the unlimited unconditional validity of this conception and of the divine demand. . . .

But what is the function of a system of ethics in regard to the central ethical question: What ought we to do? Can ethics tell us what we are to do? If it could, it would mean that the Christian ethic also is an ethical system based on law and on abstract principles. For where ethics is regarded purely as a science, there general, and to some extent timeless, propositions are stated. If these were to define what we ought to do, then the Good would be defined in legalistic terms. Therefore no such claim can be made either by or for ethics. The service it renders cannot be that of relieving us of the necessity for making moral decisions, but that it prepares the way for such decisions. How this takes place can only be made clear in the explication of the part which is played by law within a morality which is not legalistic. The significance of the law is the same as the significance of ethics, namely: that it prepares the way for a voluntary decision, or for the hearing of the divine command.

. . . *The Good consists simply and solely in the fact* that man receives and deliberately accepts his life as a gift from God, as life dependent on "grace," as the state of "being justified" because it has been granted as a gift, as "justification by faith." Only thus can we know the Will of God, that is, in this revelation of Himself in which He manifests Himself as disinterested, generous Love.

But this Divine giving is not accomplished in any magical way; it simply takes place in the fact that God *"apprehends" man;* God *claims* us for His love, for His generous giving. But this means that He claims our whole existence for Himself, for this love of His; He gives us His love. He gives us His love in such a way that He captures us completely by the power of His love. *To belong* to Him, to this love, and through His love, means that we are the *bondslaves* of this will. To believe means to become a captive, to become His property, or rather, to know that we are His property. The revelation which makes it plain that the will of God is lavish in giving *to* man, makes it equally clear that His will makes a demand *on* man. His will *for* us also means that He wants something *from* us. He claims us for His love. This is His Command. It is the *"new* commandment," because only now can man perceive that it is the command of One who gives before He demands, and who only demands something from us in the act of giving Himself to us. . . .

He claims us for *His* love, not for an *idea* of love—and not for a conception of the divine love which can be gained from merely reading the Bible. He claims us for His present, living activity of love, which can only be, and must always remain, His work. Therefore we can never know beforehand what God will require. God's command can only be perceived at the actual moment of hearing it. It would denote a breaking away from obedience if we were to think of the Divine Command as one which had been enacted once for all, to be interpreted by us in particular instances. To take this line would mean reverting to the legalistic distortion of His love. Love would then have become a "principle." The *free* love of God requires us to remain *free,* that we may be freely at His disposal. *You* cannot say what it means to love here and now; *He* alone can tell you what this means for you at this moment.

The Good is simply what *God* wills that we should do, not that which we would do on the basis of a principle of love. God wills to do something quite definite and particular through us, here and now, something which no other person could do at any other time. Just as the commandment of love is absolutely universal so also it is absolutely individual. But just as it is absolutely individual so also it is absolutely devoid of all caprice. "I will guide thee with Mine eye." No one can experience this "moment" save I myself. The Divine Command is made known to us "in the secret place." Therefore it is impossible for us to know it beforehand: to wish to know it beforehand—legalism—is an infringement of the divine honour. The fact that the holiness of God must be remembered when we dwell on His love means that we cannot have His love at our disposal, that it cannot ever be perceived as a universal principle, but only in the act in which He speaks to us Himself; even in His love He remains our *Master* and Lord. But He is our "Lord" in the sense that He tells us Himself what it means to "love," here and now. . . .

It is *His* will that God wills to accomplish in the world: He is not the servant of some purpose outside Himself. God Himself is His own End. In His love, however. He sets up an End outside Himself—without ceasing to be His own End; this "end" is the communion of the creature with Himself, the Creator. This Divine will for "community" is God's Sovereign Will. Therefore salvation, beatitude, the fulfilment of the purpose of life, both for humanity as a whole, and for the individual, is included in God's royal purpose. The tables of prohibition in the Bible may be compared with the notices on power circuits: Do Not Touch! Because God wills to control our life, He commands and He forbids. This is the "eudaemonism" of the Gospel, and at the same time its absolutely serious view of duty. God wills our true happiness; but *He* wills it, and He wills it in such a way that no one else knows what His will is. It remains outside our disposal, and indeed we do not know it. We never know what is right for us, nor what is best for the other person. We go astray when we think that we can deduce this from some principle or another, or from some experience, and we distort the thought of the divine love if we think that we know what He ought to do for us in accordance with His love. But of one thing we may be quite sure: His will is love, even when we do not understand it—when He commands as well as when He gives.

Therefore in His revelation God's will is expressed by His sanctions, by rewards and punishments. God alone gives life; to be with Him is life, to resist Him is ruin. It is impossible to exist apart from God; it is impossible to be neutral towards Him. He who is not for Him is against Him. God's Command means eternal life and

God means nothing else than this. He is Love. But His will is utterly serious; it is the will of the Lord of Life and Death. Anyone who—finally—resists Him, will only dash himself to pieces against the rock of His Being. This is the holiness of the love of God. As the divine love cannot be separated from His gift of life, so the Holiness of God cannot be separated from His judicial wrath, the denial and destruction of life. To have a share in the will of God, in the sense of union with His will, means salvation; to resist Him spells utter disaster.

Suggestions for Further Reading

Two anthologies contain a wealth of material on this subject: Gene Outka and John P. Reeder, Jr., eds., *Religion and Morality* (Garden City, N.Y.: Anchor, 1973); and Paul Helm, ed., *Divine Commands and Morality* (Oxford: Oxford University Press, 1981). Both contain articles that defend the Divine Command Theory, such as Robert Merrihew Adams's "A Modified Divine Command Theory of Ethical Wrongness," as well as critical papers. For a critical assessment, Kai Nielsen's *Ethics Without God* (London: Pemberton, 1973) is recommended.

An excellent, sympathetic discussion of the theory is Norman Kretzmann, "Abraham, Isaac, and Euthyphro" in *Hamartia,* edited by Donald Stump (Lewiston, N.Y.: Edwin Mellen Press, 1983), pp. 27–49.

Also see James Rachels, *The Elements of Moral Philosophy* (New York: Random House, 1986), ch. 4.

6 Ethics and Natural Law

Saint Thomas Aquinas

Saint Thomas Aquinas (1225–1274) is commonly regarded as the greatest of all the Christian thinkers (after, perhaps, Saint Paul). Thomas was born in Roccasecca, Italy, the son

of a count. At 19, after having attended the University of
Naples, he decided to join the Dominicans, then a new order.
This so displeased his family that they forcibly restrained him
for a year—in effect, holding him prisoner—but finally, unable to break his determination, they had to let him go. After
further studies, he became a professor of theology, first in
Rome and then in Paris. He was a prolific writer; it is said
that, in order to get his words down on paper more rapidly,
he would dictate to three or four secretaries at once.

Aquinas holds a special place among Christian theologians. He was declared a saint in 1323, 49 years after his
death. In 1567 he was named a Doctor of the Church, making
him one of five preeminent figures (along with Augustine,
Ambrose, Jerome, and Gregory). But in the respect accorded
his teachings, he clearly outranks all the others. In 1879 Pope
Leo XIII officially recognized Aquinas's preeminence among
church thinkers.

The key to understanding morality, according to Aquinas, is to understand that God has created the world according to a rational plan. Moreover, he created man as a rational
being in his own image, so that man has the capacity to
understand that plan. Thus human beings have the capacity
to discern the rational order of the world. Furthermore, it is
part of the rational order that "natural laws" determine the
moral structure of the world, just as natural laws determine
its physical structure. Man can discover these moral laws
through the use of his reason. Acting morally is, therefore,
acting in accordance with the natural law.

Question 91

Second Article: Whether there is in us a natural law?

. . . The *Gloss* on *Rom.* 2:14 (*When the Gentiles, who have not the law,
do by nature those things that are of the law*) comments as follows:
*Although they have no written law, yet they have the natural law, whereby each
one knows, and is conscious of, what is good and what is evil.* . . . Law, being

---

From Saint Thomas Aquinas, *Summa Theologica,* First Part of the Second Part. *Basic
Writings of St. Thomas Aquinas,* edited by Anton C. Pegis, vol. II (New York: Random
House, 1945). Reprinted by permission of the Estate of Anton C. Pegis.

a rule and measure, can be in a person in two ways: in one way, as in him that rules and measures; in another way, as in that which is ruled and measured, since a thing is ruled and measured in so far as it partakes of the rule or measure. Therefore, since all things subject to divine providence are ruled and measured by the eternal law ... it is evident that all things partake in some way in the eternal law, in so far as, namely, from its being imprinted on them, they derive their respective inclinations to their proper acts and ends. Now among all others, the rational creature is subject to divine providence in a more excellent way, in so far as it itself partakes of a share of providence, by being provident both for itself and for others. Therefore it has a share of the eternal reason, whereby it has a natural inclination to its proper act and end; and this participation of the eternal law in the rational creature is called the natural law. Hence the Psalmist, after saying (*Ps.* 4:6): *Offer up the sacrifice of justice*, as though someone asked what the works of justice are, adds: *Many say, Who showeth us good things?* in answer to which question he says: *The light of Thy countenance, O Lord, is signed upon us.* He thus implies that the light of natural reason, whereby we discern what is good and what is evil, which is the function of the natural law, is nothing else than an imprint on us of the divine light. It is therefore evident that the natural law is nothing else than the rational creature's participation of the eternal law.

Third Article: Whether there is a human law?
... Augustine distinguishes two kinds of law, the one eternal, the other temporal, which he calls human. ... As we have stated above, a law is a dictate of the practical reason. ... Accordingly, we conclude that, just as in the speculative reason, from naturally known indemonstrable principles we draw the conclusions of the various sciences, the knowledge of which is not imparted to us by nature, but acquired by the efforts of reason, so too it is that from the precepts of the natural law, as from common and indemonstrable principles, the human reason needs to proceed to the more particular determination of certain matters. These particular determinations, devised by human reason, are called human laws, provided that the other essential conditions of law be observed. ... Therefore Tully says in his *Rhetoric* that *justice has its source in nature; thence certain things came into custom by reason of their utility; afterwards these things which emanated from nature, and were approved by custom, were sanctioned by fear*

and reverence for the law. . . . Just as on the part of the speculative reason, by a natural participation of divine wisdom, there is in us the knowledge of certain common principles, but not a proper knowledge of each single truth, such as that contained in the divine wisdom, so, too, on the part of the practical reason, man has a natural participation of the eternal law, according to certain common principles, but not as regards the particular determinations of individual cases, which are, however, contained in the eternal law. Hence the need for human reason to proceed further to sanction them by law.

Fourth Article: Whether there was any need for a divine law?
. . . Besides the natural and the human law it was necessary for the directing of human conduct to have a divine law. And this for four reasons. First, because it is by law that man is directed how to perform his proper acts in view of his last end. Now if man were ordained to no other end than that which is proportionate to his natural ability, there would be no need for man to have any further direction, on the part of his reason, in addition to the natural law and humanly devised law which is derived from it. But since man is ordained to an end of eternal happiness which exceeds man's natural ability, . . . therefore it was necessary that, in addition to the natural and the human law, man should be directed to his end by a law given by God.

Secondly, because, by reason of the uncertainty of human judgment, especially on contingent and particular matters, different people form different judgments on human acts; whence also different and contrary laws result. In order, therefore, that man may know without any doubt what he ought to do and what he ought to avoid, it was necessary for man to be directed in his proper acts by a law given by God, for it is certain that such a law cannot err.

Thirdly, because man can make laws in those matters of which he is competent to judge. But man is not competent to judge of interior movements, that are hidden, but only of exterior acts which are observable; and yet for the perfection of virtue it is necessary for man to conduct himself rightly in both kinds of acts. Consequently, human law could not sufficiently curb and direct interior acts, and it was necessary for this purpose that a divine law should supervene.

Fourthly, because, as Augustine says, human law cannot punish or forbid all evil deeds, since, while aiming at doing away with all evils, it would do away with many good things, and would hinder the advance of the common good, which is necessary for human living. In order, therefore, that no evil might remain unforbidden and unpunished, it was necessary for the divine law to supervene, whereby all sins are forbidden.

. . . .

Question 94

Third Article: Whether all the acts of the virtues are prescribed by the natural law?

... We may speak of virtuous acts in two ways: first, in so far as they are virtuous; secondly, as such and such acts considered in their proper species. If, then, we are speaking of the acts of the virtues in so far as they are virtuous, thus all virtuous acts belong to the natural law. For it has been stated that to the natural law belongs everything to which a man is inclined according to his nature. Now each thing is inclined naturally to an operation that is suitable to it according to its form: e.g., fire is inclined to give heat. Therefore, since the rational soul is the proper form of man, there is in every man a natural inclination to act according to reason; and this is to act according to virtue. Consequently, considered thus, all the acts of the virtues are prescribed by the natural law, since each one's reason naturally dictates to him to act virtuously. But if we speak of virtuous acts, considered in themselves, i.e., in their proper species, thus not all virtuous acts are prescribed by the natural law. For many things are done virtuously, to which nature does not primarily incline, but which, through the inquiry of reason, have been found by men to be conducive to well-living. . . .

Temperance is about the natural concupiscences of food, drink and sexual matters, which are indeed ordained to the common good of nature, just as other matters of law are ordained to the moral common good. . . .

By human nature we may mean either that which is proper to man, and in this sense all sins, as being against reason, are also against nature, as Damascene states; or we may mean that nature which is common to man and other animals, and in this sense, certain special sins are said to be against nature: e.g., contrary to sexual intercourse, which is natural to all animals, is unisexual lust, which has received the special name of the unnatural crime. . . .

Fourth Article: Whether the natural law is the same in all men?
. . . As we have stated above, to the natural law belong those things
to which a man is inclined naturally; and among these it is proper
to man to be inclined to act according to reason. Now it belongs to
the reason to proceed from what is common to what is proper, as
is stated in *Physics* i. The speculative reason, however, is differently
situated, in this matter, from the practical reason. For, since the
speculative reason is concerned chiefly with necessary things, which
cannot be otherwise than they are, its proper conclusions, like the
universal principles, contain the truth without fail. The practical
reason, on the other hand, is concerned with contingent matters,
which is the domain of human actions: and, consequently, although
there is necessity in the common principles, the more we descend
towards the particular, the more frequently we encounter defects.
Accordingly, then, in speculative matters truth is the same in all
men, both as to principles and as to conclusions; although the truth
is not known to all as regards the conclusions, but only as regards
the principles which are called *common notions.* But in matters of
action, truth or practical rectitude is not the same for all as to what
is particular, but only as to the common principles; and where there
is the same rectitude in relation to particulars, it is not equally
known to all.

It is therefore evident that, as regards the common principles
whether of speculative or of practical reason, truth or rectitude is
the same for all, and is equally known by all. But as to the proper
conclusions of the speculative reason, the truth is the same for all,
but it is not equally known to all. It is true for all that the three angles
of a triangle are together equal to two right angles, although it is
not known to all. But as to the proper conclusions of the practical
reason, neither is the truth or rectitude the same for all, nor, where
it is the same, is it equally known by all. Thus, it is right and true
for all to act according to reason, and from this principle it follows,
as a proper conclusion, that goods entrusted to another should be
restored to their owner. Now this is true for the majority of cases.
But it may happen in a particular case that it would be injurious, and
therefore unreasonable, to restore goods held in trust; for instance,
if they are claimed for the purpose of fighting against one's country.
And this principle will be found to fail the more, according as we
descend further towards the particular, *e.g.,* if one were to say that
goods held in trust should be restored with such and such a guaran-

tee, or in such and such a way; because the greater the number of conditions added, the greater the number of ways in which the principle may fail, so that it be not right to restore or not to restore.

Consequently, we must say that the natural law, as to the first common principles, is the same for all, both as to rectitude and as to knowledge. But as to certain more particular aspects, which are conclusions, as it were, of those common principles, it is the same for all in the majority of cases, both as to rectitude and as to knowledge; and yet in some few cases it may fail, both as to rectitude, by reason of certain obstacles (just as natures subject to generation and corruption fail in some few cases because of some obstacle), and as to knowledge, since in some the reason is perverted by passion, or evil habit, or an evil disposition of nature. Thus at one time theft, although it is expressly contrary to the natural law, was not considered wrong among the Germans, as Julius Caesar relates.

Suggestions for Further Reading

D. J. O'Connor, *Aquinas and Natural Law* (London: Macmillan, 1968) is a good introductory treatment of the Theory of Natural Law.

A robust modern defense of Natural Law Theory may be found in John Finnis, *Natural Law and Natural Rights* (Oxford: Oxford University Press, 1980).

Also see James Rachels, *The Elements of Moral Philosophy* (New York: Random House, 1986), ch. 4.

7 The Virtue of Selfishness

Ayn Rand

Ayn Rand (1905–1982) was the best-known contemporary advocate of Ethical Egoism. Born Alice Rosenbaum in St.

Petersburg, Russia, she came to the United States a few years after the Bolshevik Revolution. She brought with her a Remington Rand typewriter, from which she took her new name. Lacking academic credentials, she nevertheless set out to become a philosopher, and by the 1960s she had succeeded in attracting a large band of followers. Rand was a passionate thinker who eschewed passions, holding that people should be guided by strictly rational principles. And reason, in her view, demands an ethic of "selfishness." She argued that altruism—the belief that one ought to be willing to sacrifice one's own interests to serve others—is a malignant idea that is responsible for much of the spiritual decay of the modern world. Her views were expounded in best-selling novels such as *The Fountainhead* (1942) and *Atlas Shrugged* (1957). The following selection is taken from a collection of her essays.

The title of this book may evoke the kind of question that I hear once in a while: "Why do you use the word 'selfishness' to denote virtuous qualities of character, when that word antagonizes so many people to whom it does not mean the things you mean?"

To those who ask it, my answer is: "For the reason that makes you afraid of it."

But there are others, who would not ask that question, sensing the moral cowardice it implies, yet who are unable to formulate my actual reason or to identify the profound moral issue involved. It is to them that I will give a more explicit answer.

It is not a mere semantic issue nor a matter of arbitrary choice. The meaning ascribed in popular usage to the word "selfishness" is not merely wrong: it represents a devastating intellectual "package-deal," which is responsible, more than any other single factor, for the arrested moral development of mankind.

In popular usage, the word "selfishness" is a synonym of evil; the image it conjures is of a murderous brute who tramples over piles of corpses to achieve his own ends, who cares for no living being and pursues nothing but the gratification of the mindless whims of any immediate moment.

Yet the exact meaning and dictionary definition of the word "selfishness" is: *concern with one's own interests.*

This concept does *not* include a moral evaluation; it does not tell us whether concern with one's own interests is good or evil; nor does it tell us what constitutes man's actual interests. It is the task of ethics to answer such questions.

The ethics of altruism has created the image of the brute, as its answer, in order to make men accept two inhuman tenets: (a) that any concern with one's own interests is evil, regardless of what these interests might be, and (b) that the brute's activities are *in fact* to one's own interest (which altruism enjoins man to renounce for the sake of his neighbors). . . .

There are two moral questions which altruism lumps together into one "package-deal": (1) What are values? (2) Who should be the beneficiary of values? Altruism substitutes the second for the first; it evades the task of defining a code of moral values, thus leaving man, in fact, without moral guidance.

Altruism declares that any action taken for the benefit of others is good, and any action taken for one's own benefit is evil. Thus the *beneficiary* of an action is the only criterion of moral value—and so long as that beneficiary is anybody other than oneself, anything goes.

Hence the appalling immorality, the chronic injustice, the grotesque double standards, the insoluble conflicts and contradictions that have characterized human relationships and human societies throughout history, under all the variants of the altruist ethics.

Observe the indecency of what passes for moral judgments today. An industrialist who produces a fortune, and a gangster who robs a bank are regarded as equally immoral, since they both sought wealth for their own "selfish" benefit. A young man who gives up his career in order to support his parents and never rises beyond the rank of grocery clerk is regarded as morally superior to the young man who endures an excruciating struggle and achieves his personal ambition. A dictator is regarded as moral, since the unspeakable atrocities he committed were intended to benefit "the people," not himself.

Observe what this beneficiary-criterion of morality does to a man's life. The first thing he learns is that morality is his enemy: he has nothing to gain from it, he can only lose; self-inflicted loss, self-inflicted pain and the gray, debilitating pall of an incomprehensible duty is all that he can expect. He may hope that others might occasionally sacrifice themselves for his benefit, as he grudgingly sacrifices himself for theirs, but he knows that the relationship will bring mutual resentment, not pleasure—and that, morally, their pursuit of values will be like an exchange of unwanted, unchosen Christmas presents, which neither is morally permitted to buy for himself. Apart from such times as he manages to perform some act of self-sacrifice, he possesses no moral significance: morality takes no cognizance of him and has nothing to say to him for guidance in the crucial issues of his life; it is only his own personal, private, "selfish" life and, as such, it is regarded either as evil or, at best, *amoral*.

Since nature does not provide man with an automatic form of survival, since he has to support his life by his own effort, the doctrine that concern with one's own interests is evil means that man's desire to live is evil—that man's life, as such, is evil. No doctrine could be more evil than that.

Yet that is the meaning of altruism, implicit in such examples as the equation of an industrialist with a robber. There is a fundamental moral difference between a man who sees his self-interest in production and a man who sees it in robbery. The evil of a robber does *not* lie in the fact that he pursues his own interests, but in *what* he regards as to his own interest; *not* in the fact that he pursues his values, but in *what* he chose to value; *not* in the fact that he wants to live, but in the fact that he wants to live on a subhuman level.

If it is true that what I mean by "selfishness" is not what is meant conventionally, then *this* is one of the worst indictments of altruism: it means that altruism *permits no concept* of a self-respecting, self-supporting man—a man who supports his life by his own effort and neither sacrifices himself nor others. It means that altruism permits no view of men except as sacrificial animals and profiteers-on-sacrifice, as victims and parasites—that it permits no concept of a benevolent coexistence among men—that it permits no concept of *justice*.

If you wonder about the reasons behind the ugly mixture of cynicism and guilt in which most men spend their lives, these are the reasons: cynicism, because they neither practice nor accept the altruist morality—guilt, because they dare not reject it.

To rebel against so devastating an evil, one has to rebel against its basic premise. To redeem both man and morality, it is the concept of *"selfishness"* that one has to redeem.

The first step is to assert *man's right to a moral existence*—that is: to recognize his need of a moral code to guide the course and the fulfillment of his own life.

. . . The reasons why man needs a moral code will tell you that the purpose of morality is to define man's proper values and interests, that *concern with his own interests* is the essence of a moral existence, and that *man must be the beneficiary of his own moral actions.*

Since all values have to be gained and/or kept by men's actions, any breach between actor and beneficiary necessitates an injustice: the sacrifice of some men to others, of the actors to the nonactors, of the moral to the immoral. Nothing could ever justify such a breach, and no one ever has.

The choice of the beneficiary of moral values is merely a preliminary or introductory issue in the field of morality. It is not a substitute for morality nor a criterion of moral value, as altruism has made it. Neither is it a moral *primary:* it has to be derived from and validated by the fundamental premises of a moral system.

The Objectivist ethics holds that the actor must always be the beneficiary of his action and that man must act for his own *rational* self-interest. But his right to do so is derived from his nature as man and from the function of moral values in human life—and, therefore, is applicable *only* in the context of a rational, objectively demonstrated and validated code of moral principles which define and determine his actual self-interest. It is not a license "to do as he pleases" and it is not applicable to the altruists' image of a "selfish" brute nor to any man motivated by irrational emotions, feelings, urges, wishes or whims.

This is said as a warning against the kind of "Nietzschean egoists" who, in fact, are a product of the altruist morality and represent the other side of the altruist coin: the men who believe that any action, regardless of its nature, is good if it is intended for one's own benefit. Just as the satisfaction of the irrational desires of others is *not* a criterion of moral value, neither is the satisfaction of one's own irrational desires. Morality is not a contest of whims. . . .

A similar type of error is committed by the man who declares that since man must be guided by his own independent judgment, any action he chooses to take is moral if *he* chooses it. One's own independent judgment is the *means* by which one must choose one's actions, but it is not a moral criterion nor a moral validation: only reference to a demonstrable principle can validate one's choices.

Just as man cannot survive by any random means, but must discover and practice the principles which his survival requires, so man's self-interest cannot be determined by blind desires or random whims, but must be discovered and achieved by the guidance of rational principles. This is why the Objectivist ethics is a morality of *rational* self-interest—or of *rational selfishness.*

Since selfishness is "concern with one's own interests," the Objectivist ethics uses that concept in its exact and purest sense. It is not a concept that one can surrender to man's enemies, nor to the unthinking misconceptions, distortions, prejudices and fears of the ignorant and the irrational. The attack on "selfishness" is an attack on man's self-esteem; to surrender one, is to surrender the other.

Suggestions for Further Reading

Most discussions of Ayn Rand are either so blindly hostile or so uncritically adulatory as to be unprofitable. For a critical assessment that has neither of these faults, see Robert Nozick, "On the Randian Argument," *The Personalist* 52 (1971): 282–304.

Alasdair MacIntyre, "Egoism and Altruism," in *The Encyclopedia of Philosophy,* edited by Paul Edwards (New York: Macmillan and the Free Press, 1967), 2: 462–466 is a good survey article.

Robert G. Olson, *The Morality of Self-Interest* (New York: Harcourt, 1965) is the best contemporary work by a philosopher sympathetic to Ethical Egoism.

The following articles amount to a more or less continuous debate about the merits of the theory: Brian Medlin, "Ultimate Principles and Ethical Egoism," *Australasian Journal of Philosophy* 35 (1957): 111–118; John Hospers, "Baier and Medlin on Ethical Egoism," *Philosophical Studies* 12 (1961): 10–16; W. H. Baumer, "Indefensible Impersonal Egoism," *Philosophical Studies* 18 (1967): 72–75; Jesse Kalin, "On Ethical Egoism," *American Philosophical Quarterly Monograph Series, No. 1: Studies in Moral Philosophy,* 1968, pp. 26–41; James Rachels, "Two Arguments Against Ethical Egoism," *Philosophia* 4 (1974): 297–314.

Also see James Rachels, *The Elements of Moral Philosophy* (New York: Random House, 1986), ch. 6.

8 *Utilitarianism*

John Stuart Mill

In the history of moral philosophy, the name of John Stuart
Mill (1806–1873) is inevitably linked with that of Jeremy Bentham (1748–1832). Bentham is the author of another selection in this book (see selection 22), so it is convenient to say
something about both men here.

Few philosophers have combined theory and practice as
successfully as Bentham. A wealthy Londoner, he studied law
but never became a lawyer, preferring instead to devote himself to writing and working for social reform. He became the
leader of a group of philosophical radicals known as the
Benthamites, who campaigned in behalf of causes ranging
from prison reform to restrictions on the use of child labor.
Bentham was a radical reformer but he was not, as many
reformers are, an "outsider." He was an effective and influential member of the British establishment, and almost all
the Benthamites' legislative proposals were eventually adopted into law.

Bentham was convinced that both law and morals must
be based on a realistic, nonsupernatural conception of man.
The very first sentence of his greatest work, *The Principles of
Morals and Legislation,* declares: "Nature has placed mankind
under the governance of two sovereign masters, *pain* and
pleasure." Some things give us pleasure, whereas other things
cause us pain. This fundamental, rock-bottom fact explains
why we behave as we do—we seek pleasure and try to avoid
pain—and it also explains why we judge some things to be
good and others evil. Therefore, he reasoned, morality must
consist in trying to bring about as much pleasure as possible,
for as many people as possible, while striving to minimize the
amount of pain in the world.

Following up on this basic insight, Bentham argued that
there is one ultimate moral principle, the Principle of Utility.
This principle requires that whenever we have a choice between alternative actions or social policies, we must choose

the one that has the best overall consequences for everyone concerned. Or, as he put it in *The Principles of Morals and Legislation:*

> By the Principle of Utility is meant that principle which approves or disapproves of every action whatsoever, according to the tendency which it appears to have to augment or diminish the happiness of the party whose interest is in question; or what is the same thing in other words, to promote or to oppose that happiness.

One of Bentham's followers as well as a friend was James Mill, the distinguished Scottish philosopher, historian, and economist. James Mill's son, John Stuart Mill, would become the leading advocate of utilitarian moral theory for the next generation, and so the Benthamite movement would continue unabated even after its founder's death.

It was no accident that John Stuart Mill became the next leading Benthamite. James Mill took no chances. He educated his son from an early age with this in mind. He had the boy studying Greek and Latin at age 3, and by the time he entered his teens John Stuart was already mastering the blend of subjects that the British call "political economy." He was 26 when Bentham died, and knew the older man well. It would be a mistake, however, to regard John Stuart Mill as "merely" a follower of the master. He became a distinguished thinker in his own right—perhaps more distinguished than Bentham—and made fundamental contributions to subjects that Bentham barely knew, such as the philosophy of science.

Unlike Bentham, the Mills were not wealthy, and John Stuart Mill earned his living working in the office of the East India Company, as had his father. In 1830 he met and fell in love with Harriet Taylor, who, alas, was married and had three children. Harriet was faithful to her husband until he died in 1849; then, two years later, she and Mill married. Probably as a result of her influence, Mill became a leader in the movement for women's rights and published an influential work on *The Subjection of Women* in 1869.

The following excerpts are from Mill's book *Utilitarianism,* in which he develops some of the basic ideas of utilitarian moral theory.

Chapter II. What Utilitarianism Is

. . . The creed which accepts as the foundation of morals, Utility, or the Greatest Happiness Principle, holds that actions are right in proportion as they tend to promote happiness, wrong as they tend to produce the reverse of happiness. By happiness is intended pleasure, and the absence of pain; by unhappiness, pain, and the privation of pleasure. To give a clear view of the moral standard set up by the theory, much more requires to be said; in particular, what things it includes in the ideas of pain and pleasure; and to what extent this is left an open question. But these supplementary explanations do not affect the theory of life on which this theory of morality is grounded—namely, that pleasure, and freedom from pain, are the only things desirable as ends; and that all desirable things (which are as numerous in the utilitarian as in any other scheme) are desirable either for the pleasure inherent in themselves, or as means to the promotion of pleasure and the prevention of pain.

Now, such a theory of life excites in many minds, and among them in some of the most estimable in feeling and purpose, inveterate dislike. To suppose that life has (as they express it) no higher end than pleasure—no better and nobler object of desire and pursuit—they designate as utterly mean and grovelling; as a doctrine worthy only of swine, to whom the followers of Epicurus were, at a very early period, contemptuously likened; and modern holders of the doctrine are occasionally made the subject of equally polite comparisons by its German, French, and English assailants.

When thus attacked, the Epicureans have always answered, that it is not they, but their accusers, who represent human nature in a degrading light; since the accusation supposes human beings to be capable of no pleasures except those of which swine are capable. If this supposition were true, the charge could not be gainsaid, but would then be no longer an imputation; for if the sources of pleasure were precisely the same to human beings and to swine, the rule of life which is good enough for the one would be good enough for the other. The comparison of the Epicurean life to that of beasts is felt as degrading, precisely because a beast's pleasures do not satisfy a human being's conceptions of happiness.

From John Stuart Mill, *Utilitarianism* (1861).

Human beings have faculties more elevated than the animal appetites, and when once made conscious of them, do not regard anything as happiness which does not include their gratification. I do
not, indeed, consider the Epicureans to have been by any means
faultless in drawing out their scheme of consequences from the
utilitarian principle. To do this in any sufficient manner, many Stoic,
as well as Christian elements require to be included. But there is no
known Epicurean theory of life which does not assign to the pleasures of the intellect, of the feelings and imagination, and of the
moral sentiments, a much higher value as pleasures than to those
of mere sensation. It must be admitted, however, that utilitarian
writers in general have placed the superiority of mental over bodily
pleasures chiefly in the greater permanency, safety, uncostliness,
& c., of the former—that is, in their circumstantial advantages rather
than in their intrinsic nature. And on all these points utilitarians
have fully proved their case; but they might have taken the other,
and, as it may be called, higher ground, with entire consistency. It
is quite compatible with the principle of utility to recognise the fact,
that some *kinds* of pleasure are more desirable and more valuable
than others. It would be absurd that while, in estimating all other
things, quality is considered as well as quantity, the estimation of
pleasures should be supposed to depend on quantity alone.

If I am asked, what I mean by difference of quality in pleasures,
or what makes one pleasure more valuable than another, merely as
a pleasure, except its being greater in amount, there is but one
possible answer. Of two pleasures, if there be one to which all or
almost all who have experience of both give a decided preference,
irrespective of any feeling of moral obligation to prefer it, that is the
more desirable pleasure. If one of the two is, by those who are
competently acquainted with both, placed so far above the other
that they prefer it, even though knowing it to be attended with a
greater amount of discontent, and would not resign it for any quantity of the other pleasure which their nature is capable of, we are
justified in ascribing to the preferred enjoyment a superiority in
quality, so far outweighing quantity as to render it, in comparison,
of small account.

Now it is an unquestionable fact that those who are equally
acquainted with, and equally capable of appreciating and enjoying,
both, do give a most marked preference to the manner of existence
which employs their higher faculties. Few human creatures would

consent to be changed into any of the lower animals, for a promise of the fullest allowance of a beast's pleasures; no intelligent human being would consent to be a fool, no instructed person would be an ignoramus, no person of feeling and conscience would be selfish and base, even though they should be persuaded that the fool, the dunce, or the rascal is better satisfied with his lot than they are with theirs. They would not resign what they possess more than he, for the most complete satisfaction of all the desires which they have in common with him. If they ever fancy they would, it is only in cases of unhappiness so extreme, that to escape from it they would exchange their lot for almost any other, however undesirable in their own eyes. A being of higher faculties requires more to make him happy, is capable probably of more acute suffering, and is certainly accessible to it at more points, than one of an inferior type; but in spite of these liabilities, he can never really wish to sink into what he feels to be a lower grade of existence. We may give what explanation we please of this unwillingness; we may attribute it to pride, a name which is given indiscriminately to some of the most and to some of the least estimable feelings of which mankind are capable; we may refer it to the love of liberty and personal independence, an appeal to which was with the Stoics one of the most effective means for the inculcation of it; to the love of power, or to the love of excitement, both of which do really enter into and contribute to it: but its most appropriate appellation is a sense of dignity, which all human beings possess in one form or other, and in some, though by no means in exact, proportion to their higher faculties, and which is so essential a part of the happiness of those in whom it is strong, that nothing which conflicts with it could be, otherwise than momentarily, an object of desire to them. Whoever supposes that this preference takes place at a sacrifice of happiness—that the superior being, in anything like the equal circumstances, is not happier than the inferior—confounds the two very different ideas, of happiness, and content. It is indisputable that the being whose capacities of enjoyment are low, has the greatest chance of having them fully satisfied; and a highly-endowed being will always feel that any happiness which he can look for, as the world is constituted, is imperfect. But he can learn to bear its imperfections, if they are at all bearable; and they will not make him envy the being who is indeed unconscious of the imperfections, but only because he feels not at all the good which those imperfections qualify. It is better to be a human being dissatisfied than a pig satisfied; better to be Socrates dissatisfied than a fool satisfied. And if the fool, or the pig, is of a different opinion, it is because they only know their own side of the question. The other party to the comparison knows both sides.

It may be objected, that many who are capable of the higher pleasures, occasionally, under the influence of temptation, postpone them to the lower. But this is quite compatible with a full appreciation of the intrinsic superiority of the higher. Men often, from infirmity of character, make their election for the nearer good, though they know it to be the less valuable; and this no less when the choice is between two bodily pleasures, than when it is between bodily and mental. They pursue sensual indulgences to the injury of health, though perfectly aware that health is the greater good. It may be further objected, that many who begin with youthful enthusiasm for everything noble, as they advance in years sink into indolence and selfishness. But I do not believe that those who undergo this very common change, voluntarily choose the lower description of pleasures in preference to the higher. I believe that before they devote themselves exclusively to the one, they have already become incapable of the other. Capacity for the nobler feelings is in most natures a very tender plant, easily killed, not only by hostile influences, but by mere want of sustenance; and in the majority of young persons it speedily dies away if the occupations to which their position in life has devoted them, and the society into which it has thrown them, are not favourable to keeping that higher capacity in exercise. Men lose their high aspirations as they lose their intellectual tastes, because they have not time or opportunity for indulging them; and they addict themselves to inferior pleasures, not because they deliberately prefer them, but because they are either the only ones to which they have access, or the only ones which they are any longer capable of enjoying. It may be questioned whether any one who has remained equally susceptible to both classes of pleasures, ever knowingly and calmly preferred the lower, though many, in all ages, have broken down in an ineffectual attempt to combine both.

From this verdict of the only competent judges, I apprehend there can be no appeal. On a question which is the best worth having of two pleasures, or which of two modes of existence is the most grateful to the feelings, apart from its moral attributes and from its consequences, the judgment of those who are qualified by knowledge of both, or, if they differ, that of the majority among them, must be admitted as final. And there needs be the less hesitation to accept this judgment respecting the quality of pleasures, since there is no other tribunal to be referred to even on the question of quantity. What means are there of determining which is the acutest of two pains, or the intensest of two pleasurable sensations, except the general suffrage of those who are familiar with both? Neither pains nor pleasures are homogeneous, and pain is always heterogeneous with pleasure. What is there to decide whether a particular pleasure is worth purchasing at the cost of a particular pain, except the feelings and judgment of the experienced? When, therefore, those feelings and judgment declare the pleasures derived from the higher faculties to be preferable *in kind,* apart from the question of intensity, to those of which the animal nature, disjoined from the higher faculties, is susceptible, they are entitled on this subject to the same regard.

I have dwelt on this point, as being a necessary part of a perfectly just conception of Utility or Happiness, considered as the directive rule of human conduct. But it is by no means an indispensable condition to the acceptance of the utilitarian standard; for that standard is not the agent's own greatest happiness, but the greatest amount of happiness altogether; and if it may possibly be doubted whether a noble character is always the happier for its nobleness, there can be no doubt that it makes other people happier, and that the world in general is immensely a gainer by it. Utilitarianism, therefore, could only attain its end by the general cultivation of nobleness of character, even if each individual were only benefitted by the nobleness of others, and his own, so far as happiness is concerned, were a sheer deduction from the benefit. But the bare enunciation of such an absurdity as this last, renders refutation superfluous.

According to the Greatest Happiness Principle, as above explained, the ultimate end, with reference to and for the sake of which all other things are desirable (whether we are considering our own good or that of other people), is an existence exempt as far as possible from pain, and as rich as possible in enjoyments, both in point of quantity and quality; the test of quality, and the rule for measuring it against quantity, being the preference felt by those who, in their opportunities of experience, to which must be added their habits of self-consciousness and self-observation, are best furnished with the means of comparison. This, being, according to the utilitarian opinion, the end of human action, is necessarily also the standard of morality; which may accordingly be defined, the rules and precepts for human conduct, by the observance of which an existence such as has been described might be, to the greatest extent possible, secured to all mankind; and not to them only, but, so far as the nature of things admits, to the whole sentient creation. . . .

I must again repeat, what the assailants of utilitarianism seldom have the justice to acknowledge, that the happiness which forms the utilitarian standard of what is right in conduct, is not the agent's own happiness, but that of all concerned. As between his own happiness and that of others, utilitarianism requires him to be as strictly impartial as a disinterested and benevolent spectator. In the golden rule of Jesus of Nazareth, we read the complete spirit of the ethics of utility. To do as one would be done by, and to love one's neighbour as oneself, constitute the ideal perfection of utilitarian morality. As the means of making the nearest approach to this ideal, utility would enjoin, first, that laws and social arrangements should place the happiness, or (as speaking practically it may be called) the interest, of every individual, as nearly as possible in harmony with the interest of the whole; and secondly, that education and opinion, which have so vast a power over human character, should so use that power as to establish in the mind of every individual an indissoluble association between his own happiness and the good of the whole; especially between his own happiness and the practice of such modes of conduct, negative and positive, as regard for the universal happiness prescribes: so that not only he may be unable to conceive the possibility of happiness to himself, consistently with conduct opposed to the general good, but also that a direct impulse to promote the general good may be in every individual one of the habitual motives of action, and the sentiments connected therewith may fill a large and prominent place in every human being's sentient existence. If the impugners of the utilitarian morality represented it to their own minds in this its true character, I know not what recommendation possessed by any other morality they could possibly affirm to be wanting to it: what more beautiful or more exalted developments of human nature any other ethical system can be supposed to foster, or what springs of action, not accessible to the utilitarian, such systems rely on for giving effect to their mandates.

. . . .

Chapter IV. Of What Sort of Proof the Principle of Utility Is Susceptible

It has already been remarked, that questions of ultimate ends do not admit of proof, in the ordinary acceptation of the term. To be incapable of proof by reasoning is common to all first principles; to the first premises of our knowledge, as well as to those of our conduct. But the former, being matters of fact, may be the subject of a direct appeal to the faculties which judge of fact—namely, our senses, and our internal consciousness. Can an appeal be made to the same faculties on questions of practical ends? Or by what other faculty is cognizance taken of them?

Questions about ends are, in other words, questions about what things are desirable. The utilitarian doctrine is, that happiness is desirable, and the only thing desirable, as an end; all other things being only desirable as means to that end. What ought to be required of this doctrine—what conditions is it requisite that the doctrine should fulfil—to make good its claim to be believed?

The only proof capable of being given that an object is visible, is that people actually see it. The only proof that a sound is audible, is that people hear it: and so of the other sources of our experience. In like manner, I apprehend, the sole evidence it is possible to produce that anything is desirable, is that people do actually desire it. If the end which the utilitarian doctrine proposes to itself were not, in theory and in practice, acknowledged to be an end, nothing could ever convince any person that it was so. No reason can be given why the general happiness is desirable, except that each person, so far as he believes it to be attainable, desires his own happiness. This, however, being a fact, we have not only all the proof which the case admits of, but all which it is possible to require, that happiness is a good: that each person's happiness is a good to that person, and the general happiness, therefore, a good to the aggregate of all persons. Happiness has made out its title as *one* of the ends of conduct, and consequently one of the criteria of morality.

But it has not, by this alone, proved itself to be the sole criterion. To do that, it would seem, by the same rule, necessary to show, not only that people desire happiness, but that they never desire anything else. Now it is palpable that they do desire things which, in common language, are decidedly distinguished from happiness. They desire, for example, virtue, and the absence of vice, no less really than pleasure and the absence of pain. The desire of virtue is not as universal, but it is as authentic a fact, as the desire of happiness. And hence the opponents of the utilitarian standard deem that they have a right to infer that there are other ends of human action besides happiness, and that happiness is not the standard of approbation and disapprobation.

But does the utilitarian doctrine deny that people desire virtue, or maintain that virtue is not a thing to be desired? The very reverse. It maintains not only that virtue is to be desired, but that it is to be desired disinterestedly, for itself. Whatever may be the opinion of utilitarian moralists as to the original conditions by which virtue is made virtue; however they may believe (as they do) that actions and dispositions are only virtuous because they promote another end than virtue; yet this being granted, and it having been decided, from considerations of this description, what *is* virtuous, they not only place virtue at the very head of the things which are good as means to the ultimate end, but they also recognise as a psychological fact the possibility of its being, to the individual, a good in itself, without looking to any end beyond it; and hold, that the mind is not in a right state, not in a state comfortable to Utility, not in the state most conducive to the general happiness, unless it does love virtue in this manner—as a thing desirable in itself, even although, in the individual instance, it should not produce those other desirable consequences which it tends to produce, and on account of which it is held to be virtue. This opinion is not, in the smallest degree, a departure from the Happiness principle. The ingredients of happiness are very various, and each of them is desirable in itself, and not merely when considered as swelling an aggregate. The principle of utility does not mean that any given pleasure, as music, for instance, or any given exemption from pain, as for example health, are to be looked upon as a means to a collective something termed happiness, and to be desired on that account. They are desired and desirable in and for themselves; besides being means, they are a part of the end. Virtue, according to the utilitarian doctrine, is not naturally and originally part of the end, but it is capable of becoming so; and in those who love it disinterestedly it has become so, and is desired and cherished, not as a means to happiness, but as a part of their happiness.

To illustrate this farther, we may remember that virtue is not the only thing, originally a means, and which if it were not a means to anything else, would be and remain indifferent, but which by association with what it is a means to, comes to be desired for itself, and that too with the utmost intensity. What, for example, shall we say of the love of money? There is nothing originally more desirable about money than about any heap of glittering pebbles. Its worth is solely that of the things which it will buy; the desires for other things than itself, which it is a means of gratifying. Yet the love of money is not only one of the strongest moving forces of human life, but money is, in many cases, desired in and for itself; the desire to possess it is often stronger than the desire to use it, and goes on increasing when all the desires which point to ends beyond it, to be encompassed by it, are falling off. It may be then said truly, that money is desired not for the sake of an end, but as part of the end. From being a means to happiness, it has come to be itself a principal ingredient of the individual's conception of happiness. The same may be said of the majority of the great objects of human life— power, for example, or fame; except that to each of these there is a certain amount of immediate pleasure annexed, which has at least the semblance of being naturally inherent in them; a thing which cannot be said of money. Still, however, the strongest natural attraction, both of power and of fame, is the immense aid they give to the attainment of our other wishes; and it is the strong association thus generated between them and all our objects of desire, which gives to the direct desire of them the intensity it often assumes, so as in some characters to surpass in strength all other desires. In these cases the means have become a part of the end, and a more important part of it than any of the things which they are means to. What was once desired as an instrument for the attainment of happiness, has come to be desired for its own sake. In being desired for its own sake it is, however, desired as *part* of happiness. The person is made, or thinks he would be made, happy by its mere possession; and is made unhappy by failure to obtain it. The desire of it is not a different thing from the desire of happiness, any more than the love of music, or the desire of health. They are included in happiness. They are some of the elements of which the desire of happiness is made up. Happiness is not an abstract idea, but a concrete whole; and these are some of its parts. And the utilitarian standard sanctions and approves their being so. Life would be a poor thing, very ill provided with sources of happiness, if there were not this provision of nature, by which things originally indifferent, but conducive to, or otherwise associated with, the satisfaction of our primitive desires, become in themselves sources of pleasure more valuable than the primitive pleasures, both in permanency, in the space of human existence that they are capable of covering, and even in intensity.

Virtue, according to the utilitarian conception, is a good of this description. There was no original desire of it, or motive to it, save its conduciveness to pleasure, and especially to protection from pain. But through the association thus formed, it may be felt a good in itself, and desired as such with as great intensity as any other good; and with this difference between it and the love of money, of power, or of fame, that all of these may, and often do, render the individual noxious to the other members of the society to which he belongs, whereas there is nothing which makes him so much a blessing to them as the cultivation of the disinterested love of virtue. And consequently, the utilitarian standard, while it tolerates and approves those other acquired desires, up to the point beyond which they would be more injurious to the general happiness than promotive of it, enjoins and requires the cultivation of the love of virtue up to the greatest strength possible, as being above all things important to the general happiness.

It results from the preceding considerations, that there is in reality nothing desired except happiness. Whatever is desired otherwise than as a means to some end beyond itself, and ultimately to happiness, is desired as itself a part of happiness, and is not desired for itself until it has become so.

Suggestions for Further Reading

J. B. Schneewind, ed., *Mill's Ethical Writings* (New York: Collier, 1965) contains several of Mill's works, including his important essay on Bentham.

In two books, the English philosopher W. D. Ross presented an uncompromising attack on Utilitarianism: *The Right and the Good* (Oxford: Oxford University Press, 1930), and *The Foundations of Ethics* (Oxford: Oxford University Press, 1939). After Ross, much of the contemporary debate was carried on in an enormous number of journal articles arguing the merits of the theory. Two useful collections contain some of the most important articles: Samuel Gorovitz, ed., *Mill: Utilitarianism. Text and Critical*

Essays (Indianapolis: Bobbs-Merrill, 1971); and Michael D. Bayles, ed., *Contemporary Utilitarianism* (Garden City, N.Y.: Anchor, 1968).

An anthology of more recent articles is *Utilitarianism and Beyond*, edited by Amartya Sen and Bernard Williams (Cambridge: Cambridge University Press, 1982).

Also recommended are J. J. C. Smart and Bernard Williams, *Utilitarianism: For and Against* (Cambridge: Cambridge University Press, 1973) and Richard B. Brandt, *A Theory of the Good and the Right* (Oxford: Clarendon, 1979).

Also see James Rachels, *The Elements of Moral Philosophy* (New York: Random House, 1986), chs. 7 and 8.

9 *The Categorical Imperative*

Immanuel Kant

Immanuel Kant, who is regarded by many commentators as the greatest philosopher of modern times, led an uneventful life. He was born in 1724 in Königsberg, East Prussia (now Kaliningrad in the Soviet Union), and died there in 1804, never having traveled more than a few miles from his home. He was a professor in the local university, popular with students, and a much sought-after dinner guest, renowned for his witty conversation. He was also known for his regular habits: a bachelor, he arose each morning at the same time (4 A.M.), prepared his lectures, taught from 7 until noon, read until 4 P.M., took a walk, had dinner, and wrote until bedtime. This routine he repeated day after day, year after year.

The only controversy in Kant's life was caused by his unorthodox views on religion. He was from a family of Pietists, who distrusted organized religion and formal religious observances. In his later years, when he was rector of the university, it was his duty to lead the faculty procession to the university chapel for religious services; he would do so, but on reaching the chapel he would stand aside and not enter. In 1786, having become the most famous philosopher of

Germany, and having argued that the existence of God cannot be proven by reason alone, Kant was ordered to publish nothing more on that subject.

Today, "Kant scholarship" is an academic specialty unto itself; many scholars spend their whole lives trying to understand what he had to say, and every year new books appear arguing new interpretations of his philosophy. The multitude of interpretations is partly due to the richness of Kant's thought and the difficulty of the topics he discussed. But it is also due, at least in part, to the fact that he was an exceedingly obscure writer. Even while reading his books, it is never easy to tell exactly what Kant had in mind.

Kant would be remembered as a major figure for his writings on metaphysics and the nature of human knowledge even if he had written nothing on ethics. But his ethical writings were among his most influential works. Like many other philosophers, Kant believed that morality can be summed up in one ultimate principle, from which all our duties and obligations are derived. He called this principle the "categorical imperative."

The following selection is from Kant's *Fundamental Principles of the Metaphysics of Morals,* the most accessible presentation of his ethical theory.

Nothing can possibly be conceived in the world, or even out of it, which can be called good without qualification, except a *good will.* Intelligence, wit, judgment, and the other *talents* of the mind, however they may be named, or courage, resolution, perseverance, as qualities of temperament, are undoubtedly good and desirable in many respects; but these gifts of nature may also become extremely bad and mischievous if the will which is to make use of them, and which, therefore, constitutes what is called *character,* is not good. It is the same with the *gifts of fortune.* Power, riches, honor, even health, and the general well-being and contentment with one's condition which is called *happiness,* inspire pride, and often presumption, if there is not a good will to correct the influence of these on the mind,

---

From Immanuel Kant, *Fundamental Principles of the Metaphysics of Morals* (1785), translated by T. K. Abbott.

and with this also to rectify the whole principle of acting, and adapt it to its end. The sight of a being who is not adorned with a single feature of a pure and good will, enjoying unbroken prosperity, can never give pleasure to an impartial rational spectator. Thus a good will appears to constitute the indispensable condition even of being worthy of happiness.

. . . .

An action done from duty derives its moral worth, *not from the purpose* which is to be attained by it, but from the maxim by which it is determined, and therefore does not depend on the realization of the object of the action, but merely on the *principle of volition* by which the action has taken place, without regard to any object of desire. It is clear from what precedes that the purposes which we may have in view in our actions, or their effects regarded as ends and springs of the will, cannot give to actions any unconditional or moral worth. In what, then, can their worth lie if it is not to consist in the will and in reference to its expected effect? It cannot lie anywhere but in the *principle of the will* without regard to the ends which can be attained by the action. For the will stands between its *a priori** principle, which is formal, and its *a posteriori*† spring, which is material, as between two roads, and as it must be determined by something, it follows that it must be determined by the formal principle of volition when an action is done from duty, in which case every material principle has been withdrawn from it.

The third proposition, which is a consequence of the two preceding, I would express thus: *Duty is the necessity of acting from respect for the law.* I may have *inclination* for an object as the effect of my proposed action, but I cannot have *respect* for it just for this reason that it is an effect and not an energy of will. Similarly, I cannot have respect for inclination, whether my own or another's; I can at most, if my own, approve it; if another's, sometimes even love it, that is, look on it as favorable to my own interest. It is only what is connected with my will as a principle, by no means as an effect—what does not subserve my inclination, but overpowers it, or at least in case of choice excludes it from its calculation—in other words, simply the law of itself, which can be an object of respect, and hence a command. Now an action done from duty must wholly

---

**a priori:* known prior to sense experience
†*a posteriori:* known as the result of sense experience

exclude the influence of inclination, and with it every object of the will, so that nothing remains which can determine the will except objectively the *law,* and subjectively *pure respect* for this practical law, and consequently the maxim that I should follow this law even to the thwarting of all of my inclinations.

Thus the moral worth of an action does not lie in the effect expected from it, nor in any principle of action which requires to borrow its motive from this expected effect. For all these effects—agreeableness of one's condition, and even the promotion of the happiness of others—could have been also brought about by other causes, so that for this there would have been no need of the will of a rational being; whereas it is in this alone that the supreme and unconditional good can be found. The pre-eminent good which we call moral can therefore consist in nothing else than *the conception of law* in itself, *which certainly is only possible in a rational being,* in so far as this conception, and not the expected effect, determines the will. This is a good which is already present in the person who acts accordingly, and we have not to wait for it to appear first in the result.

. . . .

The conception of an objective principle, in so far as it is obligatory for a will, is called a command (of reason), and the formula of the command is called an Imperative.

All imperatives are expressed by the word *ought* [or *shall*], and thereby indicate the relation of an objective law of reason to a will which from its subjective constitution is not necessarily determined by it (an obligation). They say that something would be good to do or to forbear, but they say it to a will which does not always do a thing because it is conceived to be good to do it. That is practically *good,* however, which determines the will by means of the conceptions of reason, and consequently not from subjective causes, but objectively, that is, on principles which are valid for every rational being as such. It is distinguished from the *pleasant* as that which influences the will only by means of sensation from merely subjective causes, valid only for the sense of this or that one, and not as a principle of reason which holds for every one.

A perfectly good will would therefore be equally subject to objective laws (viz., laws of good), but could not be conceived as *obliged* thereby to act lawfully, because of itself from its subjective constitution it can only be determined by the conception of good.

Therefore no imperatives hold for the Divine will, or in general for a *holy* will; *ought* is here out of place because the volition is already of itself necessarily in unison with the law. Therefore imperatives are only formulae to express the relation of objective laws of all volition to the subjective imperfection of the will of this or that rational being, for example, the human will.

Finally, there is an imperative which commands a certain conduct immediately, without having as its condition any other purpose to be attained by it. This imperative is *categorical.* It concerns not the matter of the action, or its intended result, but its form and the principle of which it is itself a result; and what is essentially good in it consists in the mental disposition, let the consequence be what it may. This imperative may be called that of *morality.*

. . . .

There is therefore but one categorical imperative, namely, this: *Act only on that maxim whereby thou canst at the same time will that it should become a universal law.*

Now if all imperatives of duty can be deduced from this one imperative as from their principle, then, although it should remain undecided whether what is called duty is not merely a vain notion, yet at least we shall be able to show what we understand by it and what this notion means.

Since the universality of the law according to which effects are produced constitutes what is properly called *nature* in the most general sense (as to form)—that is, the existence of things so far as it is determined by general laws—the imperative of duty may be expressed thus: *Act as if the maxim of thy action were to become by thy will a universal law of nature.*

We will now enumerate a few duties, adopting the usual division of them into duties to ourselves and to others, and into perfect and imperfect duties.

1. A man reduced to despair by a series of misfortunes feels wearied of life, but is still so far in possession of his reason that he can ask himself whether it would not be contrary to his duty to himself to take his own life. Now he inquires whether the maxim of his action could become a universal law of nature. His maxim is: From self-love I adopt it as a principle to shorten my life when its longer duration is likely to bring more evil than satisfaction. It is asked then simply whether this principle founded on self-love can become a universal law of nature. Now we see at once that a system

of nature of which it should be a law to destroy life by means of the very feeling whose special nature it is to impel to the improvement of life would contradict itself, and therefore could not exist as a system of nature; hence that maxim cannot possibly exist as a universal law of nature, and consequently would be wholly inconsistent with the supreme principle of all duty.

2. Another finds himself forced by necessity to borrow money. He knows that he will not be able to repay it, but sees also that nothing will be lent to him unless he promises stoutly to repay it in a definite time. He desires to make this promise, but he has still so much conscience as to ask himself: Is it not unlawful and inconsistent with duty to get out of a difficulty in this way? Suppose, however, that he resolves to do so, then the maxim of his action would be expressed thus: When I think myself in want of money, I will borrow money and promise to repay it, although I know that I never can do so. Now this principle of self-love or of one's own advantage may perhaps be consistent with my whole future welfare; but the question now is, Is it right? I change then the suggestion of self-love into a universal law, and state the question thus: How would it be if my maxim were a universal law? Then I see at once that it could never hold as a universal law of nature, but would necessarily contradict itself. For supposing it to be a universal law that everyone when he thinks himself in a difficulty should be able to promise whatever he pleases, with the purpose of not keeping his promise, the promise itself would become impossible, as well as the end that one might have in view in it, since no one would consider that anything was promised to him, but would ridicule all such statements as vain pretenses.

3. A third finds in himself a talent which with the help of some culture might make him a useful man in many respects. But he finds himself in comfortable circumstances and prefers to indulge in pleasure rather than to take pains in enlarging and improving his happy natural capacities. He asks, however, whether his maxim of neglect of his natural gifts, besides agreeing with his inclination to indulgence, agrees also with what is called duty. He sees then that a system of nature could indeed subsist with such a universal law, although men (like the South Sea islanders) should let their talents rest and resolve to devote their lives merely to idleness, amusement, and propagation of their species—in a word, to enjoyment; but he cannot possibly *will* that this should be a universal law of nature, or

be implanted in us as such by a natural instinct. For, as a rational being, he necessarily wills that his faculties be developed, since they serve him, and have been given him, for all sorts of possible purposes.

4. A fourth, who is in prosperity, while he sees that others have to contend with great wretchedness and that he could help them, thinks: What concern is it of mine? Let everyone be as happy as Heaven pleases, or as he can make himself; I will take nothing from him nor even envy him, only I do not wish to contribute anything to his welfare or to his assistance in distress! Now no doubt, if such a mode of thinking were a universal law, the human race might very well subsist, and doubtless even better than in a state in which everyone talks of sympathy and good-will, or even takes care occasionally to put it into practice, but, on the other side, also cheats when he can, betrays the rights of men, or otherwise violates them. But although it is possible that a universal law of nature might exist in accordance with that maxim, it is impossible to *will* that such a principle should have the universal validity of a law of nature. For a will which resolved this would contradict itself, inasmuch as many cases might occur in which one would have need of the love and sympathy of others, and in which, by such a law of nature, sprung from his own will, he would deprive himself of all hope of the aid he desires.

These are a few of the many actual duties, or at least what we regard as such, which obviously fall into two classes on the one principle that we have laid down. We must be *able to will* that a maxim of our action should be a universal law. This is the canon of the moral appreciation of the action generally. Some actions are of such a character that their maxim cannot without contradiction be even *conceived* as a universal law of nature, far from it being possible that we should *will* that it *should* be so. In others, this intrinsic impossibility is not found, but still it is impossible to *will* that their maxim should be raised to the universality of a law of nature, since such a will would contradict itself. It is easily seen that the former violate strict or rigorous (inflexible) duty; the latter only laxer (meritorious) duty. Thus it has been completely shown by these examples how all duties depend as regards the nature of the obligation (not the object of the action) on the same principle.

If now we attend to ourselves on occasion of any transgression of duty, we shall find that we in fact do not will that our maxim should be a universal law, for that is impossible for us; on the contrary, we will that the opposite should remain a universal law, only we assume the liberty of making an *exception* in our own favor or (just for this time only) in favor of our inclination. Consequently, if we considered all cases from one and the same point of view, namely, that of reason, we should find a contradiction in our own will, namely, that a certain principle should be objectively necessary as a universal law, and yet subjectively should not be universal, but admit of exceptions. As, however, we at one moment regard our action from the point of view of a will wholly conformed to reason, and then again look at the same action from the point of view of a will affected by inclination, there is not really any contradiction, but an antagonism of inclination to the precept of reason, whereby the universality of the principle is changed into a mere generality, so that the practical principle of reason shall meet the maxim half way. Now, although this cannot be justified in our own impartial judgment, yet it proves that we do really recognize the validity of the categorical imperative and (with all respect for it) only allow ourselves a few exceptions which we think unimportant and forced from us.

. . . .

Supposing, however, that there were something *whose existence* has *in itself* an absolute worth, something which, being *an end in itself,* could be a source of definite laws, then in this and this alone would lie the source of a possible categorical imperative, that is, a practical law.

Now I say: Man and generally any rational being *exists* as an end in himself, *not merely as a means* to be arbitrarily used by this or that will, but in all his actions, whether they concern himself or other rational beings, must be always regarded at the same time as an end. All objects of the inclinations have only a conditional worth; for if the inclinations and the wants founded on them did not exist, then their object would be without value. But the inclinations themselves, being sources of want, are so far from having an absolute worth for which they should be desired that, on the contrary, it must be the universal wish of every rational being to be wholly free from them. Thus the worth of any object which is *to be acquired* by our action is always conditional. Beings whose existence depends not on our will but on nature's, have nevertheless, if they are rational beings, only a relative value as means, and are therefore called things; rational beings, on the contrary, are called *persons*, because their very nature points them out as ends in themselves, that is, as something which must not be used merely as means, and so far therefore restricts freedom of action (and is an object of respect). These, therefore, are not merely subjective ends whose existence has a worth *for us* as an effect of our action, but *objective ends*, that is, things whose existence is an end in itself—an end, moreover, for which no other can be substituted, which they should subserve *merely* as means, for otherwise nothing whatever would possess *absolute worth;* but if all worth were conditioned and therefore contingent, then there would be no supreme practical principle of reason whatever.

If then there is a supreme practical principle or, in respect of the human will, a categorical imperative, it must be one which, being drawn from the conception of that which is necessarily an end for everyone because it is *an end in itself*, constitutes an *objective* principle of will, and can therefore serve as a universal practical law. The foundation of this principle is: *rational nature exists as an end in itself.* Man necessarily conceives his own existence as being so; so far then this is a *subjective* principle of human actions. But every other rational being regards its existence similarly, just on the same rational principle that holds for me, so that it is at the same time an objective principle from which as a supreme practical law all laws of the will must be capable of being deduced. Accordingly the practical imperative will be as follows: *So act as to treat humanity, whether in thine own person or in that of any other, in every case as an end withal, never as means only.* We will now inquire whether this can be practically carried out.

To abide by the previous examples:

First, under the head of necessary duty to oneself: He who contemplates suicide should ask himself whether his action can be consistent with the idea of humanity *as an end in itself.* If he destroys himself in order to escape from painful circumstances, he uses a person merely as a *mean* to maintain a tolerable condition up to the end of life. But a man is not a thing, that is to say, something which can be used merely as means, but must in all his actions be always considered as an end in himself. I cannot, therefore, dispose in any way of a man in my own person so as to mutilate him, to damage or kill him. (It belongs to ethics proper to define this principle more precisely, so as to avoid all misunderstanding, for example, as to the amputation of the limbs in order to preserve myself; as to exposing my life to danger with a view to preserve it, etc. This question is therefore omitted here.)

Secondly, as regards necessary duties, or those of strict obligation, towards others: He who is thinking of making a lying promise to others will see at once that he would be using another man *merely as a means,* without the latter containing at the same time the end in himself. For he whom I propose by such a promise to use for my own purposes cannot possibly assent to my mode of acting towards him, and therefore cannot himself contain the end of this action. This violation of the principle of humanity in other men is more obvious if we take in examples of attacks on the freedom and property of others. For then it is clear that he who transgresses the rights of men intends to use the person of others merely as means, without considering that as rational beings they ought always to be esteemed also as ends, that is, as beings who must be capable of containing in themselves the end of the very same action.

Thirdly, as regards contingent (meritorious) duties to oneself: It is not enough that the action does not violate humanity in our own person as an end in itself, it must also *harmonize with* it. Now there are in humanity capacities of greater perfection which belong to the end that nature has in view in regard to humanity in ourselves as the subject; to neglect these might perhaps be consistent with the *maintenance* of humanity as an end in itself, but not with the *advancement* of this end.

Fourthly, as regards meritorious duties towards others: The natural end which all men have is their own happiness. Now humanity might indeed subsist although no one should contribute anything to the happiness of others, provided he did not intentionally withdraw anything from it; but after all, this would only harmonize negatively, not positively, with *humanity as an end in itself,* if everyone does not also endeavor, as far as in him lies, to forward the ends of others. For the ends of any subject which is an end in himself ought as far as possible to be *my* ends also, if that conception is to have its *full* effect with me.

This principle that humanity and generally every rational nature is *an end in itself* (which is the supreme limiting condition of every man's freedom of action), is not borrowed from experience, *first,* because it is universal, applying as it does to all rational beings whatever, and experience is not capable of determining anything about them; *secondly* because it does not present humanity as an end to men (subjectively), that is, as an object which men do of themselves actually adopt as an end; but as an objective end which must as a law constitute the supreme limiting condition of all our subjective ends, let them be what we will; it must therefore spring from pure reason. In fact the objective principle of all practical legislation lies (according to the first principle) in *the rule* and its form of universality which makes it capable of being a law (say, for example, a law of nature); but the *subjective* principle is in the *end;* now by the second principle, the subject of all ends is each rational being inasmuch as it is an end in itself. Hence follows the third practical principle of the will, which is the ultimate condition of its harmony with the universal practical reason, viz., the idea of *the will of every rational being as a universally legislative will.*

On this principle all maxims are rejected which are inconsistent with the will being itself universal legislator. Thus the will is not subject to the law, but so subject that it must be regarded *as itself giving the law,* and on this ground only subject to the law (of which it can regard itself as the author).

Suggestions for Further Reading

The best translations of Kant's major ethical writings are *Foundations of the Metaphysics of Morals,* translated by Lewis White Beck (Indianapolis: Bobbs-Merrill, 1959); *Critique of Practical Reason,* translated by Lewis White Beck (Indianapolis: Bobbs-Merrill, 1956); *The Metaphysical Principles of Virtue,* translated by James Ellington (Indianapolis: Bobbs-Merrill, 1964); *The Metaphysical Elements of Justice,* translated by John Ladd (Indianapolis: Bobbs-Merrill, 1965); and *Lectures on Ethics,* translated by Louis Infield (New York: Harper, 1963).

H. B. Acton's *Kant's Moral Philosophy* (London: Macmillan, 1970) is a good short work on Kant. Robert Paul Wolff, ed., *Kant: Foundations of the Metaphysics of Morals. Text and Critical Essays* (Indianapolis: Bobbs-Merrill, 1969) is a helpful collection of writings on Kant's ethics by a variety of philosophers.

R. S. Downie and Elizabeth Telfer, *Respect for Persons* (London: Allen and Unwin, 1969) is a useful treatment of this concept. But perhaps the best introduction to the notion of Kantian respect is to be found in Herbert Morris's essay "Persons and Punishment," *The Monist* 52 (1968): 475–501. Even though Morris does not specifically set out to explain Kant, his argument is so clear and so Kantian that understanding Morris's point is an excellent way of coming to understand what Kant had in mind.

Also see James Rachels, *The Elements of Moral Philosophy* (New York: Random House, 1986), chs. 9 and 10.

10 *The Social Contract*

Thomas Hobbes

Thomas Hobbes (1588–1679), the foremost British philosopher of the seventeenth century, was the first to set out the Social Contract Theory in detail. Hobbes's father was a vicar who fell into disgrace after getting into a fistfight in front of his own church, and then deserted his family. Luckily, Hobbes and his mother were rescued by a wealthy uncle. After finishing school, Hobbes became a tutor in the household of the earl of Devonshire, a post that he held for 18 years. This position provided him not only with a steady income but also with time to write and the opportunity to travel all over Europe. While there Hobbes met the elderly Galileo and was invited to comment on Descartes's new book, the *Meditations.*

A fervent monarchist, Hobbes fled England in the 1630s when opposition to Charles II became intense. Charles soon had to leave England too, and in Paris Hobbes became the exiled king's tutor in mathematics. When Charles was restored to the throne in 1660, Hobbes returned to London. He was by then a renowned philosopher, but even so, his life was far from comfortable. Hobbes had openly defended materialism—the idea that all things are made of physical matter—and in Parliament a group of bishops proposed that he be burned as a heretic. Eventually Hobbes was forbidden to publish in England, and his later books were published in Holland. His *Leviathan,* the greatest of all the modern political treatises, became in his own lifetime a famous but hard-to-find volume.

Hobbes argued that morality should be viewed as the outcome of an agreement that rational, self-interested people have entered into because it is to everyone's benefit to live in a secure, peaceful society. The alternative would be the "state of nature," a war of all against all in which everyone would be much worse off. The following selection from the *Leviathan* sets out the details of his argument.

Of the Natural Condition of Mankind as Concerning Their Felicity, and Misery

Nature hath made men so equal, in the faculties of the body, and mind; as that though there be found one man sometimes manifestly stronger in body, or of quicker mind than another; yet when all is reckoned together, the difference between man, and man, is not so considerable, as that one man can thereupon claim to himself any benefit, to which another may not pretend, as well as he. For as to the strength of body, the weakest has strength enough to kill the strongest, either by secret machination, or by confederacy with others, that are in the same danger with himself.

And as to the faculties of the mind, setting aside the arts grounded upon words, and especially that skill of proceeding upon general, and infallible rules, called science; which very few have, and but in few things; as being not a native faculty, born with us; nor attained, as prudence, while we look after somewhat else, I find yet a greater equality amongst men, than that of strength. For prudence, is but experience; which equal time, equally bestows on all men, in those things they equally apply themselves unto. That which may perhaps make such equality incredible, is but a vain conceit of one's own wisdom, which almost all men think they have in a greater degree, than the vulgar; that is, than all men but themselves, and a few others, whom by fame, or for concurring with themselves, they approve. For such is the nature of men, that howsoever they may acknowledge many others to be more witty, or more eloquent, or more learned; yet they will hardly believe there be many so wise as themselves; for they see their own wit at hand, and other men's at

From Thomas Hobbes, *Leviathan* (1651), chs. 13 and 14.

a distance. But this proveth rather that men are in that point equal, than unequal. For there is not ordinarily a greater sign of the equal distribution of anything, than that every man is contented with his share.

From this equality of ability, ariseth equality of hope in the attaining of our ends. And therefore if any two men desire the same thing, which nevertheless they cannot both enjoy, they become enemies; and in the way to their end, which is principally their own conservation, and sometimes their delectation only, endeavor to destroy, or subdue one another. And from hence it comes to pass that where an invader hath no more to fear, than another man's single power; if one plant, sow, build, or possess a convenient seat, others may probably be expected to come prepared with forces united, to dispossess, and deprive him, not only of the fruit of his labour, but also of his life, or liberty. And the invader again is in the like danger of another.

And from this diffidence of one another, there is no way for any man to secure himself, so reasonable, as anticipation; that is, by force, or wiles, to master the persons of all men he can, so long, till he see no other power great enough to endanger him: and this is no more than his own conservation requireth, and is generally allowed. Also because there be some, that taking pleasure in contemplating their own power in the acts of conquest, which they pursue farther than their security requires; if others, that otherwise would be glad to be at ease within modest bounds, should not by invasion increase their power, they would not be able, long time, by standing only on their defence, to subsist. And by consequence, such augmentation of dominion over men being necessary to a man's conservation, it ought to be allowed him.

Again, men have no pleasure, but on the contrary a great deal of grief, in keeping company, where there is no power able to over-awe them all. For every man looketh that his companion should value him, at the same rate he sets upon himself: and upon all signs of contempt, or undervaluing, naturally endeavours, as far as he dares, (which amongst them that have no common power to keep them in quiet, is far enough to make them destroy each other), to extort a greater value from his contemners, by damage; and from others, by the example.

So that in the nature of man, we find three principal causes of quarrel. First, competition; secondly, diffidence; thirdly, glory.

The first, maketh men invade for gain; the second, for safety; and the third, for reputation. The first use violence, to make themselves masters of other men's persons, wives, children, and cattle; the second to defend them; the third, for trifles, as a word, a smile, a different opinion, and any other sign of undervalue, either direct in their persons, or by reflection in their kindred, their friends, their nation, their profession, or their name.

Hereby it is manifest, that during the time men live without a common power to keep them all in awe, they are in that condition which is called war; and such a war, as is of every man, against every man. For WAR, consisteth not in battle only, or the act of fighting; but in a tract of time, wherein the will to contend by battle is sufficiently known: and therefore the notion of *time*, is to be considered in the nature of war; as it is in the nature of weather. For as the nature of foul weather, lieth not in a shower or two of rain; but in an inclination thereto of many days together: so the nature of war, consisteth not in actual fighting; but in the known disposition thereto, during all the time there is no assurance to the contrary. All other time is PEACE.

Whatsoever therefore is consequent to a time of war, where every man is enemy to every man; the same is consequent to the time, wherein men live without other security, than what their own strength, and their own invention shall furnish them withal. In such condition, there is no place for industry; because the fruit thereof is uncertain: and consequently no culture of the earth; no navigation, nor use of the commodities that may be imported by sea; no commodious building; no instruments of moving, and removing, such things as require much force; no knowledge of the face of the earth; no account of time; no arts; no letters; no society; and which is worst of all, continual fear, and danger of violent death; and the life of man, solitary, poor, nasty, brutish, and short.

It may seem strange to some man, that has not well weighed these things; that nature should thus dissociate, and render men apt to invade, and destroy one another: and he may therefore, not trusting to this inference, made from the passions, desire perhaps to have the same confirmed by experience. Let him therefore consider with himself, when taking a journey, he arms himself, and seeks to go well accompanied; when going to sleep, he locks his doors; when even in his house he locks his chests; and this when he knows there be laws, and public officers, armed, to revenge all injuries shall be done him; what opinion he has of his fellow-subjects, when he rides armed; of his fellow citizens, when he locks his doors; and of his children, and servants, when he locks his chests. Does he not there as much accuse mankind by his actions, as I do by my words? But neither of us accuse man's nature in it. The desires, and other passions of man, are in themselves no sin. No more are the actions, that proceed from those passions, till they know a law that forbids them: which till laws be made they cannot know: nor can any law be made, till they have agreed upon the person that shall make it.

It may peradventure be thought, there was never such a time, nor condition of war as this; and I believe it was never generally so, over all the world: but there are many places, where they live so now. For the savage people in many places of America, except the government of small families, the concord whereof dependeth on natural lust, have no government at all; and live at this day in that brutish manner, as I said before. Howsoever, it may be perceived what manner of life there would be, where there were no common power to fear, by the manner of life, which men that have formerly lived under a peaceful government use to degenerate into, in a civil war.

But though there had never been any time, wherein particular men were in a condition of war one against another; yet in all times, kings, and persons of sovereign authority, because of their independency, are in continual jealousies, and in the state and posture of gladiators; having their weapons pointing, and their eyes fixed on one another; that is, their forts, garrisons, and guns upon the frontiers of their kingdoms; and continual spies upon their neighbours; which is a posture of war. But because they uphold thereby, the industry of their subjects; there does not follow from it, that misery, which accompanies the liberty of particular men.

To this war of every man, against every man, this also is consequent; that nothing can be unjust. The notions of right and wrong justice and injustice have there no place. Where there is no common power, there is no law: where no law, no injustice. Force, and fraud, are in war the two cardinal virtues. Justice, and injustice are none of the faculties neither of the body, nor mind. If they were, they might be in a man that were alone in the world, as well as his senses, and passions. They are qualities, that relate to men in society, not in solitude. It is consequent also to the same condition, that there be no propriety, no dominion, no *mine* and *thine* distinct; but only that to be every man's, that he can get; and for so long, as he can keep it. And thus much of the ill condition, which man by mere nature is actually placed in; though with a possibility to come out of it, consisting partly in the passions, partly in his reason.

The passions that incline men to peace, are fear of death; desire of such things as are necessary to commodious living; and a hope by their industry to obtain them. And reason suggesteth convenient articles of peace, upon which men may be drawn to agreement. These articles, are they, which otherwise are called the Laws of Nature: whereof I shall speak more particularly, in the two following chapters.

Of the First and Second Natural Laws, and of Contracts

The right of nature, which writers commonly call *jus naturale,* is liberty each man hath, to use his own power, as he will himself, for the preservation of his own nature; that is to say, of his own life; and consequently, of doing any thing, which in his own judgment, and reason, he shall conceive to be the aptest means thereunto.

By *liberty,* is understood, according to the proper signification of the word, the absence of external impediments: which impediments, may oft take away part of a man's power to do what he would; but cannot hinder him from using the power left him, according as his judgment, and reason shall dictate to him.

A *law of nature, lex naturalis,* is a precept or general rule, found out by reason, by which a man is forbidden to do that, which is destructive of his life, or taketh away the means of preserving the same; and to omit that, by which he thinketh it may be best preserved. For though they that speak of this subject, use to confound *jus,* and *lex, right* and *law:* yet they ought to be distinguished; because *right,* consisteth in liberty to do, or to forbare; whereas *law,* determineth, and bindeth to one of them: so that law, and right, differ as much, as obligation, and liberty; which in one and the same matter are inconsistent.

And because the condition of man, as hath been declared in the precedent chapter, is a condition of war of every one against every one: in which case every one is governed by his own reason; and there is nothing he can make use of, that may not be a help unto him, in preserving his life against his enemies; it followeth, that in such a condition, every man has a right to every thing; even to one another's body. And therefore, as long as this natural right of every man to every thing endureth, there can be no security to any man, how strong or wise soever he be, of living out the time, which nature ordinarily alloweth men to live, and consequently it is a precept, or general rule of reason, *that every man, ought to endeavour peace, as far as he has hope of obtaining it; and when he cannot obtain it, that he may seek, and use, all helps, and advantages of war.* The first branch of which rule, containeth the first, and fundamental law of nature; which is, *to seek peace, and follow it.* The second, the sum of the right of nature; which is, *by all means we can, to defend ourselves.*

From this fundamental law of nature, by which men are commanded to endeavour peace, is derived this second law; *that a man be willing, when others are so too, as far-forth, as for peace, and defence of himself he shall think it necessary, to lay down this right to all things; and be contented with so much liberty against other men, as he would allow other men against himself.* For as long as every man holdeth this right, of doing any thing he liketh; so long are all men in the condition of war. But if other men will not lay down their right, as well as he; then there is no reason for any one, to divest himself of his: for that were to expose himself to prey, which no man is bound to, rather than to dispose himself to peace. This is that law of the Gospel; *whatsoever you require that others should do to you, that do ye to them.* . . .

To *lay down* a man's *right* to any thing, is to *divest* himself of the *liberty,* of hindering another of the benefit of his own right to the same. For he that renounceth, or passeth away his right, giveth not to any other man a right which he had not before; because there is nothing to which every man had not right by nature: but only standeth out of his way, that he may enjoy his own original right, without hindrance from him; not without hindrance from another. So that the effect which redoundeth to one man, by another man's defect of right, is but so much diminution of impediments to the use of his own right original.

Right is laid aside, either by simply renouncing it; or by transferring it to another. By *simply renouncing;* when he cares not to whom the benefit thereof redoundeth. By *transferring;* when he intendeth the benefit thereof to some certain person, or persons. And when a man hath in either manner abandoned, or granted away his right; then he is said to be *obliged,* or *bound.* not to hinder those, to whom such right is granted, or abandoned, from the benefit of it: and that he *ought,* and it is his *duty,* not to make void that voluntary act of his own: and that such hindrance is *injustice,* and *injury,* as being *sine jure;* the right being before renounced, or transferred. So that *injury,* or *injustice,* in the controversies of the world, is somewhat like to that, which in the disputations of scholars is called *absurdity.* For as it is there called an absurdity, to contradict what one maintained in the beginning: so in the world, it is called injustice, and injury, voluntarily to undo that, which from the beginning he had voluntarily done. The way by which a man either simply renounceth, or transferreth his right, is a declaration, or signification, by some voluntary and sufficient sign, or signs, that he doth so renounce, or transfer; or hath so renounced, or transferred the same, to him that accepteth it. And these signs are either words only, or actions only; or, as it happeneth most often, both words, and actions. And the same are the *bonds,* by which men are bound, and obliged: bonds, that have their strength, not from their own nature, for nothing is more easily broken than a man's word, but from fear of some evil consequence upon that rupture.

Whensoever a man transferreth his right, or renounceth it; it is either in consideration of some right reciprocally transferred to himself; or for some other good he hopeth for thereby. For it is a voluntary act: and of the voluntary acts of every man the object is some *good to himself.* And therefore there be some rights, which no man can be understood by any words, or other signs to have abandoned, or transferred. As first a man cannot lay down the right of resisting them, that assault him by force, to take away his life; because he cannot be understood to aim thereby, at any good to himself. The same may be said of wounds, and chains, and imprisonment; both because there is no benefit consequent to such patience; as there is to the patience of suffering another to be wounded, or imprisoned: as also because a man cannot tell, when he seeth men proceed against him by violence, whether they intend his death or not. And lastly the motive, and end for which this renouncing, and transferring of right is introduced, is nothing else but the security of a man's person, in his life, and in the means of so preserving life, as not to be weary of it. And therefore if a man by words, or other signs, seem to despoil himself of the end, for which those signs were intended; he is not to be understood as if he meant it, or that it was his will; but that he was ignorant of how such words and actions were to be interpreted.

The mutual transferring of right, is that which men call *contract.*

. . . .

And though this may seem too subtle a deduction of the laws of nature, to be taken notice of by all men; whereof the most part are too busy in getting food, and the rest too negligent to understand; yet to leave all men inexcusable, they have been contracted into one easy sum, intelligible even to the meanest capacity; and that is, *Do not that to another, which thou wouldest not have done to thyself;* which sheweth him, that he has no more to do in learning the laws of nature, but, when weighing the actions of other men with his own, they seem too heavy, to put them into the other part of the balance, and his own into their place, that his passions, and self-love, may add nothing to the weight; and then there is none of these laws of nature that will not appear unto him very reasonable.

The laws of nature oblige *in foro interno;* that is to say, they bind to a desire they should take place: but *in foro externo;* that is, to the putting them in act, not always. For he that should be modest, and tractable, and perform all he promises, in such time, and place, where no man else should do so, should but make himself a prey to others, and procure his own certain ruin, contrary to the ground of all laws of nature, which tend to nature's preservation. And again, he that having sufficient security, that others shall observe the same laws towards him, observes them not himself, seeketh not peace but war; and consequently the destruction of his nature by violence.

And whatsoever laws bind *in foro interno,* may be broken, not only by a fact contrary to the law, but also by a fact according to it, in case a man think it contrary. For though his action in this case, be according to the law; yet his purpose was against the law; which, where the obligation is *in foro interno,* is a breach.

The laws of nature are immutable and eternal; for injustice, ingratitude, arrogance, pride, iniquity, acception of persons, and the rest, can never be made lawful. For it can never be that war shall preserve life, and peace destroy it.

The same laws, because they oblige only to a desire, and endeavour, I mean an unfeigned and constant endeavour, are easy to be observed. For in that they require nothing but endeavour, he that endeavoureth their performance, fulfilleth them; and he that fulfilleth the law, is just.

And the science of them, is the true and only moral philosophy. For moral philosophy is nothing else but the science of what is *good,* and *evil,* in the conversation, and society of mankind. *Good,* and *evil,* are names that signify our appetites, and aversions; which in different tempers, customs, and doctrines of men, are different: and divers men, differ not only in their judgment, on the senses of what is pleasant, and unpleasant to the taste, smell, hearing, touch, and sight; but also of what is comfortable, or disagreeable to reason, in the actions of common life. Nay, the same man in divers times, differs from himself; and one time praiseth, that is, calleth good, what another time he dispraiseth, and calleth evil: from whence arise disputes, controversies, and at least war. And therefore so long as a man is in the condition of mere nature, which is a condition of war, as private appetite is the measure of good, and evil: and consequently all men agree on this, that peace is good, and therefore also the way, or means of peace, which, as I have shewed before, are *justice, gratitude, modesty, equity, mercy,* and the rest of the laws of nature, are good; that is to say; *moral virtues;* and their contrary *vices,* evil.

Suggestions for Further Reading

In addition to Hobbes's *Leviathan* (1651), the classic works in Social Contract Theory are John Locke, *The Second Treatise of Government* (1690), and Jean Jacques Rousseau, *The Social Contract* (1762). All are available today in various editions.

David P. Gauthier, *The Logic of Leviathan: The Moral and Political Theory of Thomas Hobbes* (Oxford: Clarendon, 1969) is an excellent secondary discussion. Just as good is Gregory Kavka, *Hobbesian Moral and Political Theory* (Princeton, N.J.: Princeton University Press, 1986).

Also see James Rachels, *The Elements of Moral Philosophy* (New York: Random House, 1986), chs. 9 and 10.

Interest in the Social Contract Theory has been revived among contemporary philosophers largely through the work of the Harvard philosopher John Rawls. Rawls's *A Theory of Justice* (Cambridge, Mass.: Harvard University Press, 1971), which argues for a kind of contractarian theory, was the most acclaimed work of moral philosophy of the past three decades. Critical assessments of Rawls may be found in Brian Barry, *The Liberal Theory of Justice* (Oxford: Oxford University Press, 1973); Robert Paul Wolff, *Understanding Rawls* (Princeton, N.J.: Princeton University Press, 1977); and Norman Daniels, ed., *Reading Rawls* (New York: Basic Books, n.d.).

PART III

Philosophical Essays on Particular Moral Issues

11 *A Conservative View of Abortion*

John T. Noonan, Jr.

Although there was always some disagreement about the matter, it is fair to say that the Christian church did not traditionally regard abortion as a serious moral evil. St. Thomas Aquinas, for example, argued that an embryo does not acquire a soul until sometime between 40 and 80 days after conception. Therefore, he concluded, abortion at an early stage of pregnancy is not morally forbidden.

Because the church did not regard abortion as seriously immoral, Western law (which developed under the church's influence) did not traditionally treat abortion as a crime. Under the English common law, abortion was tolerated even if performed late in the pregnancy. In the United States, no laws prohibited it until well into the nineteenth century. When such laws were enacted, they were apparently motivated by three concerns: first, a desire to discourage illicit sexual activity; second, the general belief that abortion was an unsafe medical procedure; and third, the feeling in some circles that it is morally wrong to kill an unborn baby.

In the twentieth century every state in the United States has had laws forbidding abortion. However, those laws were all struck down by the Supreme Court in 1973 in its famous (some would say infamous) decision in *Roe* v. *Wade,* in which the Court held that laws prohibiting abortion violate women's constitutionally protected right to privacy.

The crucial question in the debate over abortion is whether a fetus should be regarded as a person. If it is a person, then killing it can be judged to be the moral equivalent of murder; if it is not a person, then a more lenient attitude toward abortion can be taken. In *Roe* v. *Wade* the Supreme Court declined to say whether the fetus is a person in the ordinary, commonsense meaning of the term; the

Court did, however, hold that a fetus is not a person in the *legal* sense, and so has no constitutionally protected rights of its own.

John T. Noonan, Jr., a distinguished Catholic legal scholar and now a United States federal court judge, is the author of a number of books on morality and the law. These include *Contraception: A History of Its Treatment by the Catholic Theologians and Canonists* (1965), *A Private Choice: Abortion in America in the Seventies* (1979), and *Bribes* (1984). In the following essay he argues that fetuses should be regarded as persons from the moment of conception, because at conception they acquire the full complement of genes that define them as distinct individuals.

The most fundamental question involved in the long history of thought on abortion is: How do you determine the humanity of a being? To phrase the question that way is to put in comprehensive humanistic terms what the theologians either dealt with as an explicitly theological question under the heading of "ensoulment" or dealt with implicitly in their treatment of abortion. The Christian position as it originated did not depend on a narrow theological or philosophical concept. It had no relation to theories of infant baptism. It appealed to no special theory of instantaneous ensoulment. It took the world's view on ensoulment as that view changed from Aristotle to Zacchia. There was, indeed, theological influence affecting the theory of ensoulment finally adopted, and, of course, ensoulment itself was a theological concept, so that the position was always explained in theological terms. But the theological notion of ensoulment could easily be translated into humanistic language by substituting "human" for "rational soul"; the problem of knowing when a man is a man is common to theology and humanism.

If one steps outside the specific categories used by the theologians, the answer they gave can be analyzed as a refusal to discriminate among human beings on the basis of their varying potentialities. Once conceived, the being was recognized as man because he had man's potential. The criterion for humanity, thus, was simple and all-embracing: if you are conceived by human parents, you are human.

The strength of this position may be tested by a review of some of the other distinctions offered in the contemporary controversy over legalizing abortion. Perhaps the most popular distinction is in terms of viability. Before an age of so many months, the fetus is not viable, that is, it cannot be removed from the mother's womb and live apart from her. To that extent, the life of the fetus is absolutely dependent on the life of the mother. This dependence is made the basis of denying recognition to its humanity.

There are difficulties with this distinction. One is that the perfection of artificial incubation may make the fetus viable at any time: it may be removed and artificially sustained. Experiments with animals already show that such a procedure is possible. This hypothetical extreme case relates to an actual difficulty: there is considerable elasticity to the idea of viability. Mere length of life is not an exact measure. The viability of the fetus depends on the extent of its anatomical and functional development. The weight and length of the fetus are better guides to the state of its development than age, but weight and length vary. Moreover, different racial groups have different ages at which their fetuses are viable. Some evidence, for example, suggests that Negro fetuses mature more quickly than white fetuses. If viability is the norm, the standard would vary with race and with many individual circumstances.

The most important objection to this approach is that dependence is not ended by viability. The fetus is still absolutely dependent on someone's care in order to continue existence; indeed a child of one or three or even five years of age is absolutely dependent on another's care for existence; uncared for, the older fetus or the younger child will die as surely as the early fetus detached from the mother. The unsubstantial lessening in dependence at viability does not seem to signify any special acquisition of humanity.

A second distinction has been attempted in terms of experience. A being who has had experience, has lived and suffered, who possesses memories, is more human than one who has not. Humanity depends on formation by experience. The fetus is thus "unformed" in the most basic human sense.

This distinction is not serviceable for the embryo which is already experiencing and reacting. The embryo is responsive to touch after eight weeks and at least at that point is experiencing. At an earlier stage the zygote is certainly alive and responding to its environment. The distinction may also be challenged by the rare case where aphasia has erased adult memory: has it erased humanity? More fundamentally, this distinction leaves even the older fetus or the younger child to be treated as an unformed inhuman thing. Finally, it is not clear why experience as such confers humanity. It could be argued that certain central experiences such as loving or learning are necessary to make a man human. But then human beings who have failed to love or to learn might be excluded from the class called man.

A third distinction is made by appeal to the sentiments of adults. If a fetus dies, the grief of the parents is not the grief they would have for a living child. The fetus is an unnamed "it" till birth, and is not perceived as personality until at least the fourth month of existence when movements in the womb manifest a vigorous presence demanding joyful recognition by the parents.

Yet feeling is notoriously an unsure guide to the humanity of others. Many groups of humans have had difficulty in feeling that persons of another tongue, color, religion, sex, are as human as they. Apart from reactions to alien groups, we mourn the loss of a ten-year-old boy more than the loss of his one-day-old brother or his 90-year-old grandfather. The difference felt and the grief expressed vary with the potentialities extinguished, or the experience wiped out; they do not seem to point to any substantial difference in the humanity of baby, boy, or grandfather.

Distinctions are also made in terms of sensation by the parents. The embryo is felt within the womb only after about the fourth month. The embryo is seen only at birth. What can be neither seen nor felt is different from what is tangible. If the fetus cannot be seen or touched at all, it cannot be perceived as man.

Yet experience shows that sight is even more untrustworthy than feeling in determining humanity. By sight, color became an appropriate index for saying who was a man, and the evil of racial discrimination was given foundation. Nor can touch provide the test; a being confined by sickness, "out of touch" with others, does not thereby seem to lose his humanity. To the extent that touch still has appeal as a criterion, it appears to be a survival of the old English idea of "quickening"—a possible mistranslation of the Latin *animatus* used in the canon law. To that extent touch as a criterion seems to be dependent on the Aristotelian notion of en-soulment, and to fall when this notion is discarded.

Finally, a distinction is sought in social visibility. The fetus is not socially perceived as human. It cannot communicate with others. Thus, both subjectively and objectively, it is not a member of society. As moral rules are rules for the behavior of members of society to each other, they cannot be made for behavior toward what is not yet a member. Excluded from the society of men, the fetus is excluded from the humanity of men.

By force of the argument from the consequences, this distinction is to be rejected. It is more subtle than that founded on an appeal to physical sensation, but it is equally dangerous in its implications. If humanity depends on social recognition, individuals or whole groups may be dehumanized by being denied any status in their society. Such a fate is fictionally portrayed in *1984* and has actually been the lot of many men in many societies. In the Roman empire, for example, condemnation to slavery meant the practical denial of most human rights; in the Chinese Communist world, landlords have been classified as enemies of the people and so treated as nonpersons by the state. Humanity does not depend on social recognition, though often the failure of society to recognize the prisoner, the alien, the heterodox as human has led to the destruction of human beings. Anyone conceived by a man and a woman is human. Recognition of this condition by society follows a real event in the objective order, however imperfect and halting the recognition. Any attempt to limit humanity to exclude some group runs the risk of furnishing authority and precedent for excluding other groups in the name of the consciousness or perception of the controlling group in the society.

A philosopher may reject the appeal to the humanity of the fetus because he views "humanity" as a secular view of the soul and because he doubts the existence of anything real and objective which can be identified as humanity. One answer to such a philosopher is to ask how he reasons about moral questions without supposing that there is a sense in which he and the others of whom he speaks are human. Whatever group is taken as the society which determines who may be killed is thereby taken as human. A second answer is to ask if he does not believe that there is a right and wrong way of deciding moral questions. If there is such a difference, experience may be appealed to: to decide who is human on the basis of the sentiment of a given society has led to consequences which rational men would characterize as monstrous.

The rejection of the attempted distinctions based on viability and visibility, experience and feeling, may be buttressed by the following considerations: Moral judgments often rest on distinctions, but if the distinctions are not to appear arbitrary fiat, they should relate to some real difference in probabilities. There is a kind of continuity in all life, but the earlier stages of the elements of human life possess tiny probabilities of development. Consider for example, the spermatozoa in any normal ejaculate: There are about 200,000,000 in any single ejaculate, of which one has a chance of developing into a zygote. Consider the oocytes which may become ova: there are 100,000 to 1,000,000 oocytes in a female infant, of which a maximum of 390 are ovulated. But once spermatozoon and ovum meet and the conceptus is formed, such studies as have been made show that roughly in only 20 percent of the cases will spontaneous abortion occur. In other words, the chances are about 4 out of 5 that this new being will develop. At this stage in the life of the being there is a sharp shift in probabilities, an immense jump in potentialities. To make a distinction between the rights of spermatozoa and the rights of the fertilized ovum is to respond to an enormous shift in possibilities. For about twenty days after conception the egg may split to form twins or combine with another egg to form a chimera, but the probability of either event happening is very small.

It may be asked, What does a change in biological probabilities have to do with establishing humanity? The argument from probabilities is not aimed at establishing humanity but at establishing an objective discontinuity which may be taken into account in moral discourse. As life itself is a matter of probabilities, as most moral reasoning is an estimate of probabilities, so it seems in accord with the structure of reality and the nature of moral thought to found a moral judgment on the change in probabilities at conception. The appeal to probabilities is the most commonsensical of arguments, to a greater or smaller degree all of us base our actions on probabilities, and in morals, as in law, prudence and negligence are often measured by the account one has taken of the probabilities. If the chance is 200,000,000 to 1 that the movement in the bushes into which you shoot is a man's, I doubt if many persons would hold you careless in shooting; but if the chances are 4 out of 5 that the movement is a human being's, few would acquit you of blame.

Would the argument be different if only one out of ten children conceived came to term? Of course this argument would be different. This argument is an appeal to probabilities that actually exist, not to any and all states of affairs which may be imagined.

The probabilities as they do exist do not show the humanity of the embryo in the sense of a demonstration in logic any more than the probabilities of the movement in the bush being a man demonstrate beyond all doubt that the being is a man. The appeal is a "buttressing" consideration, showing the plausibility of the standard adopted. The argument focuses on the decisional factor in any moral judgment and assumes that part of the business of a moralist is drawing lines. One evidence of the nonarbitrary character of the line drawn is the difference of probabilities on either side of it. If a spermatozoon is destroyed, one destroys a being which had a chance of far less than 1 in 200 million of developing into a reasoning being, possessed of the genetic code, a heart and other organs, and capable of pain. If a fetus is destroyed, one destroys a being already possessed of the genetic code, organs, and sensitivity to pain, and one which had an 80 percent chance of developing further into a baby outside the womb who, in time, would reason.

The positive argument for conception as the decisive moment of humanization is that at conception the new being receives the genetic code. It is this genetic information which determines his characteristics, which is the biological carrier of the possibility of human wisdom, which makes him a self-evolving being. A being with a human genetic code is man.

This review of current controversy over the humanity of the fetus emphasizes what a fundamental question the theologians resolved in asserting the inviolability of the fetus. To regard the fetus as possessed of equal rights with other humans was not, however, to decide every case where abortion might be employed. It did decide the case where the argument was that the fetus should be aborted for its own good. To say a being was human was to say it had a destiny to decide for itself which could not be taken from it by another man's decision. But human beings with equal rights often come in conflict with each other, and some decision must be made as whose claims are to prevail. Cases of conflict involving the fetus are different only in two respects: the total inability of the fetus to speak for itself and the fact that the right of the fetus regularly at stake is the right to life itself.

The approach taken by the theologians to these conflicts was articulated in terms of "direct" and "indirect." Again, to look at what they were doing from outside their categories, they may be said to have been drawing lines or "balancing values." "Direct" and "indirect" are spatial metaphors; "line-drawing" is another. "To weigh" or "to balance" values is a metaphor of a more complicated mathematical sort hinting at the process which goes on in moral judgments. All the metaphors suggest that, in the moral judgments made, comparisons were necessary, that no value completely controlled. The principle of double effect was no doctrine fallen from heaven, but a method of analysis appropriate where two relative values were being compared. In Catholic moral theology, as it developed, life even of the innocent was not taken as an absolute. Judgments on acts affecting life issued from a process of weighing. In the weighing, the fetus was always given a value greater than zero, always a value separate and independent from its parents. This valuation was crucial and fundamental in all Christian thought on the subject and marked it off from any approach which considered that only the parents' interests needed to be considered.

Even with the fetus weighed as human, one interest could be weighed as equal or superior: that of the mother in her own life. The casuists between 1450 and 1895 were willing to weigh this interest as superior. Since 1895, that interest was given decisive weight only in the two special cases of the cancerous uterus and the ectopic pregnancy. In both of these cases the fetus itself had little chance of survival even if the abortion were not performed. As the balance was once struck in favor of the mother whenever her life was endangered, it could be so struck again. The balance reached between 1895 and 1930 attempted prudentially and pastorally to forestall a multitude of exceptions for interests less than life.

The perception of the humanity of the fetus and the weighing of fetal rights against other human rights constituted the work of the moral analysts. But what spirit animated their abstract judgments? For the Christian community it was the injunction of Scripture to love your neighbor as yourself. The fetus as human was a neighbor; his life had parity with one's own. The commandment gave life to what otherwise would have been only rational calculation.

The commandment could be put in humanistic as well as theological terms: Do not injure your fellow man without reason. In these terms, once the humanity of the fetus is perceived, abortion is never right except in self-defense. When life must be taken to save life, reason alone cannot say that a mother must prefer a child's life to her own. With this exception, now of great rarity, abortion violates the rational humanist tenet of the equality of human lives.

For Christians the commandment to love had received a special imprint in that the exemplar proposed of love was the love of the Lord for his disciples. In the light given by this example, self-sacrifice carried to the point of death seemed in the extreme situations not without meaning. In the less extreme cases, preference for one's own interests to the life of another seemed to express cruelty or selfishness irreconcilable with the demands of love.

Suggestions for Further Reading

See page 132.

12 *A Liberal View of Abortion*

Mary Anne Warren

Mary Anne Warren, a philosopher who teaches at San Francisco State University, is well known for her writings on current moral issues, particularly issues related to feminism. In this selection she discusses the central issue of whether fetuses should be regarded as persons. In her view, the possession of physical characteristics, such as genes, is never enough to make one a full-fledged person. Persons, she says, are defined by their *psychological* capacities, such as self-awareness and the ability to communicate. Because they lack such psychological characteristics, she concludes, fetuses are not persons, and so abortion is not morally objectionable.

The question which we must answer in order to produce a satisfactory solution to the problem of the moral status of abortion is this: How are we to define the moral community, the set of beings with full and equal moral rights, such that we can decide whether a human fetus is a member of this community or not? What sort of entity, exactly, has the inalienable rights to life, liberty, and the pursuit of happiness? Jefferson attributed these rights to all *men,* and it may or may not be fair to suggest that he intended to attribute them *only* to men. Perhaps he ought to have attributed them to all human beings. If so, then we arrive, first, at Noonan's problem of defining what makes a being human, and, second, at the equally vital question which Noonan does not consider, namely, What reason is there for identifying the moral community with the set of all human beings, in whatever way we have chosen to define that term?

1. On the Definition of "Human"

One reason why this vital second question is so frequently overlooked in the debate over the moral status of abortion is that the term "human" has two distinct, but not often distinguished, senses. This fact results in a slide of meaning, which serves to conceal the fallaciousness of the traditional argument that since (1) it is wrong to kill innocent human beings, and (2) fetuses are innocent human beings, then (3) it is wrong to kill fetuses. For if "human" is used in the same sense in both (1) and (2) then, whichever of the two senses is meant, one of these premises is question-begging. And if it is used in two different senses then of course the conclusion doesn't follow.

Thus, (1) is a self-evident moral truth,[1] and avoids begging the question about abortion, only if "human being" is used to mean something like "a full-fledged member of the moral community." (It may or may not also be meant to refer exclusively to members of the species *Homo sapiens.*) We may call this the *moral* sense of "human." It is not to be confused with what we will call the *genetic* sense, i.e., the sense in which *any* member of the species is a human being, and no member of any other species could be. If (1) is

---

acceptable only if the moral sense is intended, (2) is non-question-begging only if what is intended is the genetic sense.

In "Deciding Who Is Human," Noonan argues for the classification of fetuses with human beings by pointing to the presence of the full genetic code, and the potential capacity for rational thought.[2] It is clear that what he needs to show, for his version of the traditional argument to be valid, is that fetuses are human in the moral sense, the sense in which it is analytically true that all human beings have full moral rights. But, in the absence of any argument showing that whatever is genetically human is also morally human, and he gives none, nothing more than genetic humanity can be demonstrated by the presence of the human genetic code. And, as we will see, the *potential* capacity for rational thought can at most show that an entity has the potential for *becoming* human in the moral sense.

2. Defining the Moral Community

Can it be established that genetic humanity is sufficient for moral humanity? I think that there are very good reasons for not defining the moral community in this way. I would like to suggest an alternative way of defining the moral community, which I will argue for only to the extent of explaining why it is, or should be, self-evident. The suggestion is simply that the moral community consists of all and only *people*, rather than all and only human beings;[3] and probably the best way of demonstrating its self-evidence is by considering the concept of personhood, to see what sorts of entity are and are not persons, and what the decision that a being is or is not a person implies about its moral rights.

What characteristics entitle an entity to be considered a person? This is obviously not the place to attempt a complete analysis of the concept of personhood, but we do not need such a fully adequate analysis just to determine whether and why a fetus is or isn't a person. All we need is a rough and approximate list of the most basic criteria of personhood, and some idea of which, or how many, of these an entity must satisfy in order to properly be considered a person.

In searching for such criteria, it is useful to look beyond the set of people with whom we are acquainted, and ask how we would decide whether a totally alien being was a person or not. (For we have no right to assume that genetic humanity is necessary for personhood.) Imagine a space traveler who lands on an unknown planet and encounters a race of beings utterly unlike any he has ever seen or heard of. If he wants to be sure of behaving morally toward these beings, he has to somehow decide whether they are people, and hence have full moral rights, or whether they are the sort of thing which he need not feel guilty about treating as, for example, a source of food.

How should he go about making this decision? If he has some anthropological background, he might look for such things as religion, art, and the manufacturing of tools, weapons, or shelters, since these factors have been used to distinguish our human from our prehuman ancestors, in what seems to be closer to the moral than the genetic sense of "human." And no doubt he would be right to consider the presence of such factors as good evidence that the alien beings were people, and morally human. It would, however, be overly anthropocentric of him to take the absence of these things as adequate evidence that they were not, since we can imagine people who have progressed beyond, or evolved without ever developing, these cultural characteristics.

I suggest that the traits which are most central to the concept of personhood, or humanity in the moral sense, are, very roughly, the following:

1. consciousness (of objects and events external and/or internal to the being), and in particular the capacity to feel pain;
2. reasoning (the *developed* capacity to solve new and relatively complex problems);
3. self-motivated activity (activity which is relatively independent of either genetic or direct external control);
4. the capacity to communicate, by whatever means, messages of an indefinite variety of types, that is, not just with an indefinite number of possible contents, but on indefinitely many possible topics;
5. the presence of self-concepts, and self-awareness, either individual or racial, or both.

Admittedly, there are apt to be a great many problems involved in formulating precise definitions of these criteria, let alone in developing universally valid behavioral criteria for deciding when they apply. But I will assume that both we and our explorer know approximately what (1)–(5) mean, and that he is also able to determine whether or not they apply. How, then, should he use his findings to decide whether or not the alien beings are people? We needn't suppose that an entity must have *all* of these attributes to be properly considered a person; (1) and (2) alone may well be sufficient for personhood, and quite probably (1)–(3) are sufficient. Neither do we need to insist that any one of these criteria is *necessary* for personhood, although once again (1) and (2) look like fairly good candidates for necessary conditions, as does (3), if "activity" is construed so as to include the activity of reasoning.

All we need to claim, to demonstrate that a fetus is not a person, is that any being which satisfies *none* of (1)–(5) is certainly not a person. I consider this claim to be so obvious that I think anyone who denied it, and claimed that a being which satisfied none of (1)–(5) was a person all the same, would thereby demonstrate that he had no notion at all of what a person is—perhaps because he had confused the concept of a person with that of genetic humanity. If the opponents of abortion were to deny the appropriateness of these five criteria, I do not know what further arguments would convince them. We would probably have to admit that our conceptual schemes were indeed irreconcilably different, and that our dispute could not be settled objectively.

I do not expect this to happen, however, since I think that the concept of a person is one which is very nearly universal (to people), and that it is common to both proabortionists and antiabortionists, even though neither group has fully realized the relevance of this concept to the resolution of their dispute. Furthermore, I think that on reflection even the antiabortionists ought to agree not only that (1)–(5) are central to the concept of personhood, but also that it is a part of this concept that all and only people have full moral rights. The concept of a person is in part a moral concept; once we have admitted that x is a person we have recognized, even if we have not agreed to respect, x's right to be treated as a member of the moral community. It is true that the claim that x is a *human being* is more commonly voiced as part of an appeal to treat x decently than is the claim that x is a person, but this is either because "human being" is here used in the sense which implies personhood, or because the genetic and moral senses of "human" have been confused.

Now if (1)–(5) are indeed the primary criteria of personhood, then it is clear that genetic humanity is neither necessary nor sufficient for establishing that an entity is a person. Some human beings are not people, and there may well be people who are not human beings. A man or woman whose consciousness has been permanently obliterated but who remains alive is a human being which is no longer a person; defective human beings, with no appreciable mental capacity, are not and presumably never will be people; and a fetus is a human being which is not yet a person, and which therefore cannot coherently be said to have full moral rights. Citizens of the next century should be prepared to recognize highly advanced, self-aware robots or computers, should such be developed, and intelligent inhabitants of other worlds, should such be found, as people in the fullest sense, and to respect their moral rights. But to ascribe full moral rights to an entity which is not a person is as absurd as to ascribe moral obligations and responsibilities to such an entity.

3. Fetal Development and the Right to Life

Two problems arise in the application of these suggestions for the definition of the moral community to the determination of the precise moral status of a human fetus. Given that the paradigm example of a person is a normal adult human being, then (1) How like this paradigm, in particular how far advanced since conception, does a human being need to be before it begins to have a right to life by virtue, not of being fully a person as of yet, but of being *like* a person? and (2) To what extent, if any, does the fact that a fetus has the *potential* for becoming a person endow it with some of the same rights? Each of these questions requires some comment.

In answering the first question, we need not attempt a detailed consideration of the moral rights of organisms which are not developed enough, aware enough, intelligent enough, etc., to be considered people, but which resemble people in some respects. It does seem reasonable to suggest that the more like a person, in the relevant respects, a being is, the stronger is the case for regarding it as having a right to life, and indeed the stronger its right to life is. Thus we ought to take seriously the suggestion that, insofar as "the human individual develops biologically in a continuous fashion . . . the rights of a human person might develop in the same way."[4] But we must keep in mind that the attributes which are relevant in determining whether or not an entity is enough like a person to be regarded as having some of the same moral rights are no different from those which are relevant to determining whether or not it is fully a person—i.e., are no different from (1)–(5)—and that being genetically human, or having recognizably human facial and other physical features, or detectable brain activity, or the capacity to survive outside the uterus, are simply not among these relevant attributes.

Thus it is clear that even though a seven- or eight-month fetus has features which make it apt to arouse in us almost the same powerful protective instinct as is commonly aroused by a small infant, nevertheless it is not significantly more personlike than is a very small embryo. It is *somewhat* more personlike; it can apparently feel and respond to pain, and it may even have a rudimentary form of consciousness, insofar as its brain is quite active. Nevertheless, it seems safe to say that it is not fully conscious, in the way that an infant of a few months is, and that it cannot reason, or communicate messages of indefinitely many sorts, does not engage in self-motivated activity, and has no self-awareness. Thus, in the *relevant* respects, a fetus, even a fully developed one, is considerably less personlike than is the average mature mammal, indeed the average fish. And I think that a rational person must conclude that if the right to life of a fetus is to be based upon its resemblance to a person, then it cannot be said to have any more right to life than, let us say, a newborn guppy (which also seems to be capable of feeling pain), and that a right of that magnitude could never override a woman's right to obtain an abortion, at any stage of her pregnancy.

There may, of course, be other arguments in favor of placing legal limits upon the stage of pregnancy in which an abortion may be performed. Given the relative safety of the new techniques of artificially inducing labor during the third trimester, the danger to the woman's life or health is no longer such an argument. Neither is the fact that people tend to respond to the thought of abortion in the later stages of pregnancy with emotional repulsion, since mere emotional responses cannot take the place of moral reasoning in determining what ought to be permitted. Nor, finally, is the frequently heard argument that legalizing abortion, especially late in the pregnancy, may erode the level of respect for human life, leading, perhaps, to an increase in unjustified euthanasia and other crimes. For this threat, if it is a threat, can be better met by educating people to the kinds of moral distinctions which we are making here than by limiting access to abortion (which limitation may, in its disregard for the rights of women, be just as damaging to the level of respect for human rights).

Thus, since the fact that even a fully developed fetus is not personlike enough to have any significant right to life on the basis of its personlikeness shows that no legal restrictions upon the stage of pregnancy in which an abortion may be performed can be justified on the grounds that we should protect the rights of the older fetus, and since there is no other apparent justification for such restrictions, we may conclude that they are entirely unjustified. Whether or not it would be *indecent* (whatever that means) for a woman in her seventh month to obtain an abortion just to avoid having to postpone a trip to Europe, it would not, in itself, be *immoral*, and therefore it ought to be permitted.

4. Potential Personhood and the Right to Life

We have seen that a fetus does not resemble a person in any way which can support the claim that it has even some of the same rights. But what about its *potential*, the fact that if nurtured and allowed to develop naturally it will very probably become a person? Doesn't that alone give it at least some right to life? It is hard to deny that the fact that an entity is a potential person is a strong prima facie reason for not destroying it; but we need not conclude from this that a potential person has a right to life, by virtue of that potential. It may be that our feeling that it is better, other things being equal, not to destroy a potential person is better explained by the fact that potential people are still (felt to be) an invaluable resource, not to be lightly squandered. Surely, if every speck of dust were a potential person, we would be much less apt to conclude that every potential person has a right to become actual.

Still, we do not need to insist that a potential person has no right to life whatever. There may well be something immoral, and not just imprudent, about wantonly destroying potential people, when doing so isn't necessary to protect anyone's rights. But even if a potential person does have some prima facie right to life, such a right could not possibly outweigh the right of a woman to obtain an abortion, since the rights of any actual person invariably outweigh those of any potential person, whenever the two conflict. Since this may not be immediately obvious in the case of a human fetus, let us look at another case.

Suppose that our space explorer falls into the hands of an alien culture, whose scientists decide to create a few hundred thousand or more human beings, by breaking his body into its component cells, and using these to create fully developed human beings, with, of course, his genetic code. We may imagine that each of these newly created men will have all of the original man's abilities, skills, knowledge, and so on, and also have an individual self-concept, in short that each of them will be a bona fide (though hardly unique) person. Imagine that the whole project will take only seconds, and that its chances of success are extremely high, and that our explorer knows all of this, and also knows that these people will be treated fairly. I maintain that in such a situation he would have every right to escape if he could, and thus to deprive all of these potential people of their potential lives; for his right to life outweighs all of theirs together, in spite of the fact that they are all genetically human, all innocent, and all have a very high probability of becoming people very soon, if only he refrains from acting.

Indeed, I think he would have a right to escape even if it were not his life which the alien scientists planned to take, but only a year of his freedom, or, indeed, only a day. Nor would he be obligated to stay if he had gotten captured (thus bringing all these people-potentials into existence) because of his own carelessness, or even if he had done so deliberately, knowing the consequences. Regardless of how he got captured, he is not morally obligated to remain in captivity for *any* period of time for the sake of permitting any number of potential people to come into actuality, so great is the margin by which one actual person's right to liberty outweighs whatever right to life even a hundred thousand potential people have. And it seems reasonable to conclude that the rights of a woman will outweigh by a similar margin whatever right to life a fetus may have by virtue of its potential personhood.

Thus, neither a fetus's resemblance to a person, nor its potential for becoming a person provides any basis whatever for the claim that it has any significant right to life. Consequently, a woman's right to protect her health, happiness, freedom, and even her life, by terminating an unwanted pregnancy, will always override whatever right to life it may be appropriate to ascribe to a fetus, even a fully developed one. And thus, in the absence of any overwhelming social need for every possible child, the laws which restrict the right to obtain an abortion, or limit the period of pregnancy during which an abortion may be performed, are a wholly unjustified violation of a woman's most basic moral and constitutional rights.

Notes

1. Of course, the principle that it is (always) wrong to kill innocent human beings is in need of many other modifications, e.g., that it may be permissible to do so to save a greater number of other innocent human beings, but we may safely ignore these complications here.

2. John Noonan, "Deciding Who Is Human," *Natural Law Forum,* 13 (1968), 135.

3. From here on, we will use "human" to mean genetically human, since the moral sense seems closely connected to, and perhaps derived from, the assumption that genetic humanity is sufficient for membership in the moral community.

4. Thomas L. Hayes, "A Biological View," *Commonweal,* 85 (March 17, 1967), 677–78; quoted by Daniel Callahan, in *Abortion: Law, Choice and Morality* (London: Macmillan & Co., 1970).

Suggestions for Further Reading

The literature on abortion is vast. Some of the best philosophical articles are collected in Joel Feinberg, ed., *The Problem of Abortion,* 2nd ed. (Belmont, Calif.: Wadsworth, 1984). Perhaps the easiest way into the philosophical debate is through the sixth chapter of Peter Singer's *Practical Ethics* (Cambridge: Cambridge University Press, 1979). One of the most important, but also most difficult, philosophical studies of abortion is Michael Tooley, *Abortion and Infanticide* (Oxford: Clarendon Press, 1983). See, too, Joel Feinberg's essay "Abortion" in *Matters of Life and Death,* 2nd ed., edited by Tom Regan (New York: Random House, 1985).

13 *On Letting Handicapped Babies Die*

Peter Singer and Helga Kuhse

The ancient Greeks did not believe that all human life is precious, or that it should be preserved at all costs. In both Athens and Sparta it was common for deformed infants to be put to death—this was considered better than an unhappy life for them and their parents. The Romans agreed. Describing the Roman attitude, the Stoic philosopher Seneca wrote, "We destroy monstrous births, and drown our children if they are born weakly and unnaturally formed."

The coming of Christianity caused a great change in this attitude. The Christians taught that all human life, no matter how "weakly or unnaturally formed," is precious (is made in the image of God) and must be protected without qualification. With the spread of Christianity, this idea came to dominate the thinking of Western moralists, and today the destruction of innocent babies seems to most people in our culture to be an uncontroversial example of immoral behavior. Tales of infanticidal societies seem no more than stories from the childhood of our civilization.

Recently, however, this situation has begun to change. Many people are now arguing that, in some cases at least, defective infants should be allowed to die. This new attitude is prompted by advances in medical technology that make it possible to "save" many babies that previously could not have been kept alive. Some of these babies are so severely malformed that they have little hope for a meaningful life. In such cases, some parents and doctors have quietly decided against treating the infants. Not much publicity was given to this until 1973, when three doctors "went public" in a pair of articles in the prestigious *New England Journal of Medicine*.

These articles caused great public controversy. In one of them, Drs. Raymond Duff and A. G. M. Campbell described how they had let 43 defective babies die in the Yale–

New Haven Special Care Nursery. In the other, Dr. Anthony
Shaw of the University of Virginia Medical Center discussed
his own handling of such cases. Like Duff and Campbell,
Shaw said that he had sometimes allowed defective babies to
die when the parents refused permission for needed treatment. When these articles appeared, there was some fear that
the doctors would be arrested. But that did not happen, and
despite continuing controversy, such practices have now
become commonplace.

Shaw argued that the new medical techniques pose a
new dilemma: does it follow from the fact that we *have* a new
life-preserving technique that we should *use* it? In some instances, wouldn't we be better off without it? He wrote:

> Each year it becomes possible to remove yet another type of
> malformation from the "unsalvageable" category. All pediatric
> surgeons, including myself, have "triumphs"—infants who, if
> they had been born 25 or even five years ago, would not have
> been salvageable. . . . But how about the infant whose gastroin-
> testinal tract has been removed after volvulus and infarction?
> Although none of us regard the insertion of a central venous
> catheter as a "heroic" procedure, is it right to insert a "lifeline"
> to feed this baby in the light of our present technology, which can
> support him, tethered to an infusion pump, for a maximum of
> one year and some months?

By the late 1970s it seemed that our society was slowly
coming to accept the idea that the decision whether to treat
such infants, or let them die, should be left up to the parents
and physicians. However, with the election of Ronald Reagan
things changed dramatically. President Reagan and his ap-
pointees were determined to reverse this trend, and they set
out to use the power of the federal government to compel
treatment even when the parents and physicians did not wish
it. Reagan's actions were applauded by many people, including many religious groups, but denounced by others, including the American Medical Association, the American
Hospital Association, and other representatives of the medical profession.

The controversy in the 1980s has centered on a pair of
cases involving babies known as Baby Doe and Baby Jane
Doe. In the following selection Peter Singer and Helga

Kuhse describe this controversy and examine some of the
moral issues involved in it. Singer is a professor of philosophy and director of the Centre for Human Bioethics
at Monash University in Australia, where Kuhse is a research fellow. Together they wrote a book-length treatment of these issues, *Should the Baby Live?* (1985). Helga
Kuhse is also the author of *The Sanctity of Life Doctrine in
Medicine: A Critique* (1985). For more information about
Peter Singer, see the editor's comments preceding selection 16.

The original Baby Doe was born on April 9, 1982, in Bloomington,
Indiana, with Down's syndrome (also known as mongolism) and a
blockage in the digestive system. Without surgery to remove the
blockage, such a baby will die. The prospects for successful surgery
were fair, but even if surgery were successful, of course, the underlying mental retardation would be unaffected. For this reason the
parents refused to consent to surgery. Both the county court and the
Indiana Supreme Court upheld the parents' right to make this decision. Before an appeal to the United States Supreme Court could
be mounted, Baby Doe died.

Public reaction to this case began with outraged protests from
the "right-to-life" movement, but soon spread beyond these circles,
with *The Washington Post* and *The New York Times* both editorially
deploring the decision. Letters of protest began to flow into Congress and the White House. The White House responded with
unusual speed. In a memorandum dated April 30, 1982, President
Reagan ordered Richard Schweiker, Secretary of Health and
Human Services, to ensure that federal laws protecting the rights of
handicapped citizens were being adequately enforced. In particular,
the president instructed Secretary Schweiker to notify all who provide health care that section 504 of the Rehabilitation Act of 1973
forbids medical institutions receiving federal funds to withhold
from handicapped citizens, simply because they are handicapped,

---

From *The New York Review of Books*, March 1, 1984. Reprinted by permission of the
authors.

any benefit or service that would ordinarily be provided to people without handicaps. Regulations under this law, the president continued, prohibit hospitals receiving federal assistance from discriminating against the handicapped. President Reagan then instructed the attorney general to report on constitutional and legal means of preventing the withholding from the handicapped of potentially life-saving treatment. His memorandum concluded with the following words:

> Our Nation's commitment to equal protection of the law will have little meaning if we deny such protection to those who have not been blessed with the same physical or mental gifts we too often take for granted. I support Federal laws prohibiting discrimination against the handicapped, and remain determined that such laws will be vigorously enforced.

In accordance with the president's instructions, the Secretary of Health and Human Services sent 6,800 hospitals a "Notice to Health Care Providers." The notice told hospital administrators that it was

> unlawful for a recipient of Federal financial assistance to withhold from a handicapped infant nutritional sustenance or medical or surgical treatment required to correct a life-threatening condition if
> (1) the withholding is based on the fact that the infant is handicapped; and
> (2) the handicap does not render treatment or nutritional sustenance contra-indicated.

Hospital administrators were told that they would have federal government funds cut off if they allowed handicapped infants to die when nonhandicapped infants in similar circumstances would be saved. The "Notice" was saying, in effect, that no matter how severe an infant's handicap might be, the efforts made to preserve its life must be no less than the efforts that would be made to preserve the life of a nonhandicapped infant in an otherwise similar condition. . . .

When confronted with complex ethical questions, one is tempted to look for a simple answer. The Reagan administration has found its simple answer in the idea that all human life is of equal worth.

. . . .

We shall soon see that this position cannot be taken seriously. No one, not even Reagan's own surgeon general, Dr. C. Everett Koop, a man much admired by right-to-life groups . . . can carry it out in practice. But to appreciate this, we must first return to the story of the administration's response to the Baby Doe case.

Strong as its language was, the "Notice" was not sufficient for the White House. In March 1983 the Department of Health and Human Services therefore issued a more forceful follow-up regulation. Officially, the new regulation had the contradictory title "Interim Final Rule," but it has become known as the "Baby Doe guidelines." These guidelines specified that a poster was to be conspicuously displayed in each delivery ward, maternity ward, pediatric ward, and intensive care nursery. The department sent out large, seventeen-by-fourteen-inch posters with heavy black lettering which read as follows:

NOTICE

Department of Health and Human Services
Office for Civil Rights
DISCRIMINATORY FAILURE TO FEED AND CARE FOR
HANDICAPPED INFANTS IN THIS FACILITY IS
PROHIBITED BY FEDERAL LAW. SECTION 504 OF THE
REHABILITATION ACT OF 1973 STATES THAT

"NO OTHERWISE QUALIFIED HANDICAPPED INDIVID-
UAL SHALL, SOLELY BY REASON OF HANDICAP, BE EX-
CLUDED FROM PARTICIPATION IN, BE DENIED THE
BENEFITS OF, OR BE SUBJECTED TO DISCRIMINATION
UNDER ANY PROGRAM OR ACTIVITY RECEIVING FED-
ERAL FINANCIAL ASSISTANCE."

Any person having knowledge that a handicapped infant is being discriminatorily denied food or customary medical care should immediately contact:

Handicapped Infant Hotline
US Department of Health and Human Services
Washington, D.C. 20201
Phone 800-368-1019

(Available 24 hours a day)
TTY Capability
In Washington, D.C., call 863-0100
OR
Your State Child Protective Agency.
Federal Law prohibits retaliation or intimidation against any person who provides information about possible violations of the Rehabilitation Act of 1973.
Identity of callers will be held confidential.
Failure to feed and care for infants may also violate the criminal and civil laws of your state.

Later in the year, the administration worked out the finer details of how to enforce the notice. It was decided to set up a special "Baby Doe Squad." According to a March 4, 1983, memo from the deputy director of program operations to Betty Lou Dotson, director of the Office for Civil Rights within Health and Human Services, the Baby Doe Squad was to consist of "cadres especially selected and trained" who would be provided with individually numbered copies of "Baby Doe complaint" investigation procedures, which were not to be duplicated or released outside the Office for Civil Rights. Depending on the nature of the complaint, one, two, or three squad members would be immediately dispatched to the hospital site, where they would have power to demand hospital records and to interview all relevant personnel. These "special squad assignments" were to "take precedence over any and all assignments."

The Baby Doe guidelines incensed many of the nation's most senior pediatricians—not surprisingly, since they invited all and sundry to make confidential complaints about the way doctors treated their patients. As a result the American Academy of Pediatrics, an association of twenty-four thousand pediatricians, joined with the National Association of Children's Hospitals and the Children's Hospital National Medical Center, in Washington, DC, to contest the regulations in the courts.

Among the grounds for opposition to the guidelines was the question of their scope. The American Academy of Pediatrics submitted affidavits describing medical conditions which are, it said, "simply not treatable"; should we still try to prolong the lives of these infants, as we would, of course, if the infants did not have the conditions in question? In other words, the academy was asking, are doctors now supposed to do everything in their power to prolong all infant lives, no matter what the prospects?

The affidavits referred to three conditions. The first is anencephaly. This means "no brain" and refers to a condition that occurs approximately once in every two thousand births. The infant is born with most or all of its brain missing. Many of these babies die at birth or very soon after, but some have lived for a week or two, and it would be possible, with modern artificial support systems, to keep them alive even longer. The absence, or virtual absence, of a brain means that even if such infants could be kept alive indefinitely, they would never become conscious or respond in any way to other human beings.

The second condition is an intracranial hemorrhage—less technically, a bleeding in the head. Dr. Robert Parrott, director of the Children's Hospital National Medical Center, described some cases as "infants who have such severe bleeding in their heads that they will never breathe without mechanical respiratory assistance yet [sic] never will have the capacity for cognitive behavior." . . .

The third condition is one in which the infant lacks a substantial part of its digestive tract, for instance its intestine and bowels. The infant cannot be fed by mouth, for it will not obtain anything of nutritional value. It is not possible to correct the condition by surgery. Feeding such infants by means of a drip directly into the bloodstream will keep them alive, but nutritional deficiencies are likely and the long-term prospects are poor.

In mentioning these three conditions, the academy was suggesting that the guidelines were, at best, unclear on whether in these cases infants might be allowed to die without receiving life-sustaining treatment; or at worst, the guidelines would direct that such life-sustaining treatment be given, despite the apparent futility of such treatment.

The hearing took place before Judge Gerhard Gesell. . . .

Judge Gerhard Gesell found in favor of the Academy of Pediatrics and its coplaintiffs on the grounds that the department had, by issuing the regulation without allowing a period for public comment, failed to comply with the requirements of the Administrative Procedure Act, an act designed to curb bureaucratic actions taken without consultation and notice to those affected. The department therefore issued, on July 5, 1983, a new "Proposed Rule." The new rule was essentially similar to the ill-fated Interim Final Rule, but it was issued with considerably more information on the circumstances in which it was to apply. In particular, it was stated that:

> Section 504 does not compel medical personnel to attempt to perform impossible or futile acts or therapies. Thus, Section 504 does not require the imposition of futile therapies which merely temporarily prolong the process of dying of an infant born terminally will [sic], such as a child born with anencephaly or intra-cranial bleeding. Such medical decisions, by medical personnel and parents, concerning whether to treat, and if so, what form the treatment should take, are outside the scope of Section 504. The Department recognizes that reasonable medical judgments can differ when evaluating these difficult, individual cases.

Here the department takes the commonsense view that it is not obligatory to keep alive infants with anencephaly or intracranial bleeding. It is interesting to see how the department tries to take this view without basing it on the fact that infants with these conditions have no prospect of a reasonable quality of life. What the department suggests is that in these cases treatment is "futile" and will "merely temporarily prolong the process of dying" of an infant born terminally ill. Whether a treatment is futile in this way is, the department states, a "medical decision" and "reasonable medical judgments can differ" in these cases. The department seems to be saying that it does not wish to interfere in these "medical decisions." Since this remains the position of the department in the final version of its rule, published on January 9, 1984, its approach requires close scrutiny.

The department's position cannot be maintained. As we have seen, sophisticated modern medical techniques could indefinitely prolong the lives of children with anencephaly or intracranial bleeding. The judgment that someone whose life could be indefinitely prolonged by available medical means is "terminally ill" and therefore should not have his or her life prolonged is not a *medical* judgment; it is an ethical judgment about the desirability of prolonging that particular life.

Could the department defend its view by saying that whether a patient is dying is a medical judgment, based on the fact that the patient can survive only with the help of medical treatment? Such a test would be far too broad. By this standard, a patient suffering from diabetes would be "terminally ill" and it would not be required to provide "futile" insulin therapy. The fact that no one in his or her right mind would regard insulin therapy for a diabetic as "futile" should make us realize that judgments about the futility of treatment are not purely medical judgments based on the prospect of the underlying condition being cured. At present we cannot cure diabetes, any more than we can cure anencephaly, or intracranial bleeding, or the absence of an intestine. In all these conditions, the patient will remain, for his or her entire life, dependent for survival on continuing medical treatment. The difference between diabetes and the other three conditions is, of course, that the diabetic will be able to enjoy a near-normal life, while no matter how much we prolong the life of the infant with severe intracranial bleeding, for instance, the infant's life will always remain devoid of everything that we regard as making life worthwhile.

As we read on through the "supplementary information" issued by the Department of Health and Human Services it becomes still more clear that, despite protestations to the contrary, the department's position is based on thinly veiled judgments that some lives are not worth living. The department's statement continues:

> Section 504 simply preserves the decision-making process customarily undertaken by physicians in any treatment decision: will the treatment be medically beneficial to the patient and are those benefits outweighed by any medical risk associated with the treatment? It is only when non-medical considerations, such as subjective judgments that an unrelated handicap makes a person's life not worth living, are interjected in the decision-making process that the Section 504 concerns arise.

In issuing the January 9 "Final Rule," the department indicated that so far as the provision of all "medically beneficial treatment" is concerned, "the Department's position remains unchanged." The problem with this unchanged position is that we need to decide what treatments are "medically beneficial to the patient." The simple answer, and the only answer that is consistent with the idea that all human life is of equal worth, is that all treatments which prolong life are beneficial. Yet this is clearly not the answer the department would give: it does not regard it as beneficial to prolong the lives of infants born with virtually no brain, or who have suffered severe intracranial bleeding. Why is this not "medically beneficial to the patient" in the same way that giving insulin is medically beneficial to the diabetic?

Once again, the answer must be that it is not medically beneficial to prolong the lives of infants who will never experience anything, and will remain alive but in a state without feelings or awareness, unable to enjoy their lives in any way. Plainly, the prolongation of such a life is not "medically beneficial" because it is not beneficial in any sense. . . .

Prolonging the life of an infant without a brain does the infant no good because it is not possible for the infant to benefit from the additional period of life. This is not, however, a medical judgment. It is, quite obviously, a "nonmedical consideration" based on the judgment that the handicap—in this case, the virtual absence of a brain—"makes a person's life not worth living." The department seems to think that such judgments are "subjective" and must not be "interjected in the decision-making process"; yet its own position is based on just this type of judgment.

Admittedly, the department does refer to judgments about "an unrelated handicap," and in criticizing its position we have not taken account of the stipulation that the judgment be about a handicap that is "unrelated." But it is difficult to see exactly what this means or how it can make a difference. Presumably it is supposed to be wrong to take account of a handicap unrelated to the treatment needed to keep the infant alive; but how do we define what the handicap is? This may seem clear enough in a case like that of Baby Doe, where Down's syndrome is the reason for not operating on the blockage in the digestive system. But what about the case of, say, an intracranial bleeding? The treatment needed to keep the infant alive might be artificial respiration. A baby who was having breathing problems, but was otherwise normal, would certainly be put on a respirator; the baby who, as Dr. Parrott put it, "never will have the capacity for cognitive behavior" would not be put on a respirator.

But if the lack of any "capacity for cognitive behavior" is a factor in the decision to put the baby on the respirator, this would have to be a "subjective judgment that an unrelated handicap makes a person's life not worth living." As such, it should give rise to what the department calls "Section 504 concerns." Yet apparently the department does not think it does. On the other hand, the department presumably would think that "Section 504 concerns" arise even in some cases where the decision not to sustain life is made because of a handicap that *is* directly related to the form of treatment—for instance, if a doctor did not give insulin to a diabetic patient because in the doctor's judgment diabetes is a handicap that makes life not worth living. Thus, whether the life-sustaining treatment is or is not related to the patient's handicap cannot be, even in the department's view, a crucial factor in whether a decision not to prolong life is a case of discriminating against the handicap.

The Department of Health and Human Services received 16,739 comments on the proposed rule it issued on July 5, 1983. Ninety-seven percent were in support of the rule, many written in virtually identical terms as a response to appeals by groups like the "Christian Action Council." One hundred and forty-one pediatricians or newborn care specialists sent in comments: of these, 72 percent opposed the rule. The American Academy of Pediatrics has also made a lengthy submission, which includes documentation of the harm done to hospitals trying to cope with medical and human crises by sudden descents of the "Baby Doe Squad." For instance, at Vanderbilt University Hospital, a "hotline" call led to three investigators and a neonatologist examining, after midnight, each infant in the facility, and diverting the hard-pressed hospital staff from patient care for a total of fifty-four staff-hours. The neonatologist described the hospital's care as "exemplary." More dramatic still is a comment quoted from a New Mexico pediatrician:

> Because of the fear I had in being "reported," I recently spent one agonizing hour trying to resuscitate a newborn who had no larynx, and many other congenital anomalies. The sad part was that both the parents in the delivery room watched this most difficult ordeal. It was obvious to me that this was in no way a viable child but I felt compelled to carry on this way out of fear someone in the hospital would "turn me in." I am sure that you who sit in Washington are not faced with such difficult decisions at two o'clock AM.

Comments like this appear to have had some effect on the wording of the Final Rule issued on January 9. Chastened by the hostile reaction to its earlier attempts, the department retreated from the heavy-handed intimidation that had characterized previous versions of the rule. This gradual retreat is reflected in the size and positioning of the notice to be posted in hospitals: the notice sent out with the March 1983 Interim Rule measured seventeen inches by fourteen; the July Proposed Rule required the notice to be no smaller than eleven by eight and a half inches; now the notice can be as small as seven by five inches. Moreover the notice does not have to be posted where parents and visitors can see it, but only at nurses' stations where it can be seen by health care professionals. The wording of the notice has been toned down: for instance, the reference to violations of state criminal and civil laws has been deleted on the grounds that the statement is "unnecessary" and "potentially inflammatory."

The most significant innovation in the new rule of January 9 is the suggestion that hospitals may wish to set up "Infant Care Review Committees" which would discuss problem cases, and with which the department would consult, in the first instance, if any alleged violations were reported to it. This suggestion picks up a recommendation of the American Academy of Pediatrics, and is clearly another attempt to conciliate.

That the department should seek the views of those on the spot before rushing to its own decision is, of course, desirable; but the department makes it clear, beneath its conciliatory language, that it is still the boss. As Dr. Koop said at the press conference at which the Final Rule was announced: "The rules do no more than continue to provide an effective method of enforcing Section 504 in connection with the health care of handicapped infants."

The new rule itself says that "the Department does not seek to take over medical decision-making regarding health care for handicapped infants" but then adds that the parents and physicians must act within the framework set by law, including the Section 504 prohibition of discrimination. The department specifically rejects the suggestion that with the review boards in place, the government could refrain from playing a role in enforcing this statute with regard to handicapped infants.

. . . .

Spina bifida is one of the most common birth defects. It is controversial because in many countries, including Britain and Australia, it is standard practice to allow the more severely afflicted babies to die. Less severe cases are operated on and given every available assistance, often with the result that the children go on to lead fulfilling lives; the remainder, if the parents agree, are not operated upon, and if infections appear or pneumonia develops, these children are not given antibiotics.

There is no hypocrisy or pretense about this practice of selection, which has been accepted by the British Department of Health and Social Service. The practice derives largely from the work of Dr. John Lorber of Sheffield. For several years Lorber and his colleagues in Sheffield treated every case of spina bifida as vigorously as possible. Then, looking back on the results of more than a thousand cases, Lorber decided that this was a mistake; in many cases, the lives he had saved were not worth living and the burden on families was sometimes barely tolerable. Lorber switched to treating about 25 percent of the cases brought before him, obtaining the parents' consent for whatever course he followed: in advocating this policy in medical journals he has stated candidly that he does not operate on the more severely affected infants because he thinks it better that they do not survive beyond infancy.

The Reagan administration is now insisting that treatment for spina bifida infants may be withheld only if there is a medical judgment that it is "futile" and "not of medical benefit to the infant." If this were taken seriously in Great Britain, thousands of infants who would be allowed to die there would survive, often against the wishes of the parents. Apparently the Reagan administration believes that infants must be treated even if in the opinion of the parents, the doctors, *and* the hospital Infant Care Review Committee the life thus "saved" will be so miserable that the infant would be better off dead. "Medical benefit," remember, is not supposed to involve considerations of the quality of life.

In practice it is very likely that the new rule will simply widen the already considerable gap between appearance and reality in American medicine. American doctors will start to disguise their inevitable judgments about quality of life under the cloak of "medical judgments" about the "futility" of treatment. A cynic might see the new rule as an open invitation to doctors to do just this, thus defusing the politically damaging war of words between pediatricians and pro-life forces.

Those who reject judgments about quality of life should not forget that pregnant women who run an abnormal risk of carrying a defective child are standardly advised to have a prenatal test with a view to abortion if the test does reveal that the infant will be handicapped. These women are obviously making quality-of-life judgments, and presumably will continue to be allowed to do so. . . . The pro-life groups are right about one thing: the location of the baby inside or outside the womb cannot make such a crucial moral difference. We cannot coherently hold that it is all right to kill a fetus a week before birth, but as soon as the baby is born everything must be done to keep it alive. The solution, however, is not to accept the pro-life view that the fetus is a human being with the same moral status as yours or mine. The solution is the very opposite: to abandon the idea that all human life is of equal worth.

The statement will assuredly bring letters saying that once we abandon our belief in the equal worth of all human life we are well on the way to Nazism and to ridding the world of all social undesirables, political undesirables, and racial undesirables. The Nazi parallel is an old bogey which has no historical basis. But history apart, the unequal worth of human life is really so obvious that we have only to cast off our religious or ideological blinkers to see it as plain as day. If the life of a human being is more valuable than the life of, say, a cabbage, this must be because the human being has qualities like consciousness, rationality, autonomy, and self-awareness which distinguish human beings from cabbages. How, then, can we pretend that the life of a human being *with* all these distinctive qualities is of no greater value than the life of a human being who, tragically, has never had and never will have these qualities? As we said earlier: in practice, not even Dr. C. Everett Koop treats the life of a baby without a brain as if it were of the same value as the life of a normal child.

Suggestions for Further Reading

Singer and Kuhse's book-length treatment of these matters is *Should the Baby Live?* (Oxford: Oxford University Press, 1985). But for a view of Baby Jane Doe very different from Singer and Kuhse's, see Nat Hentoff, "The Awful Privacy of Baby Doe," *The Atlantic,* January 1985, pp. 54ff.

Marvin Kohl, ed., *Infanticide and the Value of Life* (Buffalo, N.Y.: Prometheus Books, 1978) is an excellent collection of articles.

Fred M. Frohock, *Special Care* (Chicago: University of Chicago Press,

1986) is an extended case study of decision making in a particular special-care nursery; it is highly recommended for its picture of what such facilities are actually like.

Also see Donald VanDeVeer, "Whither Baby Doe?" in *Matters of Life and Death*, 2nd ed., edited by Tom Reagan (New York: Random House, 1985).

14 *Gay Basics: Some Questions, Facts, and Values*

Richard D. Mohr

Richard D. Mohr, who teaches philosophy at the University of Illinois, is a scholar specializing in ancient Greek thought. His extensive writing on gay rights includes the book *Gays/Justice: A Study of Ethics, Society, and Law* (1988). In the following essay, written especially for this volume, he discusses a variety of issues connected with the position of homosexuals in American society.

I. Who Are Gays Anyway?

A recent Gallup poll found that only one in five Americans reports having a gay or lesbian acquaintance.[1] This finding is extraordinary given the number of practicing homosexuals in America. Alfred Kinsey's 1948 study of the sex lives of 12,000 white males shocked the nation: 37 percent had at least one homosexual experience to

148   RICHARD D. MOHR

orgasm in their adult lives; an additional 13 percent had homosexual fantasies to orgasm; 4 percent were exclusively homosexual in
their practices; another 5 percent had virtually no heterosexual
experience; and nearly 20 percent had at least as many homosexual
as heterosexual experiences.[2]

Two out of five men one passes on the street have had orgas-
mic sex with men. Every second family in the country has a member
who is essentially homosexual and many more people regularly
have homosexual experiences. Who are homosexuals? They are
your friends, your minister, your teacher, your bank teller, your
doctor, your mail carrier, your officemate, your roommate, your
congressional representative, your sibling, parent, and spouse.
They are everywhere, virtually all ordinary, virtually all unknown.

Several important consequences follow. First, the country is
profoundly ignorant of the actual experience of gay people. Second,
social attitudes and practices that are harmful to gays have a much
greater overall harmful impact on society than is usually realized.
Third, most gay people live in hiding—in the closet—making the
"coming out" experience the central fixture of gay consciousness
and invisibility the chief characteristic of the gay community.

II. Ignorance, Stereotype, and Morality

Ignorance about gays, however, has not stopped people from having strong opinions about them. The void which ignorance leaves
has been filled with stereotypes. Society holds chiefly two groups of
anti-gay stereotypes; the two are an oddly contradictory lot. One set
of stereotypes revolves around alleged mistakes in an individual's
gender identity: lesbians are women that want to be, or at least look
and act like, men—bull dykes, diesel dykes; while gay men are those
who want to be, or at least look and act like, women—queens,
fairies, limp-wrists, nellies. These stereotypes of mismatched gen-
ders provide the materials through which gays and lesbians become
the butts of ethniclike jokes. These stereotypes and jokes, though
derisive, basically view gays and lesbians as ridiculous.

Another set of stereotypes revolves around gays as a pervasive,
sinister, conspiratorial threat. The core stereotype here is the gay
person as child molester, and more generally as sex-crazed maniac.
These stereotypes carry with them fears of the very destruction of
family and civilization itself. Now, that which is essentially ridiculous

can hardly have such a staggering effect. Something must be afoot in this incoherent amalgam.

Sense can be made of this incoherence if the nature of stereotypes is clarified. Stereotypes are not *simply* false generalizations from a skewed sample of cases examined. Admittedly, false generalizing plays some part in the stereotypes a society holds. If, for instance, one takes as one's sample homosexuals who are in psychiatric hospitals or prisons, as was done in nearly all early investigations, not surprisingly one will probably find homosexuals to be of a crazed and criminal cast. Such false generalizations, though, simply confirm beliefs already held on independent grounds, ones that likely led the investigator to the prison and psychiatric ward to begin with. Evelyn Hooker, who in the late fifties carried out the first rigorous studies to use nonclinical gays, found that psychiatrists, when presented with case files including all the standard diagnostic psychological profiles—but omitting indications of sexual orientation—were unable to distinguish files of gays from those of straights, even though they believed gays to be crazy and supposed themselves to be experts in detecting craziness.[3] These studies proved a profound embarrassment to the psychiatric establishment, the financial well-being of which has been substantially enhanced by "curing" allegedly insane gays. The studies led the way to the American Psychiatric Association finally in 1973 dropping homosexuality from its registry of mental illnesses.[4] Nevertheless, the stereotype of gays as sick continues apace in the mind of America.

False generalizations *help maintain* stereotypes; they do not *form* them. As the history of Hooker's discoveries shows, stereotypes have a life beyond facts; their origin lies in a culture's ideology—the general system of beliefs by which it lives—and they are sustained across generations by diverse cultural transmissions, hardly any of which, including slang and jokes, even purport to have a scientific basis. Stereotypes, then, are not the products of bad science but are social constructions that perform central functions in maintaining society's conception of itself.

On this understanding, it is easy to see that the anti-gay stereotypes surrounding gender identification are chiefly means of reinforcing still powerful gender roles in society. If, as this stereotype presumes and condemns, one is free to choose one's social roles independently of gender, many guiding social divisions, both domestic and commercial, might be threatened. The socially gender-linked distinctions between breadwinner and homemaker, boss and secretary, doctor and nurse, protector and protected would blur. The accusations "dyke" and "fag" exist in significant part to keep women in their place and to prevent men from breaking ranks and ceding away theirs.

The stereotypes of gays as child molesters, sex-crazed maniacs, and civilization destroyers function to displace (socially irresolvable) problems from their actual source to a foreign (and so, it is thought, manageable) one. Thus the stereotype of child molester functions to give the family unit a false sheen of absolute innocence. It keeps the unit from being examined too closely for incest, child abuse, wife-battering, and the terrorism of constant threats. The stereotype teaches that the problems of the family are not internal to it, but external.[5]

One can see these cultural forces at work in society's and the media's treatment of current reports of violence, especially domestic violence. When a mother kills her child or a father rapes his daughter—regular Section B fare even in major urban papers—this is never taken by reporters, columnists, or pundits as evidence that there is something wrong with heterosexuality or with traditional families. These issues are not even raised. But when a homosexual child molestation is reported it is taken as confirming evidence of the way homosexuals are. One never hears of heterosexual murders, but one regularly hears of "homosexual" ones. Compare the social treatment of Richard Speck's sexually motivated mass murder of Chicago nurses with that of John Wayne Gacy's murders of Chicago youths. Gacy was in the culture's mind taken as symbolic of gay men in general. To prevent the possibility that The Family was viewed as anything but an innocent victim in this affair, the mainstream press knowingly failed to mention that most of Gacy's adolescent victims were homeless hustlers. That knowledge would be too much for the six o'clock news and for cherished beliefs.

Because "the facts" largely don't matter when it comes to the generation and maintenance of stereotypes, the effects of scientific and academic research and of enlightenment generally will be, at best, slight and gradual in the changing fortunes of lesbians and gay men. If this account of stereotypes holds, society has been profoundly immoral. For its treatment of gays is a grand scale rationalization, a moral sleight-of-hand. The problem is not that society's usual standards of evidence and procedure in coming to judgments of social policy have been misapplied to gays; rather when it comes to gays, the standards themselves have simply been ruled out of court and disregarded in favor of mechanisms that encourage unexamined fear and hatred.

III. Are Gays Discriminated Against? Does It Matter?

Partly because lots of people suppose they don't know any gay people and partly through willful ignorance of its own workings, society at large is unaware of the many ways in which gays are subject to discrimination in consequence of widespread fear and hatred. Contributing to this social ignorance of discrimination is the difficulty for gay people, as an invisible minority, even to complain of discrimination. For if one is gay, to register a complaint would suddenly target one as a stigmatized person, and so in the absence of any protections against discrimination, would simply invite additional discrimination. Further, many people, especially those who are persistently downtrodden and so lack a firm sense of self to begin with, tend either to blame themselves for their troubles or to view injustice as a matter of bad luck rather than as indicating something wrong with society. The latter recognition would require doing something to rectify wrong and most people, especially the already beleaguered, simply aren't up to that. So for a number of reasons discrimination against gays, like rape, goes seriously underreported.

First, gays are subject to violence and harassment based simply on their perceived status rather than because of any actions they have performed. A recent extensive study by the National Gay Task Force found that over 90 percent of gays and lesbians had been victimized in some form on the basis of their sexual orientation.[6] Greater than one in five gay men and nearly one in ten lesbians had been punched, hit, or kicked; a quarter of all gays had had objects thrown at them; a third had been chased; a third had been sexually harassed; and 14 percent had been spit on—all just for being perceived as gay.

The most extreme form of anti-gay violence is "queerbashing"—where groups of young men target a person who they suppose is a gay man and beat and kick him unconscious and sometimes to death amid a torrent of taunts and slurs. Such seemingly random but in reality socially encouraged violence has the same social origin and function as lynchings of blacks—to keep a whole stigmatized group in line. As with lynchings of the recent past, the police and courts have routinely averted their eyes, giving their implicit approval to the practice.

Few such cases with gay victims reach the courts. Those that do are marked by inequitable procedures and results. Frequently judges will describe "queerbashers" as "just all-American boys." Recently a District of Columbia judge handed suspended sentences to queerbashers whose victim had been stalked, beaten, stripped at knife point, slashed, kicked, threatened with castration, and pissed on, because the judge thought the bashers were good boys at heart—after all, they went to a religious prep school.[7]

Police and juries will simply discount testimony from gays; they typically construe assaults on and murders of gays as "justified" self-defense—the killer need only claim his act was a panicked response to a sexual overture. Alternatively, when guilt seems patent, juries will accept highly implausible "diminished capacity" defenses, as in the case of Dan White's 1978 assassination of openly gay San Francisco city councilman Harvey Milk: Hostess Twinkies made him do it.[8]

These inequitable procedures and results collectively show that the life and liberty of gays, like those of blacks, simply count for less than the life and liberty of members of the dominant culture.

The equitable rule of law is the heart of an orderly society. The collapse of the rule of law for gays shows that society is willing to perpetrate the worst possible injustices against them. Conceptually there is only a difference in degree between the collapse of the rule of law and systematic extermination of members of a population simply for having some group status independent of any act an individual has performed. In the Nazi concentration camps, gays were forced to wear pink triangles as identifying badges, just as Jews were forced to wear yellow stars. In remembrance of that collapse of the rule of law, the pink triangle has become the chief symbol of the gay rights movement.[9]

Gays are subject to widespread discrimination in employment—the very means by which one puts bread on one's table and one of the chief means by which individuals identify themselves to themselves and achieve personal dignity. Governments are leading offenders here. They do a lot of discriminating themselves, require that others do it (e.g., government contractors), and set precedents favoring discrimination in the private sector. The federal government explicitly discriminates against gays in the armed forces, the CIA, FBI, National Security Agency, and the state department. The federal government refuses to give security clearances to gays and so forces the country's considerable private sector military and aerospace contractors to fire known gay employees. State and local governments regularly fire gay teachers, policemen, firemen, social workers, and anyone who has contact with the public. Further, through licensing laws states officially bar gays from a vast array of occupations and professions—everything from doctors, lawyers, accountants, and nurses to hairdressers, morticians, and used car dealers. The American Civil Liberties Union's handbook *The Rights of Gay People* lists 307 such prohibited occupations.[10]

Gays are subject to discrimination in a wide variety of other ways, including private-sector employment, public accommodations, housing, immigration and naturalization, insurance of all types, custody and adoption, and zoning regulations that bar "singles" or "nonrelated" couples. All of these discriminations affect central components of a meaningful life; some even reach to the means by which life itself is sustained. In half the states, where gay sex is illegal, the central role of sex to meaningful life is officially denied to gays.

All these sorts of discriminations also affect the ability of people to have significant intimate relations. It is difficult for people to live together as couples without having their sexual orientation perceived in the public realm and so becoming targets for discrimination. Illegality, discrimination, and the absorption by gays of society's hatred of them all interact to impede or block altogether the ability of gays and lesbians to create and maintain significant personal relations with loved ones. So every facet of life is affected by discrimination. Only the most compelling reasons could justify it.

IV. But Aren't They Immoral?

Many people think society's treatment of gays is justified because they think gays are extremely immoral. To evaluate this claim, different senses of "moral" must be distinguished. Sometimes by "morality" is meant the overall beliefs affecting behavior in a society—its mores, norms, and customs. On this understanding, gays certainly are not moral: lots of people hate them and social customs are designed to register widespread disapproval of gays. The problem here is that this sense of morality is merely a *descriptive* one. On this understanding *every* society has a morality—even Nazi society, which had racism and mob rule as central features of its "morality," understood in this sense. What is needed in order to use the notion of morality to praise or condemn behavior is a sense of morality that is *prescriptive* or *normative*—a sense of morality whereby, for instance, the descriptive morality of the Nazis is found wanting.

As the Nazi example makes clear, that something is descriptively moral is nowhere near enough to make it normatively moral. A lot of people in a society saying something is good, even over eons, does not make it so. Our rejection of the long history of socially approved and state-enforced slavery is another good example of this principle at work. Slavery would be wrong even if nearly everyone liked it. So consistency and fairness require that we abandon the belief that gays are immoral simply because most people dislike or disapprove of gays or gay acts, or even because gay sex acts are illegal.

Furthermore, recent historical and anthropological research has shown that opinion about gays has been by no means universally negative. Historically, it has varied widely even within the larger part of the Christian era and even within the church itself.[11] There are even societies—current ones—where homosexuality is not only tolerated but a universal compulsory part of social maturation.[12] Within the last thirty years, American society has undergone a grand turnabout from deeply ingrained, near total condemnation to near total acceptance on two emotionally charged "moral" or "family" issues: contraception and divorce. Society holds its current descriptive morality of gays not because it has to, but because it chooses to.

If popular opinion and custom are not enough to ground moral condemnation of homosexuality, perhaps religion can. Such argument proceeds along two lines. One claims that the condemnation is a direct revelation of God, usually through the Bible; the other claims to be able to detect condemnation in God's plan as manifested in nature.

One of the more remarkable discoveries of recent gay research is that the Bible may not be as univocal in its condemnation of homosexuality as has been usually believed.[13] Christ never mentions homosexuality. Recent interpreters of the Old Testament have pointed out that the story of Lot at Sodom is probably intended to condemn inhospitality rather than homosexuality. Further, some of the Old Testament condemnations of homosexuality seem simply to be ways of tarring those of the Israelites' opponents who happened to accept homosexual practices when the Israelites themselves did not. If so, the condemnation is merely a quirk of history and rhetoric rather than a moral precept.

What does seem clear is that those who regularly cite the Bible to condemn an activity like homosexuality do so by reading it selectively. Do ministers who cite what they take to be condemnations of homosexuality in Leviticus maintain in their lives all the hygienic and dietary laws of Leviticus? If they cite the story of Lot at Sodom to condemn homosexuality, do they also cite the story of Lot in the cave to praise incestuous rape? It seems then not that the Bible is being used to ground condemnations of homosexuality as much as society's dislike of homosexuality is being used to interpret the Bible.[14]

Even if a consistent portrait of condemnation could be gleaned from the Bible, what social significance should it be given? One of the guiding principles of society, enshrined in the Constitution as a check against the government, is that decisions affecting social policy are not made on religious grounds. If the real ground of the alleged immorality invoked by governments to discriminate against gays is religious (as it has explicitly been even in some recent court cases involving teachers and guardians), then one of the major commitments of our nation is violated.

V. But Aren't They Unnatural?

The most noteworthy feature of the accusation of something being unnatural (where a moral rather than an advertising point is being made) is that the plaint is so infrequently made. One used to hear the charge leveled against abortion, but that has pretty much faded as anti-abortionists have come to lay all their chips on the hope that people will come to view abortion as murder. Incest used to be considered unnatural but discourse now usually assimilates it to the moral machinery of rape and violated trust. The charge comes up now in ordinary discourse only against homosexuality. This suggests that the charge is highly idiosyncratic and has little, if any, explanatory force. It fails to put homosexuality in a class with anything else so that one can learn by comparison with clear cases of the class just exactly what it is that is allegedly wrong with it.

Though the accusation of unnaturalness looks whimsical, in actual ordinary discourse when applied to homosexuality, it is usually delivered with venom aforethought. It carries a high emotional charge, usually expressing disgust and evincing queasiness. Probably it is nothing but an emotional charge. For people get equally disgusted and queasy at all sorts of things that are perfectly natural—to be expected in nature apart from artifice—and that could hardly be fit subjects for moral condemnation. Two typical examples in current American culture are some people's responses to mothers' suckling in public and to women who do not shave body hair. When people have strong emotional reactions, as they do in these cases, without being able to give good reasons for them, we think of them not as operating morally, but rather as being obsessed and manic. So the feelings of disgust that some people have to gays will hardly ground a charge of immorality. People fling the term "unnatural" against gays in the same breath and with the same force as when they call gays "sick" and "gross." When they do this, they give every appearance of being neurotically fearful and incapable of reasoned discourse.

When "nature" is taken in *technical* rather than ordinary usages, it looks like the notion also will not ground a charge of homosexual immorality. When unnatural means "by artifice" or "made by humans," it need only be pointed out that virtually everything that is good about life is unnatural in this sense, that the chief feature that distinguishes people from other animals is their very ability to make over the world to meet their needs and desires, and that their well-being depends upon these departures from nature. On this understanding of human nature and the natural, homosexuality is perfectly unobjectionable.

Another technical sense of natural is that something is natural and so, good, if it fulfills some function in nature. Homosexuality on this view is unnatural because it allegedly violates the function of genitals, which is to produce babies. One problem with this view is that lots of bodily parts have lots of functions and just because some one activity can be fulfilled by only one organ (say, the mouth for eating) this activity does not condemn other functions of the organ to immorality (say, the mouth for talking, licking stamps, blowing bubbles, or having sex). So the possible use of the genitals to produce children does not, without more, condemn the use of the genitals for other purposes, say, achieving ecstasy and intimacy.

The functional view of nature will only provide a morally condemnatory sense to the unnatural if a thing which might have many uses has but one proper function to the exclusion of other possible functions. But whether this is so cannot be established simply by looking at the thing. For what is seen is all its possible functions. The notion of function seemed like it might ground moral authority, but instead it turns out that moral authority is needed to define proper function. Some people try to fill in this moral authority by appeal to the "design" or "order" of an organ, saying, for instance, that the genitals are designed for the purpose of procreation. But these people cheat intellectually if they do not make explicit *who* the designer and orderer is. If it is God, we are back to square one—holding others accountable for religious beliefs.

Further, ordinary moral attitudes about childbearing will not provide the needed supplement which in conjunction with the natural function view of bodily parts would produce a positive obligation to use the genitals for procreation. Society's attitude toward a childless couple is that of pity not censure—even if the couple could have children. The pity may be an unsympathetic one, that is, not registering a course one would choose *for oneself,* but this does not make it a course one would *require* of others. The couple who discovers they cannot have children are viewed not as having thereby had a debt canceled, but rather as having to forgo some of the richness of life, just as a quadriplegic is viewed not as absolved from some moral obligation to hop, skip, and jump, but as missing some of the richness of life. Consistency requires then that, at most, gays who do not or cannot have children are to be pitied rather than condemned. What *is* immoral is the willful preventing of people from achieving the richness of life. Immorality in this regard lies with those social customs, regulations, and statutes that prevent lesbians and gay men from establishing blood or adoptive families, not with gays themselves.

Sometimes people attempt to establish authority for a moral obligation to use bodily parts in a certain fashion simply by claiming that moral laws are natural laws and vice versa. On this account, inanimate objects and plants are good in that they follow natural laws by necessity, animals by instinct, and persons by a rational will. People are special in that they must first discover the laws that govern them. Now, even if one believes the view—dubious in the post-Newtonian, post-Darwinian world—that natural laws in the usual sense ($E = mc^2$, for instance) have some moral content, it is not at all clear how one is to discover the laws in nature that apply to people.

On the one hand, if one looks to people themselves for a model—and looks hard enough—one finds amazing variety, including homosexuality as a social ideal (upper-class fifth-century Athens) and even as socially mandatory (Melanesia today). When one looks to people, one is simply unable to strip away the layers of social custom, history, and taboo in order to see what's really there to any degree more specific than that people are the creatures that make over their world and are capable of abstract thought. That this is so should raise doubts that neutral principles are to be found in human nature that will condemn homosexuality.

On the other hand, if one looks to nature apart from people for models, the possibilities are staggering. There are fish that change gender over their lifetimes: should we "follow nature" and be operative transsexuals? Orangutans, genetically our next of kin, live completely solitary lives without social organization of any kind: ought we to "follow nature" and be hermits? There are many species where only two members per generation reproduce: should we be bees? The search in nature for people's purpose, far from finding sure models for action, is likely to leave one morally rudderless.

VI. But Aren't Gays Willfully the Way They Are?

It is generally conceded that if sexual orientation is something over which an individual—for whatever reason—has virtually no control, then discrimination against gays is especially deplorable, as it is against racial and ethnic classes, because it holds people accountable without regard for anything they themselves have done. And to hold a person accountable for that over which the person has no control is a central form of prejudice.

Attempts to answer the question whether or not sexual orientation is something that is reasonably thought to be within one's own control usually appeal simply to various claims of the biological or "mental" sciences. But the ensuing debate over genes, hormones, twins, early childhood development, and the like, is as unnecessary as it is currently inconclusive.[15] All that is needed to answer the question is to look at the actual experience of gays in current society and it becomes fairly clear that sexual orientation is not likely a matter of choice. For coming to have a homosexual identity simply does not have the same sort of structure that decision making has.

On the one hand, the "choice" of the gender of a sexual partner does not seem to express a trivial desire that might be as easily well fulfilled by a simple substitution of the desired object. Picking the gender of a sex partner is decidedly dissimilar, that is, to such activities as picking a flavor of ice cream. If an ice-cream parlor is out of one's flavor, one simply picks another. And if people were persecuted, threatened with jail terms, shattered careers, loss of family and housing, and the like, for eating, say, rocky road ice cream, no one would ever eat it; everyone would pick another easily available flavor. That gay people abide in being gay even in the face of persecution shows that being gay is not a matter of easy choice.

On the other hand, even if establishing a sexual orientation is not like making a relatively trivial choice, perhaps it is nevertheless relevantly like making the central and serious life choices by which individuals try to establish themselves as being of some type. Again, if one examines gay experience, this seems not to be the case. For one never sees anyone setting out to become a homosexual, in the way one does see people setting out to become doctors, lawyers, and bricklayers. One does not find "gays-to-be" picking some end— "At some point in the future, I want to become a homosexual"—and then setting about planning and acquiring the ways and means to that end, in the way one does see people deciding that they want to become lawyers, and then sees them plan what courses to take and what sort of temperaments, habits, and skills to develop in order to become lawyers. Typically gays-to-be simply find themselves having homosexual encounters and yet at least initially resisting quite strongly the identification of being homosexual. Such a person even very likely resists having such encounters, but ends up having them anyway. Only with time, luck, and great personal effort, but sometimes never, does the person gradually come to accept her or his orientation, to view it as a given material condition of life, coming as materials do with certain capacities and limitations. The person begins to act in accordance with his or her orientation and its capacities, seeing its actualization as a requisite for an integrated personality and as a central component of personal well-being. As a result, the experience of coming out to oneself has for gays the basic structure of a discovery, not the structure of a choice. And far from signaling immorality, coming out to others affords one of the few remaining opportunities in ever more bureaucratic, mechanistic, and socialistic societies to manifest courage.

VII. How Would Society at Large Be Changed If Gays Were Socially Accepted?

Suggestions to change social policy with regard to gays are invariably met with claims that to do so would invite the destruction of civilization itself: after all, isn't that what did Rome in? Actually Rome's decay paralleled not the flourishing of homosexuality but its repression under the later Christianized emperors.[16] Predictions of American civilization's imminent demise have been as premature as they have been frequent. Civilization has shown itself rather resilient here, in large part because of the country's traditional commitments to a respect for privacy, to individual liberties, and especially to people minding their own business. These all give society an open texture and the flexibility to try out things to see what works. And because of this one now need not speculate about what changes reforms in gay social policy might bring to society at large. For many reforms have already been tried.

Half the states have decriminalized homosexual acts. Can you guess which of the following states still have sodomy laws: Wisconsin, Minnesota; New Mexico, Arizona; Vermont, New Hampshire; Nebraska, Kansas. One from each pair does and one does not have sodomy laws. And yet one would be hard pressed to point out any substantial difference between the members of each pair. (If you're interested, it is the second of each pair with them.) Empirical studies have shown that there is no increase in other crimes in states that have decriminalized.[17] Further, sodomy laws are virtually never enforced. They remain on the books not to "protect society" but to insult gays, and for that reason need to be removed.

Neither has the passage of legislation barring discrimination against gays ushered in the end of civilization. Some 50 counties and municipalities, including some of the country's largest cities (like Los Angeles and Boston), have passed such statutes and among the states and colonies Wisconsin and the District of Columbia have model protective codes. Again, no more brimstone has fallen in these places than elsewhere. Staunchly anti-gay cities, like Miami and Houston, have not been spared the AIDS crisis.

Berkeley, California, has even passed domestic partner legislation giving gay couples the same rights to city benefits as married couples, and yet Berkeley has not become more weird than it already was.

Seemingly hysterical predictions that the American family would collapse if such reforms would pass proved false, just as the same dire predictions that the availability of divorce would lessen the ideal and desirability of marriage proved completely unfounded. Indeed if current discriminations, which drive gays into hiding and into anonymous relations, were lifted, far from seeing gays raze American families, one would see gays forming them.

Virtually all gays express a desire to have a permanent lover. Many would like to raise or foster children—perhaps those alarming numbers of gay kids who have been beaten up and thrown out of their "families" for being gay. But currently society makes gay coupling very difficult. A life of hiding is a pressure-cooker existence not easily shared with another. Members of non-gay couples are here asked to imagine what it would take to erase every trace of their own sexual orientation for even just a week.

Even against oppressive odds, gays have shown an amazing tendency to nest. And those gay couples who have survived the odds show that the structure of more usual couplings is not a matter of destiny but of personal responsibility. The so-called basic unit of society turns out not to be a unique immutable atom, but can adopt different parts, be adapted to different needs, and even be improved. Gays might even have a thing or two to teach others about division of labor, the relation of sensuality and intimacy, and stages of development in such relations.

If discrimination ceased, gay men and lesbians would enter the mainstream of the human community openly and with self-respect. The energies that the typical gay person wastes in the anxiety of leading a day-to-day existence of systematic disguise would be released for use in personal flourishing. From this release would be generated the many spinoff benefits that accrue to a society when its individual members thrive.

Society would be richer for acknowledging another aspect of human richness and diversity. Families with gay members would develop relations based on truth and trust rather than lies and fear.

And the heterosexual majority would be better off for knowing that they are no longer trampling their gay friends and neighbors.

Finally and perhaps paradoxically, in extending to gays the rights and benefits it has reserved for its dominant culture, America would confirm its deeply held vision of itself as a morally progressing nation, a nation itself advancing and serving as a beacon for others—especially with regard to human rights. The words with which our national pledge ends—"with liberty and justice for all"— are not a description of the present but a call for the future. Ours is a nation given to a prophetic political rhetoric which acknowledges that morality is not arbitrary and that justice is not merely the expression of the current collective will. It is this vision that led the black civil rights movement to its successes. Those congressmen who opposed that movement and its centerpiece, the 1964 Civil Rights Act, on obscurantist grounds, but who lived long enough and were noble enough, came in time to express their heartfelt regret and shame at what they had done. It is to be hoped and someday to be expected that those who now grasp at anything to oppose the extension of that which is best about America to gays will one day feel the same.

Notes

1. "Public Fears—And Sympathies," *Newsweek,* August 12, 1985, p. 23.

2. Alfred C. Kinsey, *Sexual Behavior in the Human Male* (Philadelphia: Saunders, 1948), pp. 650–651. On the somewhat lower incidences of lesbianism, see Alfred C. Kinsey, *Sexual Behavior in the Human Female* (Philadelphia: Saunders, 1953), pp. 472–475.

3. Evelyn Hooker, "The Adjustment of the Male Overt Homosexual," *Journal of Projective Techniques* 21 (1957): 18–31, reprinted in Hendrik M. Ruitenbeek, ed., *The Problem of Homosexuality* (New York: Dutton, 1963), pp. 141–161.

4. See Ronald Bayer, *Homosexuality and American Psychiatry* (New York: Basic Books, 1981).

5. For studies showing that gay men are no more likely—indeed, are less likely—than heterosexuals to be child molesters and that the largest groups of sexual abusers of children and the people most persistent in their molestation of children are the children's fathers or stepfathers or mother's

boyfriends, see Vincent De Francis, *Protecting the Child Victim of Sex Crimes Committed by Adults* (Denver: The American Humane Association, 1969), pp. vii, 38, 69–70; A. Nicholas Groth, "Adult Sexual Orientation and Attraction to Underage Persons," *Archives of Sexual Behavior* 7 (1978): 175–181; Mary J. Spencer, "Sexual Abuse of Boys," *Pediatrics* 78, no. 1 (July 1986): 133–138.

6. See National Gay Task Force, *Anti-Gay/Lesbian Victimization* (New York: NGTF, 1984).

7. "2 St. John's Students Given Probation in Assault on Gay," *The Washington Post,* May 15, 1984, p. 1.

8. See Randy Shilts, *The Mayor of Castro Street: The Life and Times of Harvey Milk* (New York: St. Martin's, 1982), pp. 308–325.

9. See Richard Plant, *The Pink Triangle: The Nazi War Against Homosexuals* (New York: Holt, 1986).

10. E. Carrington Boggan, *The Rights of Gay People: The Basic ACLU Guide to a Gay Person's Rights* (New York: Avon, 1975), pp. 211–235.

11. John Boswell, *Christianity, Social Tolerance and Homosexuality: Gay People in Western Europe from the Beginning of the Christian Era to the Fourteenth Century* (Chicago: University of Chicago Press, 1980).

12. See Gilbert Herdt, *Guardians of the Flute: Idioms of Masculinity* (New York: McGraw-Hill, 1981), pp. 232–239, 284–288; and see generally Gilbert Herdt, ed., *Ritualized Homosexuality in Melanesia* (Berkeley: University of California Press, 1984). For another eye-opener, see Walter L. Williams, *The Spirit and the Flesh: Sexual Diversity in American Indian Culture* (Boston: Beacon, 1986).

13. See especially Boswell, *Christianity,* ch. 4.

14. For Old Testament condemnations of homosexual acts, see Leviticus 18:22, 21:3. For hygienic and dietary codes, see, for example, Leviticus 15:19–27 (on the uncleanliness of women) and Leviticus 11:1–47 (on not eating rabbits, pigs, bats, finless water creatures, legless creeping creatures, etc.). For Lot at Sodom, see Genesis 19:1–25. For Lot in the cave, see Genesis 19:30–38.

15. The preponderance of the scientific evidence supports the view that homosexuality is either genetically determined or a permanent result of early childhood development. See the Kinsey Institute's study by Alan Bell, Martin Weinberg, and Sue Hammersmith, *Sexual Preference: Its Development in Men and Women* (Bloomington: Indiana University Press, 1981); Frederick Whitam and Robin Mathy, *Male Homosexuality in Four Societies* (New York: Praeger, 1986), ch. 7.

16. See Boswell, *Christianity,* ch. 3.

17. See Gilbert Geis, "Reported Consequences of Decriminalization of Consensual Adult Homosexuality in Seven American States," *Journal of Homosexuality* 1, no. 4 (1976): 419–426; Ken Sinclair and Michael Ross,

"Consequences of Decriminalization of Homosexuality: A Study of Two Australian States," *Journal of Homosexuality* 12, no. 1 (1985): 119–127.

Suggestions for Further Reading

See page 173.

---

15 *Is Homosexuality Unnatural?*

Burton M. Leiser

As in so many matters, Western attitudes toward homosexuality have been shaped largely by Christianity; and within the Christian tradition, homosexuality has been condemned time and again. Saint Paul declared that "idolators, thieves, homosexuals, drunkards, and robbers" cannot inherit the Kingdom of God. But why? What was so bad about them? Later theologians decided it was because homosexuality is *unnatural,* and this concept became the key term in the debate. Saint Thomas Aquinas, who after Saint Paul was the most influential of all Christian thinkers, held that morality is a matter of acting in accordance with "the laws of nature," and he cited "unisexual lust" as a particularly obnoxious "sin against nature." (see selection 6)

Burton M. Leiser is professor of philosophy at Pace University and the author of *Liberty, Justice, and Morals* (3rd ed., 1986). In the following selection he discusses the argument that gay sex is "unnatural." As he points out, this term can have several different meanings, and it is important to separate them and to analyze closely what is meant by this opaque notion.

Theologians and other moralists have said homosexual acts violate the "natural law," and that they are therefore immoral and ought to be prohibited by the state.

The word *nature* has a built-in ambiguity that can lead to serious misunderstandings. When something is said to be "natural" or in conformity with "natural law" or the "law of nature," this may mean either (1) that it is in conformity with the descriptive laws of nature, or (2) that it is not artificial, that man has not imposed his will or his devices upon events or conditions as they exist or would have existed without such interference.

1. *The descriptive laws of nature.* The laws of nature, as these are understood by the scientist, differ from the laws of man. The former are purely descriptive, where the latter are prescriptive. When a scientist says that water boils at 212° Fahrenheit or that the volume of a gas varies directly with the heat that is applied to it and inversely with the pressure, he means merely that as a matter of recorded and observable fact, pure water under standard conditions always boils at precisely 212° Fahrenheit and that as a matter of observed fact, the volume of a gas rises as it is heated and falls as pressure is applied to it. These "laws" merely *describe* the manner in which physical substances *actually behave.* They differ from municipal and federal laws in that they *do not prescribe behavior.* Unlike man-made laws, natural laws are not passed by any legislator or group of legislators; they are not proclaimed or announced; they impose no obligation upon anyone or anything; their violation entails no penalty, and there is no reward for following them or abiding by them. When a scientist says that the air in a tire obeys the laws of nature that govern gases, he does *not* mean that the air, having been informed that it *ought* to behave in a certain way, behaves appropriately under the right conditions. He means, rather, that as a matter of fact, the air in a tire *will* behave like all other gases. In saying that Boyle's law governs the behavior of gases, he means merely that gases do, as a matter of fact, behave in accordance with Boyle's law, and that Boyle's law enables one to predict accurately what will happen to a given quantity of a gas as its pressure is raised; he does *not* mean to suggest that some heavenly voice has proclaimed that all gases should henceforth behave in accordance with the terms of Boyle's law and that a ghostly policeman patrols the world, ready

to mete out punishments to any gases that violate the heavenly decree. In fact, according to the scientist, it does not make sense to speak of a natural law being violated. For if there were a true exception to a so-called law of nature, the exception would require a change in the description of those phenomena, and the law would have been shown to be no law at all. The laws of nature are revised as scientists discover new phenomena that require new refinements in their descriptions of the way things actually happen. In this respect they differ fundamentally from human laws, which are revised periodically by legislators who are not so interested in *describing* human behavior as they are in *prescribing* what human behavior *should* be.

2. *The artificial as a form of the unnatural.* On occasion when we say that something is not natural, we mean that it is a product of human artifice. A typewriter is not a natural object, in this sense, for the substances of which it is composed have been removed from their natural state—the state in which they existed before men came along—and have been transformed by a series of chemical and physical and mechanical processes into other substances. They have been rearranged into a whole that is quite different from anything found in nature. In short, a typewriter is an artificial object. In this sense, clothing is not natural, for it has been transformed considerably from the state in which it was found in nature; and wearing clothing is also not natural, in this sense, for in one's natural state, before the application of anything artificial, before any human interference with things as they are, one is quite naked. Human laws, being artificial conventions designed to exercise a degree of control over the natural inclinations and propensities of men, may in this sense be considered to be unnatural.

When theologians and moralists speak of homosexuality, contraception, abortion, and other forms of human behavior as being unnatural and say that for that reason such behavior must be considered to be wrong, in what sense are they using the word *unnatural?* Are they saying that homosexual behavior and the use of contraceptives are contrary to the scientific laws of nature, are they saying that they are artificial forms of behavior, or are they using the terms *natural* and *unnatural* in some third sense?

They cannot mean that homosexual behavior (to stick to the subject presently under discussion) violates the laws of nature in the first sense, for, as has been pointed out, in *that* sense it is impossible to violate the laws of nature. Those laws, being merely descriptive of what actually does happen, would have to *include* homosexual behavior if such behavior does actually take place. Even if the defenders of the theological view that homosexuality is unnatural were to appeal to a statistical analysis by pointing out that such behavior is not normal from a statistical point of view, and therefore not what the laws of nature require, it would be open to their critics to reply that any descriptive law of nature must account for and incorporate all statistical deviations, and that the laws of nature, in this sense, do not *require* anything. These critics might also note that the best statistics available reveal that about half of all American males engage in homosexual activity at some time in their lives, and that a very large percentage of American males have exclusively homosexual relations for a fairly extensive period of time; from which it would follow that such behavior is natural, for them, at any rate, in this sense of the word *natural.*

If those who say that homosexual behavior is unnatural are using the term *unnatural* in the second sense as artificial, it is difficult to understand their objection. That which is artificial is often far better than what is natural. Artificial homes seem, at any rate, to be more suited to human habitation and more conducive to longer life and better health than are caves and other natural shelters. There are distinct advantages to the use of such unnatural (artificial) amenities as clothes, furniture, and books. Although we may dream of an idyllic return to nature in our more wistful moments, we would soon discover, as Thoreau did in his attempt to escape from the artificiality of civilization, that needles and thread, knives and matches, ploughs and nails, and countless other products of human artifice are essential to human life. We would discover, as Plato pointed out in the *Republic,* that no man can be truly self-sufficient. Some of the by-products of industry are less than desirable, but neither industry nor the products of industry are intrinsically evil, even though both are unnatural in this sense of the word.

Interference with nature is not evil in itself. Nature, as some writers have put it, must be tamed. In some respects man must look upon it as an enemy to be conquered. If nature were left to its own devices, without the intervention of human artifice, men would be consumed by disease, they would be plagued by insects, they would be chained to the places where they were born with no means of swift communication or transport, and they would suffer the discomforts and the torments of wind and weather and flood and fire with no practical means of combating any of them. Interfering with nature, doing battle with nature, using human will and reason and skill to thwart what might otherwise follow from the conditions that prevail in the world is a peculiarly human enterprise, one that can hardly be condemned merely because it does what is not natural.

Homosexual behavior can hardly be considered to be unnatural in this sense. There is nothing artificial about such behavior. On the contrary, it is quite natural, in this sense, to those who engage in it. And even if it were not, even if it were quite artificial, this is not in itself a ground for condemning it.

It would seem, then, that those who condemn homosexuality as an unnatural form of behavior must mean something else by the word *unnatural,* something not covered by either of the preceding definitions. A third possibility is this:

3. *Anything uncommon or abnormal is unnatural.* If this is what is meant by those who condemn homosexuality on the ground that it is unnatural, it is quite obvious that their condemnation cannot be accepted without further argument. The fact that a given form of behavior is uncommon provides no justification for condemning it. Playing viola in a string quartet may be an uncommon form of human behavior. Yet there is no reason to suppose that such uncommon behavior is, by virtue of its uncommonness, deserving of condemnation or ethically or morally wrong. On the contrary, many forms of behavior are praised precisely because they are so uncommon. Great artists, poets, musicians, and scientists are uncommon in this sense; but clearly the world is better off for having them, and it would be absurd to condemn them or their activities for their failure to be common and normal. If homosexual behavior is wrong, then, it must be for some reason other than its unnaturalness in this sense of the word.

4. *Any use of an organ or an instrument that is contrary to its principal purpose or function is unnatural.* Every organ and every instrument— perhaps even every creature—has a function to perform, one for which it is particularly designed. Any use of those instruments and organs that is consonant with their purposes is natural and proper, but any use that is inconsistent with their principal functions is unnatural and improper, and to that extent, evil or harmful. Human teeth, for example, are admirably designed for their principal functions—biting and chewing the kinds of food suitable for human

consumption. But they are not particularly well suited for prying the caps from beer bottles. If they are used for that purpose, which is not natural to them, they are likely to crack or break under the strain. The abuse of one's teeth leads to their destruction and to a consequent deterioration in one's overall health. If they are used only for their proper function, however, they may continue to serve well for many years. Similarly, a given drug may have a proper function. If used in the furtherance of that end, it can preserve life and restore health. But if it is abused and employed for purposes for which it was never intended, it may cause serious harm and even death. The natural uses of things are good and proper, but their unnatural uses are bad and harmful.

What we must do, then, is to find the proper use, or the true purpose, of each organ in our bodies. Once we have discovered that, we will know what constitutes the natural use of each organ and what constitutes an unnatural, abusive, and potentially harmful employment of the various parts of our bodies. If we are rational, we will be careful to confine behavior to the proper functions and to refrain from unnatural behavior. According to those philosophers who follow this line of reasoning, the way to discover the proper use of any organ is to determine what it is peculiarly suited to do. The eye is suited for seeing, the ear for hearing, the nerves for transmitting impulses from one part of the body to another, and so on.

What are the sex organs peculiarly suited to do? Obviously, they are peculiarly suited to enable men and women to reproduce their own kind. No other organ in the body is capable of fulfilling that function. It follows, according to those who follow the natural-law line, that the proper or natural function of the sex organs is reproduction, and that strictly speaking, any use of those organs for other purposes is unnatural, abusive, potentially harmful, and therefore wrong. The sex organs have been given to us in order to enable us to maintain the continued existence of mankind on this earth. All perversions—including masturbation, homosexual behavior, and heterosexual intercourse that deliberately frustrates the design of the sexual organs—are unnatural and bad. As Pope Pius XI once said, "Private individuals have no other power over the members of their bodies than that which pertains to their natural ends."

But the problem is not so easily resolved. Is it true that every organ has one and only one proper function? A hammer may have been designed to pound nails, and it may perform that particular job best. But it is not sinful to employ a hammer to crack nuts if you have no other more suitable tool immediately available. The hammer, being a relatively versatile tool, may be employed in a number of ways. It has no one proper or natural function. A woman's eyes are well adapted to seeing, it is true. But they seem also to be well adapted to flirting. Is a woman's use of her eyes for the latter purpose sinful merely because she is not using them, at that moment, for their "primary" purpose of seeing? Our sexual organs are uniquely adapted for procreation, but that is obviously not the only function for which they are adapted. Human beings may—and do— use those organs for a great many other purposes, and it is difficult to see why any *one* use should be considered to be the only proper one. The sex organs seem to be particularly well adapted to give their owners and others intense sensations of pleasure. Unless one believes that pleasure itself is bad, there seems to be little reason to believe that the use of the sex organs for the production of pleasure in oneself or in others is evil. In view of the peculiar design of these organs, with their great concentration of nerve endings, it would seem that they were designed (if they *were* designed) with that very goal in mind, and that their use for such purposes would be no more unnatural than their use for the purpose of procreation.

Nor should we overlook the fact that human sex organs may be and are used to express, in the deepest and most intimate way open to man, the love of one person for another. Even the most ardent opponents of "unfruitful" intercourse admit that sex does serve this function. They have accordingly conceded that a man and his wife may have intercourse even though she is pregnant, or past the age of child bearing, or in the infertile period of her menstrual cycle.

Human beings are remarkably complex and adaptable creatures. Neither they nor their organs can properly be compared to hammers or to other tools. The analogy quickly breaks down. The generalization that a given organ or instrument has one and only one proper function does not hold up, even with regard to the simplest manufactured tools, for, as we have seen, a tool may be used for more than one purpose—less effectively than one especially designed for a given task, perhaps, but properly and certainly not *sinfully*. A woman may use her eyes not only to see and to flirt, but also to earn money—if she is, for example, an actress or a model. Though neither of the latter functions seems to have been a part of the original design, if one may speak sensibly of *design* in this context, of the eye, it is difficult to see why such a use of the eyes of a woman should be considered sinful, perverse, or unnatural. Her sex organs have the unique capacity of producing ova and nurturing human embryos, under the right conditions; but why should any other use of those organs, including their use to bring pleasure to their owner or to someone else, or to manifest love to another person, or even, perhaps, to earn money, be regarded as perverse, sinful, or unnatural? Similarly, a man's sexual organs possess the unique capacity of causing the generation of another human being, but if a man chooses to use them for pleasure, or for the expression of love, or for some other purpose—so long as he does not interfere with the rights of some other person—the fact that his sex organs do have their unique capabilities does not constitute a convincing justification for condemning their other uses as being perverse, sinful, unnatural, or criminal. If a man "perverts" himself by wiggling his ears for the entertainment of his neighbors instead of using them exclusively for their "natural" function of hearing, no one thinks of consigning him to prison. If he abuses his teeth by using them to pull staples from memos—a function for which teeth were clearly not designed—he is not accused of being immoral, degraded, and degenerate. The fact that people *are* condemned for using their sex organs for their own pleasure or profit, or for that of others, may be more revealing about the prejudices and taboos of our society than it is about our perception of the true nature or purpose of our bodies.

In this connection, it may be worthwhile to note that with the development of artificial means of reproduction (that is, test tube babies), the sex organs may become obsolete for reproductive purposes but would still contribute greatly to human pleasure. In addition, studies of animal behavior and anthropological reports indicate that such nonreproductive sex acts as masturbation, homosexual intercourse, and mutual fondling of genital organs are widespread, both among human beings and among lower animals. Under suitable circumstances, many animals reverse their sex roles, males assuming the posture of females and presenting themselves to others for intercourse, and females mounting other females and going through all the actions of a male engaged in intercourse. Many peoples all around the world have sanctioned and even ritualized homosexual relations. It would seem that an excessive readiness to insist that human sex organs are designed only for reproductive purposes and therefore ought to be used only for such purposes must be based upon a very narrow conception that is conditioned by our own society's peculiar history and taboos.

To sum up, then, the proposition that any use of an organ that is contrary to its principal purpose or function is unnatural assumes that organs *have* a principal purpose or function, but this may be denied on the ground that the purpose or function of a given organ may vary according to the needs or desires of its owner. It may be denied on the ground that a given organ may have more than one principal purpose or function, and any attempt to call one use or another the only natural one seems to be arbitrary, if not question-begging. Also, the proposition suggests that what is unnatural is evil or depraved. This goes beyond the pure description of things, and enters into the problem of the evaluation of human behavior, which leads us to the fifth meaning of *natural.*

5. *That which is natural is good, and whatever is unnatural is bad.* When one condemns homosexuality or masturbation or the use of contraceptives on the ground that it is unnatural, one implies that whatever is unnatural is bad, wrongful, or perverse. But as we have seen, in some senses of the word, the unnatural (the artificial) is often very good, whereas that which is natural (that which has not been subjected to human artifice or improvement) may be very bad indeed. Of course, interference with nature may be bad. Ecologists have made us more aware than we have ever been of the dangers of unplanned and uninformed interference with nature. But this is not to say that *all* interference with nature is bad. Every time a man cuts down a tree to make room for a home for himself, or catches a fish to feed himself or his family, he is interfering with nature. If men did not interfere with nature, they would have no homes, they could eat no fish, and, in fact, they could not survive. What, then, can be meant by those who say that whatever is natural is good and whatever is unnatural is bad? Clearly, they cannot have intended merely to reduce the word *natural* to a synonym of *good, right,* and *proper,* and *unnatural* to a synonym of *evil, wrong, improper, corrupt,* and *depraved.* If that were all they had intended to do, there would be very little to discuss as to whether a given form of behavior might be proper even though it is not in strict conformity with someone's views of what is natural; for *good* and *natural* being synonyms, it would follow inevitably

that whatever is good must be natural, and vice versa, by definition. This is certainly not what the opponents of homosexuality have been saying when they claim that homosexuality, being unnatural, is evil. For if it were, their claim would be quite empty. They would be saying merely that homosexuality, being evil, is evil—a redundancy that could as easily be reduced to the simpler assertion that homosexuality is evil. This assertion, however, is not an argument. Those who oppose homosexuality and other sexual "perversions" on the ground that they are "unnatural" are saying that there is some objectively identifiable quality in such behavior that is unnatural; and that that quality, once it has been identified by some kind of scientific observation, can be seen to be detrimental to those who engage in such behavior, or to those around them; and that *because* of the harm (physical, mental, moral, or spiritual) that results from engaging in any behavior possessing the attribute of unnaturalness, such behavior must be considered to be wrongful, and should be discouraged by society. "Unnaturalness" and "wrongfulness" are not synonyms, then, but different concepts. The problem with which we are wrestling is that we are unable to find a meaning for *unnatural* that enables us to arrive at the conclusion that homosexuality is unnatural or that if homosexuality is unnatural, it is therefore wrongful behavior. We have examined four common meanings of *natural* and *unnatural,* and have seen that none of them performs the task that it must perform if the advocates of this argument are to prevail.

Suggestions for Further Reading

Philosophers have not written a great deal about homosexuality. Richard Mohr's writings include "Gay Rights," *Social Theory and Practice* 8 (1982): 31–41; "Invisible Minorities, Civic Rights, Democracy," *Philosophical Forum* 16 (1985): pp. 1–24; and "AIDS, Gays, and State Coercion," *Bioethics* 1 (1987): 35–50.

Also see Robert Baker and Frederick Elliston, eds., *Philosophy and Sex* (Buffalo, N.Y.: Prometheus Books, 1975); and C. H. Whiteley and Winifred M. Whiteley, *Sex and Morals* (New York: Basic Books, 1967).

Two articles defending anti-gay positions are Samuel McCracken, "Are Homosexuals Gay?" *Commentary* 67 (1979): 23–28; and Paul Cameron, "A Case Against Homosexuality," *Human Life Review* 4 (1978): 17–49.

16 *Famine, Affluence, and Morality*

Peter Singer

Peter Singer is professor of philosophy and director of the
Centre for Human Bioethics at Monash University in Australia. His best-known work is *Animal Liberation* (1975), which
is widely credited with having launched the modern animal-
rights movement. A prolific author, he has also written
books about civil disobedience, reproductive technologies,
sociobiology, Marx, and Hegel.

In the following essay Singer considers the question of
whether it is morally defensible for affluent people to spend
money on luxuries for themselves while less fortunate people
are starving.

As I write this, in November 1971, people are dying in East Bengal from lack of food, shelter, and medical care. The suffering and
death that are occurring there now are not inevitable, not unavoidable in any fatalistic sense of the term. Constant poverty, a
cyclone, and a civil war have turned at least nine million people
into destitute refugees; nevertheless, it is not beyond the capacity
of the richer nations to give enough assistance to reduce any further suffering to very small proportions. The decisions and actions
of human beings can prevent this kind of suffering. Unfortunately,
human beings have not made the necessary decisions. At the individual level, people have, with very few exceptions, not responded
to the situation in any significant way. Generally speaking, people
have not given large sums to relief funds; they have not written to

Singer, Peter, "Famine, Affluence, and Morality," *Philosophy and Public Affairs* 1, No.
3 (Spring 1972). Copyright © 1972 by Princeton University Press. Excerpts pp.
229–33, 234–35, 238–43 reprinted with permission of Princeton University Press.

their parliamentary representatives demanding increased government assistance; they have not demonstrated in the streets, held
symbolic fasts, or done anything else directed toward providing the
refugees with the means to satisfy their essential needs. At the
government level, no government has given the sort of massive aid
that would enable the refugees to survive for more than a few days.
Britain, for instance, has given rather more than most countries. It
has, to date, given £14,750,000. For comparative purposes, Britain's share of the nonrecoverable development costs of the Anglo-
French Concorde project is already in excess of £275,000,000, and
on present estimates will reach £440,000,000. The implication is
that the British government values a supersonic transport more
than thirty times as highly as it values the lives of the nine million
refugees. Australia is another country which, on a per capita basis,
is well up in the "aid to Bengal" table. Australia's aid, however,
amounts to less than one-twelfth of the cost of Sydney's new opera
house. The total amount given, from all sources, now stands at
about £65,000,000. The estimated cost of keeping the refugees alive
for one year is £464,000,000. Most of the refugees have now been
in the camps for more than six months. The World Bank has said
that India needs a minimum of £300,000,000 in assistance from
other countries before the end of the year. It seems obvious that
assistance on this scale will not be forthcoming. India will be forced
to choose between letting the refugees starve or diverting funds
from her own development program, which will mean that more of
her own people will starve in the future.[1]

These are the essential facts about the present situation in
Bengal. So far as it concerns us here, there is nothing unique about
this situation except its magnitude. The Bengal emergency is just
the latest and most acute of a series of major emergencies in various
parts of the world, arising both from natural and from man-made
causes. There are also many parts of the world in which people die
from malnutrition and lack of food independent of any special
emergency. I take Bengal as my example only because it is the
present concern, and because the size of the problem has ensured
that it has been given adequate publicity. Neither individuals nor
governments can claim to be unaware of what is happening there.

What are the moral implications of a situation like this? In what
follows, I shall argue that the way people in relatively affluent countries react to a situation like that in Bengal cannot be justified;

indeed, the whole way we look at moral issues—our moral conceptual scheme—needs to be altered, and with it, the way of life that has come to be taken for granted in our society.

In arguing for this conclusion I will not, of course, claim to be morally neutral. I shall, however, try to argue for the moral position that I take, so that anyone who accepts certain assumptions, to be made explicit, will, I hope, accept my conclusion.

I begin with the assumption that suffering and death from lack of food, shelter, and medical care are bad. I think most people will agree about this, although one may reach the same view by different routes. I shall not argue for this view. People can hold all sorts of eccentric positions, and perhaps from some of them it would not follow that death by starvation is in itself bad. It is difficult, perhaps impossible, to refute such positions, and so for brevity I will henceforth take this assumption as accepted. Those who disagree need read no further.

My next point is this: if it is in our power to prevent something bad from happening, without thereby sacrificing anything of comparable moral importance, we ought, morally, to do it. By "without sacrificing anything of comparable moral importance" I mean without causing anything else comparably bad to happen, or doing something that is wrong in itself, or failing to promote some moral good, comparable in significance to the bad thing that we can prevent. This principle seems almost as uncontroversial as the last one. It requires us only to prevent what is bad, and not to promote what is good, and it requires this of us only when we can do it without sacrificing anything that is, from the moral point of view, comparably important. I could even, as far as the application of my argument to the Bengal emergency is concerned, qualify the point so as to make it: if it is in our power to prevent something very bad from happening, without thereby sacrificing anything morally significant, we ought, morally, to do it. An application of this principle would be as follows: if I am walking past a shallow pond and see a child drowning in it, I ought to wade in and pull the child out. This will mean getting my clothes muddy, but this is insignificant, while the death of the child would presumably be a very bad thing.

The uncontroversial appearance of the principle just stated is deceptive. If it were acted upon, even in its qualified form, our lives, our society, and our world would be fundamentally changed. For the principle takes, firstly, no account of proximity or distance. It makes no moral difference whether the person I can help is a neighbor's child ten yards from me or a Bengali whose name I shall never know, ten thousand miles away. Secondly, the principle makes no distinction between cases in which I am the only person who could possibly do anything and cases in which I am just one among millions in the same position.

I do not think I need to say much in defense of the refusal to take proximity and distance into account. The fact that a person is physically near to us, so that we have personal contact with him, may make it more likely that we *shall* assist him, but this does not show that we *ought* to help him rather than another who happens to be further away. If we accept any principle of impartiality, universalizability, equality, or whatever, we cannot discriminate against someone merely because he is far away from us (or we are far away from him). Admittedly, it is possible that we are in a better position to judge what needs to be done to help a person near to us than one far away, and perhaps also to provide the assistance we judge to be necessary. If this were the case, it would be a reason for helping those near to us first. This may once have been a justification for being more concerned with the poor in one's town than with famine victims in India. Unfortunately for those who like to keep their moral responsibilities limited, instant communication and swift transportation have changed the situation. From the moral point of view, the development of the world into a "global village" has made an important, though still unrecognized, difference to our moral situation. Expert observers and supervisors, sent out by famine relief organizations or permanently stationed in famine-prone areas, can direct our aid to a refugee in Bengal almost as effectively as we could get it to someone in our own block. There would seem, therefore, to be no possible justification for discriminating on geographical grounds.

There may be a greater need to defend the second implication of my principle—that the fact that there are millions of other people in the same position, in respect to the Bengali refugees, as I am, does not make the situation significantly different from a situation in which I am the only person who can prevent something very bad from occurring. Again, of course, I admit that there is a psychological difference between the cases; one feels less guilty about doing nothing if one can point to others, similarly placed, who have also done nothing. Yet this can make no real difference to our moral obligations. Should I consider that I am less obliged to pull the drowning child out of the pond if on looking around I see other people, no further away than I am, who have also noticed the child but are doing nothing? One has only to ask this question to see the absurdity of the view that numbers lessen obligation. It is a view that is an ideal excuse for inactivity; unfortunately most of the major evils—poverty, overpopulation, pollution—are problems in which everyone is almost equally involved.

The view that numbers do make a difference can be made plausible if stated in this way: if everyone in circumstances like mine gave £5 to the Bengal Relief Fund, there would be enough to provide food, shelter, and medical care for the refugees; there is no reason why I should give more than anyone else in the same circumstances as I am; therefore I have no obligation to give more than £5. Each premise in this argument is true, and the argument looks sound. It may convince us, unless we notice that it is based on a hypothetical premise, although the conclusion is not stated hypothetically. The argument would be sound if the conclusion were: if everyone in circumstances like mine were to give £5, I would have no obligation to give more than £5. If the conclusion were so stated, however, it would be obvious that the argument has no bearing on a situation in which it is not the case that everyone else gives £5. This, of course, is the actual situation. It is more or less certain that not everyone in circumstances like mine will give £5. So there will not be enough to provide the needed food, shelter, and medical care. Therefore by giving more than £5 I will prevent more suffering than I would if I gave just £5.

. . . .

If my argument so far has been sound, neither our distance from a preventable evil nor the number of other people who, in respect to that evil, are in the same situation as we are, lessens our obligation to mitigate or prevent that evil. I shall therefore take as established the principle I asserted earlier. As I have already said, I need to assert it only in its qualified form: if it is in our power to prevent something very bad from happening, without thereby sacrificing anything else morally significant, we ought, morally, to do it.

The outcome of this argument is that our traditional moral categories are upset. The traditional distinction between duty and charity cannot be drawn, or at least, not in the place we normally draw it. Giving money to the Bengal Relief Fund is regarded as an act of charity in our society. The bodies which collect money are known as "charities." These organizations see themselves in this way—if you send them a check, you will be thanked for your "generosity." Because giving money is regarded as an act of charity, it is not thought that there is anything wrong with not giving. The charitable man may be praised, but the man who is not charitable is not condemned. People do not feel in any way ashamed or guilty about spending money on new clothes or a new car instead of giving it to famine relief. (Indeed, the alternative does not occur to them.) This way of looking at the matter cannot be justified. When we buy new clothes not to keep ourselves warm but to look "well-dressed" we are not providing for any important need. We would not be sacrificing anything significant if we were to continue to wear our old clothes, and give the money to famine relief. By doing so, we would be preventing another person from starving. It follows from what I have said earlier that we ought to give money away, rather than spend it on clothes which we do not need to keep us warm. To do so is not charitable, or generous. Nor is it the kind of act which philosophers and theologians have called "supererogatory"—an act which it would be good to do, but not wrong not to do. On the contrary, we ought to give the money away, and it is wrong not to do so. . . .

It may still be thought that my conclusions are so wildly out of line with what everyone else thinks and has always thought that there must be something wrong with the argument somewhere. In order to show that my conclusions, while certainly contrary to contemporary Western moral standards, would not have seemed so extraordinary at other times and in other places, I would like to quote a passage from a writer not normally thought of as a way-out radical, Thomas Aquinas.

> Now, according to the natural order instituted by divine providence, material goods are provided for the satisfaction of human needs. Therefore the division and appropriation of property, which proceeds from human law, must not hinder the satisfaction of man's necessity from such goods. Equally, whatever a man has in superabundance is owed, of natural right, to the poor for their sustenance. So Ambrosius says, and it is also to be found in the *Decretum Gratiani*: "The bread which you withhold belongs to the hungry; the clothing you shut away, to

the naked; and the money you bury in the earth is the redemp-
tion and freedom of the penniless."[2]

I now want to consider a number of points, more practical than
philosophical, which are relevant to the application of the moral
conclusion we have reached. These points challenge not the idea
that we ought to be doing all we can to prevent starvation, but the
idea that giving away a great deal of money is the best means to this
end.

It is sometimes said that overseas aid should be a government
responsibility, and that therefore one ought not to give to privately
run charities. Giving privately, it is said, allows the government and
the noncontributing members of society to escape their responsibilities.

This argument seems to assume that the more people there
are who give to privately organized famine relief funds, the less
likely it is that the government will take over full responsibility for
such aid. This assumption is unsupported, and does not strike me
as at all plausible. The opposite view—that if no one gives voluntarily, a government will assume that its citizens are uninterested in
famine relief and would not wish to be forced into giving aid—
seems more plausible. In any case, unless there were a definite
probability that by refusing to give one would be helping to bring
about massive government assistance, people who do refuse to
make voluntary contributions are refusing to prevent a certain
amount of suffering without being able to point to any tangible
beneficial consequence of their refusal. So the onus of showing how
their refusal will bring about government action is on those who
refuse to give.

I do not, of course, want to dispute the contention that governments of affluent nations should be giving many times the amount
of genuine, no-strings-attached aid that they are giving now. I agree,
too, that giving privately is not enough, and that we ought to be
campaigning actively for entirely new standards for both public and
private contributions to famine relief. Indeed, I would sympathize
with someone who thought that campaigning was more important
than giving oneself, although I doubt whether preaching what one
does not practice would be very effective. Unfortunately, for many
people the idea that "it's the government's responsibility" is a rea-

son for not giving which does not appear to entail any political action either.

Another, more serious reason for not giving to famine relief funds is that until there is effective population control, relieving famine merely postpones starvation. If we save the Bengal refugees now, others, perhaps the children of these refugees, will face starvation in a few years' time. In support of this, one may cite the now well-known facts about the population explosion and the relatively limited scope for expanded production.

This point, like the previous one, is an argument against relieving suffering that is happening now, because of a belief about what might happen in the future; it is unlike the previous point in that very good evidence can be adduced in support of this belief about the future. I will not go into the evidence here. I accept that the earth cannot support indefinitely a population rising at the present rate. This certainly poses a problem for anyone who thinks it important to prevent famine. Again, however, one could accept the argument without drawing the conclusion that it absolves one from any obligation to do anything to prevent famine. The conclusion that should be drawn is that the best means of preventing famine, in the long run, is population control. It would then follow from the position reached earlier that one ought to be doing all one can to promote population control (unless one held that all forms of population control were wrong in themselves, or would have significantly bad consequences). Since there are organizations working specifically for population control, one would then support them rather than more orthodox methods of preventing famine.

A third point raised by the conclusion reached earlier relates to the question of just how much we all ought to be giving away. One possibility, which has already been mentioned, is that we ought to give until we reach the level of marginal utility—that is, the level at which, by giving more, I would cause as much suffering to myself or my dependents as I would relieve by my gift. This would mean, of course, that one would reduce oneself to very near the material circumstances of a Bengali refugee. It will be recalled that earlier I put forward both a strong and a moderate version of the principle of preventing bad occurrences. The strong version, which required us to prevent bad things from happening unless in doing so we would be sacrificing something of comparable moral significance, does seem to require reducing ourselves to the level of marginal utility. I should also say that the strong version seems to me to be the correct one. I proposed the more moderate version—that we should prevent bad occurrences unless, to do so, we had to sacrifice something morally significant—only in order to show that even on this surely undeniable principle a great change in our way of life is required. On the more moderate principle, it may not follow that we ought to reduce ourselves to the level of marginal utility, for one might hold that to reduce oneself and one's family to this level is to cause something significantly bad to happen. Whether this is so I shall not discuss, since, as I have said, I can see no good reason for holding the moderate version of the principle rather than the strong version. Even if we accepted the principle only in its moderate form, however, it should be clear that we would have to give away enough to ensure that the consumer society, dependent as it is on people spending on trivia rather than giving to famine relief, would slow down and perhaps disappear entirely. There are several reasons why this would be desirable in itself. The value and necessity of economic growth are now being questioned not only by conservationists, but by economists as well. There is no doubt, too, that the consumer society has had a distorting effect on the goals and purposes of its members. Yet looking at the matter purely from the point of view of overseas aid, there must be a limit to the extent to which we should deliberately slow down our economy; for it might be the case that if we gave away, say, 40 percent of our Gross National Product, we would slow down the economy so much that in absolute terms we would be giving less than if we gave 25 percent of the much larger GNP that we would have if we limited our contribution to this smaller percentage.

I mention this only as an indication of the sort of factor that one would have to take into account in working out an ideal. Since Western societies generally consider one percent of the GNP an acceptable level for overseas aid, the matter is entirely academic. Nor does it affect the question of how much an individual should give in a society in which very few are giving substantial amounts.

It is sometimes said, though less often now than it used to be, that philosophers have no special role to play in public affairs, since most public issues depend primarily on an assessment of facts. On questions of fact, it is said, philosophers as such have no special expertise, and so it has been possible to engage in philosophy without committing oneself to any position on major public issues. No doubt there are some issues of social policy and foreign policy about which it can truly be said that a really expert assessment of the facts is required before taking sides or acting, but the issue of famine is surely not one of these. The facts about the existence of suffering are beyond dispute. Nor, I think, is it disputed that we can do something about it, either through orthodox methods of famine relief or through population control or both. This is therefore an issue on which philosophers are competent to take a position. The issue is one which faces everyone who has more money than he needs to support himself and his dependents, or who is in a position to take some sort of political action. These categories must include practically every teacher and student of philosophy in the universities of the Western world. If philosophy is to deal with matters that are relevant to both teachers and students, this is an issue that philosophers should discuss.

Discussion, though, is not enough. What is the point of relating philosophy to public (and personal) affairs if we do not take our conclusions seriously? In this instance, taking our conclusion seriously means acting upon it. The philosopher will not find it any easier than anyone else to alter his attitudes and way of life to the extent that, if I am right, is involved in doing everything that we ought to be doing. At the very least, though, one can make a start. The philosopher who does so will have to sacrifice some of the benefits of the consumer society, but he can find compensation in the satisfaction of a way of life in which theory and practice, if not yet in harmony, are at least coming together.

Notes

1. There was also a third possibility: that India would go to war to enable the refugees to return to their lands. Since I wrote this paper, India has taken this way out. The situation is no longer that described above, but this does not affect my argument, as the next paragraph indicates.

2. *Summa Theologica*, II–II, Question 66, Article 7, in *Aquinas, Selected Political Writings,* ed. A. P. d'Entreves, trans. J. G. Dawson (Oxford: Basil Blackwell, 1948), p. 171.

Suggestions for Further Reading

See page 191.

17 On Not Feeding the Starving

Garrett Hardin

Do we have an obligation to feed the starving in foreign countries? Most people would say that we do, even though they might be a little embarrassed that in fact they give relatively little money themselves to support famine-relief efforts. Few are willing to say, simply, No, let them starve.

Garrett Hardin, professor of human ecology at the University of California in Santa Barbara, has become famous in recent years for saying precisely that. Hardin argues that nothing we can do will make any real difference to the starving. The problem, he says, is that certain countries are overpopulated and the resources available in those countries cannot support the number of people living there. It is misguided to think that we can change this fundamental situation. Our "aid" will only postpone the inevitable, and possibly even make it worse. Moreover, he says, in trying to help we only weaken our own position, and expose ourselves to the danger of a similar fate. If Hardin is right, the problem of world hunger is intractable and it is a foolish mistake to think that we can do anything about it.

No generation has viewed the problem of the survival of the human species as seriously as we have. Inevitably, we have entered this world of concern through the door of metaphor. Environmentalists have emphasized the image of the earth as a spaceship—Spaceship Earth. Kenneth Boulding is the principal architect of this metaphor. It is time, he says, that we replace the wasteful "cowboy economy" of the past with the frugal "spaceship economy" required for continued survival in the limited world we now see ours to be. The metaphor is notably useful in justifying pollution control measures.

Unfortunately, the image of a spaceship is also used to promote measures that are suicidal. One of these is a generous immigration policy, which is only a particular instance of a class of policies that are in error because they lead to the tragedy of the commons. These suicidal policies are attractive because they mesh with what we unthinkingly take to be the ideals of "the best people." What is missing in the idealistic view is an insistence that rights and responsibilities must go together. The "generous" attitude of all too many people results in asserting inalienable rights while ignoring or denying matching responsibilities.

For the metaphor of a spaceship to be correct the aggregate of people on board would have to be under unitary sovereign control. A true ship always has a captain. It is conceivable that a ship could be run by a committee. But it could not possibly survive if its course were determined by bickering tribes that claimed rights without responsibilities.

What about Spaceship Earth? It certainly has no captain, and no executive committee. The United Nations is a toothless tiger, because the signatories of its charter wanted it that way. The spaceship metaphor is used only to justify spaceship demands on common resources without acknowledging corresponding spaceship responsibilities.

An understandable fear of decisive action leads people to embrace "incrementalism"—moving toward reform in tiny stages. As we shall see, this strategy is counterproductive in the area discussed here if it means accepting rights before responsibilities. Where human survival is at stake, the acceptance of responsibilities is a precondition to the acceptance of rights, if the two cannot be introduced simultaneously.

Lifeboat Ethics

Before taking up certain substantive issues let us look at an alternative metaphor, that of a lifeboat. In developing some relevant examples the following numerical values are assumed. Approximately two-thirds of the world is desperately poor, and only one-third is comparatively rich. The people in poor countries have an average per capita GNP (Gross National Product) of about $200 per year; the rich, of about $3,000. (For the United States it is nearly $5,000 per year.) Metaphorically, each rich nation amounts to a lifeboat full of comparatively rich people. The poor of the world are in other, much more crowded lifeboats. Continuously, so to speak, the poor fall out of their lifeboats and swim for a while in the water outside, hoping to be admitted to a rich lifeboat, or in some other way to benefit from the "goodies" on board. What should the passengers on a rich lifeboat do? This is the central problem of "the ethics of a lifeboat."

First we must acknowledge that each lifeboat is effectively limited in capacity. The land of every nation has a limited carrying capacity. The exact limit is a matter for argument, but the energy crunch is convincing more people every day that we have already exceeded the carrying capacity of the land. We have been living on "capital"—stored petroleum and coal—and soon we must live on income alone.

Let us look at only one lifeboat—ours. The ethical problem is the same for all, and is as follows. Here we sit, say 50 people in a lifeboat. To be generous, let us assume our boat has a capacity of 10 more, making 60. (This, however, is to violate the engineering principle of the "safety factor." A new plant disease or a bad change in the weather may decimate our population if we don't preserve some excess capacity as a safety factor.)

The 50 of us in the lifeboat see 100 others swimming in the water outside, asking for admission to the boat, or for handouts. How shall we respond to their calls? There are several possibilities.

One. We may be tempted to try to live by the Christian ideal of being "our brother's keeper," or by the Marxian ideal of "from each according to his abilities, to each according to his needs." Since the needs of all are the same, we take all the needy into our boat, making a total of 150 in a boat with a capacity of 60. The boat is swamped, and everyone drowns. Complete justice, complete catastrophe.

Two. Since the boat has an unused excess capacity of 10, we admit just 10 more to it. This has the disadvantage of getting rid of the safety factor, for which action we will sooner or later pay dearly. Moreover, *which* 10 do we let in? "First come, first served?" The best 10? The neediest 10? How do we *discriminate?* And what do we say to the 90 who are excluded?

Three. Admit no more to the boat and preserve the small safety factor. Survival of the people in the lifeboat is then possible (though we shall have to be on our guard against boarding parties).

The last solution is abhorrent to many people. It is unjust, they say. Let us grant that it is.

"I feel guilty about my good luck," say some. The reply to this is simple: *Get out and yield your place to others.* Such a selfless action might satisfy the conscience of those who are addicted to guilt but it would not change the ethics of the lifeboat. The needy person to whom a guilt-addict yields his place will not himself feel guilty about his sudden good luck. (If he did he would not climb aboard.) The net result of conscience-stricken people relinquishing their unjustly held positions is the elimination of their kind of conscience from the lifeboat. The lifeboat, as it were, purifies itself of guilt. The ethics of the lifeboat persist, unchanged by such momentary aberrations.

This then is the basic metaphor within which we must work out our solutions. Let us enrich the image step by step with substantive additions from the real world.

Reproduction

The harsh characteristics of lifeboat ethics are heightened by reproduction, particularly by reproductive differences. The people inside the lifeboats of the wealthy nations are doubling in numbers every 87 years; those outside are doubling every 35 years, on the average. And the relative difference in prosperity is becoming greater.

Let us, for a while, think primarily of the U.S. lifeboat. As of 1973 the United States had a population of 210 million people, who were increasing by 0.8% per year, that is, doubling in number every 87 years.

Although the citizens of rich nations are outnumbered two to one by the poor, let us imagine an equal number of poor people outside our lifeboat—a mere 210 million poor people reproducing at a quite different rate. If we imagine these to be the combined populations of Colombia, Venezuela, Ecuador, Morocco, Thailand, Pakistan, and the Philippines, the average rate of increase of the people "outside" is 3.3% per year. The doubling time of this population is 21 years.

Suppose that all these countries, and the United States, agreed to live by the Marxian ideal, "to each according to his needs," the ideal of most Christians as well. Needs, of course, are determined by population size, which is affected by reproduction. Every nation regards its rate of reproduction as a sovereign right. If our lifeboat were big enough in the beginning it might be possible to live *for a while* by Christian-Marxian ideals. *Might.*

Initially, in the model given, the ratio of non-Americans to Americans would be one to one. But consider what the ratio would be 87 years later. By this time Americans would have doubled to a population of 420 million. The other group (doubling every 21 years) would now have swollen to 3,540 million. Each American would have more than eight people to share with. How could the lifeboat possibly keep afloat?

All this involves extrapolation of current trends into the future, and is consequently suspect. Trends may change. Granted: but the change will not necessarily be favorable. If—as seems likely—the rate of population increase falls faster in the ethnic group presently inside the lifeboat than it does among those now outside, the future will turn out to be even worse than mathematics predicts, and sharing will be even more suicidal.

Ruin in the Commons

The fundamental error of the sharing ethics is that it leads to the tragedy of the commons. Under a system of private property the man (or group of men) who own property recognize their responsibility to care for it, for if they don't they will eventually suffer. A farmer, for instance, if he is intelligent, will allow no more cattle in a pasture than its carrying capacity justifies. If he overloads the pasture, weeds take over, erosion sets in, and the owner loses in the long run.

But if a pasture is run as a commons open to all, the right of each to use it is not matched by an operational responsibility to take care of it. It is no use asking independent herdsmen in a commons to act responsibly, for they dare not. The considerate herdsman who refrains from overloading the commons suffers more than a selfish one who says his needs are greater. (As Leo Durocher says, "Nice guys finish last.") Christian-Marxian idealism is counterproductive. That it *sounds* nice is no excuse. With distribution systems, as with individual morality, good intentions are no substitute for good performance.

A social system is stable only if it is insensitive to errors. To the Christian-Marxian idealist a selfish person is a sort of "error." Prosperity in the system of the commons cannot survive errors. If *everyone* would only restrain himself, all would be well; but it takes *only one less than everyone* to ruin a system of voluntary restraint. In a crowded world of less than perfect human beings—and we will never know any other—mutual ruin is inevitable in the commons. This is the core of the tragedy of the commons. . . .

World Food Banks

In the international arena we have recently heard a proposal to create a new commons, namely an international depository of food reserves to which nations will contribute according to their abilities, and from which nations may draw according to their needs. Nobel laureate Norman Borlaug has lent the prestige of his name to this proposal.

A world food bank appeals powerfully to our humanitarian impulses. We remember John Donne's celebrated line, "Any man's death diminishes me." But before we rush out to see for whom the bell tolls let us recognize where the greatest political push for international granaries comes from, lest we be disillusioned later. Our experience with Public Law 480 clearly reveals the answer. This was the law that moved billions of dollars worth of U.S. grain to food-short, population-long countries during the past two decades. When P.L. 480 first came into being, a headline in the business magazine *Forbes* revealed the power behind it: "Feeding the World's Hungry Millions: How it will mean billions for U.S. business."

And indeed it did. In the years 1960 to 1970 a total of $7.9 billion was spent on the "Food for Peace" program, as P.L. 480 was called. During the years of 1948 to 1970 an additional $49.9 billion were extracted from American taxpayers to pay for other economic aid programs, some of which went for food and food-producing machinery. (This figure does *not* include military aid.) That P.L. 480 was a give-away program was concealed. Recipient countries went through the motions of paying for P.L. 480 food—with IOU's. In December 1973 the charade was brought to an end as far as India was concerned when the United States "forgave" India's $3.2 billion debt. Public announcement of the cancellation of the debt was delayed for two months: one wonders why. . . .

What happens if some organizations budget for emergencies and others do not? If each organization is solely responsible for its own well-being, poorly managed ones will suffer. But they should be able to learn from experience. They have a chance to mend their ways and learn to budget for infrequent but certain emergencies. The weather, for instance, always varies and periodic crop failures are certain. A wise and competent government saves out of the production of the good years in anticipation of bad years that are sure to come. This is not a new idea. The Bible tells us that Joseph taught this policy to Pharaoh in Egypt more than 2,000 years ago. Yet it is literally true that the vast majority of the governments of the world today have no such policy. They lack either the wisdom or the competence, or both. Far more difficult than the transfer of wealth from one country to another is the transfer of wisdom between sovereign powers or between generations.

"But it isn't their fault! How can we blame the poor people who are caught in an emergency? Why must we punish them?" The concepts of blame and punishment are irrelevant. The question is, what are the operational consequences of establishing a world food bank? If it is open to every country every time a need develops, slovenly rulers will not be motivated to take Joseph's advice. Why should they? Others will bail them out whenever they are in trouble.

Some countries will make deposits in the world food bank and others will withdraw from it: there will be almost no overlap. Calling such a depository-transfer unit a "bank" is stretching the metaphor of *bank* beyond its elastic limits. The proposers, of course, never call attention to the metaphorical nature of the word they use.

Suggestions for Further Reading

Three anthologies provide a wide range of views on this subject: William Aiken and Hugh LaFollette, eds., *World Hunger and Moral Obligation* (Englewood Cliffs, N.J.: Prentice-Hall, 1977); George R. Lucas, Jr., ed., *Lifeboat Ethics* (New York: Harper and Row, 1976); and Peter G. Brown and Henry Shue, eds., *Food Policy* (New York: Free Press, 1977).

Also see Onora O'Neill, "The Moral Perplexities of Famine Relief," in *Matters of Life and Death,* 2nd ed., edited by Tom Regan (New York: Random House, 1985).

18 *The Morality of Euthanasia*

James Rachels

The single most powerful argument in support of euthanasia is the argument from mercy. It is also an exceptionally simple argument, at least in its main idea, which makes one uncomplicated point. Terminally ill patients sometimes suffer pain so horrible that it is beyond the comprehension of those who have not actually experienced it. Their suffering can be so terrible that we do not like even to read about it or think about it; we recoil even from the descriptions of such agony. The argument from mercy says euthanasia is justified because it provides an end to *that.*

The great Irish satirist Jonathan Swift took eight years to die, while, in the words of Joseph Fletcher, "His mind crumbled to pieces." At times the pain in his blinded eyes was so intense he had to be restrained from tearing them out with his own hands. Knives and other potential instruments of suicide had to be kept from him. For the last three years of his life, he could do nothing but sit and drool: and when he finally died it was only after convulsions that lasted thirty-six hours.

Swift died in 1745. Since then, doctors have learned how to eliminate much of the pain that accompanies terminal illness, but the victory has been far from complete. So, here is a more modern example.

Stewart Alsop was a respected journalist who died in 1975 of a rare form of cancer. Before he died, he wrote movingly of his experiences as a terminal patient. Although he had not thought much about euthanasia before, he came to approve of it after rooming briefly with someone he called Jack:

> The third night that I roomed with Jack in our tiny double room in the solid-tumor ward of the cancer clinic of the National Institutes of Health in Bethesda, Md., a terrible thought occurred to me.
>
> Jack had a melanoma in his belly, a malignant solid tumor that the doctors guessed was about the size of a softball. The cancer had started a few months before with a small tumor in his left shoulder, and there had been several operations since. The doctors planned to remove the softball-sized tumor, but they knew Jack would soon die. The cancer had metastasized— it had spread beyond control.
>
> Jack was good-looking, about 28, and brave. He was in constant pain, and his doctor had prescribed an intravenous shot of a synthetic opiate—a pain-killer, or analgesic—every four hours. His wife spent many of the daylight hours with him, and she would sit or lie on his bed and pat him all over, as one pats a child, only more methodically, and this seemed to help control the pain. But at night, when his pretty wife had left (wives cannot stay overnight at the NIH clinic) and darkness fell, the pain would attack without pity.
>
> At the prescribed hour, a nurse would give Jack a shot of the synthetic analgesic, and this would control the pain for perhaps two hours or a bit more. Then he would begin to moan, or whimper, very low, as though he didn't want to wake me. Then he would begin to howl, like a dog.
>
> When this happened, either he or I would ring for a nurse, and ask for a pain-killer. She would give him some co-

deine or the like by mouth, but it never did any real good—it affected him no more than half an aspirin might affect a man who had just broken his arm. Always the nurse would explain as encouragingly as she could that there was not long to go before the next intravenous shot—"Only about 50 minutes now." And always poor Jack's whimpers and howls would become more loud and frequent until at last the blessed relief came.

The third night of this routine, the terrible thought occurred to me. "If Jack were a dog," I thought, "what would be done with him?" The answer was obvious: the pound, and chloroform. No human being with a spark of pity could let a living thing suffer so, to no good end.

The NIH clinic is, of course, one of the most modern and best-equipped hospitals we have. Jack's suffering was not the result of poor treatment in some backward rural facility; it was the inevitable product of his disease, which medical science was powerless to prevent.

I have quoted Alsop at length not for the sake of indulging in gory details but to give a clear idea of the kind of suffering we are talking about. We should not gloss over these facts with euphemistic language or squeamishly avert our eyes from them. For only by keeping them firmly and vividly in mind can we appreciate the full force of the argument from mercy: If a person prefers—and even begs for—death as the only alternative to lingering on *in this kind of torment,* only to die anyway after a while, then surely it is not immoral to help this person die sooner. As Alsop put it, "No human being with a spark of pity could let a living thing suffer so, to no good end."

The Utilitarian Version of the Argument

In connection with this argument, the utilitarians deserve special mention. They argued that actions and social policies should be judged right or wrong *exclusively* according to whether they cause happiness or misery; and they argued that when judged by this standard, euthanasia turns out to be morally acceptable. The utilitarian argument may be elaborated as follows:

1. Any action or social policy is morally right if it serves to increase the amount of happiness in the world or

to decrease the amount of misery. Conversely, an action or social policy is morally wrong if it serves to decrease happiness or to increase misery.

2. The policy of killing, at their own request, hopelessly ill patients who are suffering great pain would decrease the amount of misery in the world. (An example could be Alsop's friend Jack.)

3. Therefore, such a policy would be morally right.

The first premise of this argument, (1), states the Principle of Utility, which is the basic utilitarian assumption. Today most philosophers think that this principle is wrong, because they think that the promotion of happiness and the avoidance of misery are not the *only* morally important things. Happiness, they say, is only one among many values that should be promoted: freedom, justice, and a respect for people's rights are also important. To take one example; people *might* be happier if there were no freedom of religion, for if everyone adhered to the same religious beliefs, there would be greater harmony among people. There would be no unhappiness caused within families by Jewish girls marrying Catholic boys, and so forth. Moreover, if people were brainwashed well enough, no one would mind not having freedom of choice. Thus happiness would be increased. But, the argument continues, even if happiness *could* be increased this way, it would not be right to deny people freedom of religion, because people have a right to make their own choices. Therefore, the first premise of the utilitarian argument is unacceptable.

There is a related difficulty for utilitarianism, which connects more directly with the topic of euthanasia. Suppose a person is leading a miserable life—full of more unhappiness than happiness—but does *not* want to die. This person thinks that a miserable life is better than none at all. Now I assume that we would all agree that the person should not be killed; that would be plain, unjustifiable murder. Yet it *would* decrease the amount of misery in the world if we killed this person—it would lead to an increase in the balance of happiness over unhappiness—and so it is hard to see how, on strictly utilitarian grounds, it could be wrong. Again, the Principle of Utility seems to be an inadequate guide for determining right and wrong. So we are on shaky ground if we rely on *this* version of the argument from mercy for a defense of euthanasia.

Doing What Is in Everyone's Best Interests

Although the foregoing utilitarian argument is faulty, it is neverthe-less based on a sound idea. For even if the promotion of happiness and avoidance of misery are not the *only* morally important things, they are still very important. So, when an action or a social policy would decrease misery, that is *a* very strong reason in its favor. In the cases of voluntary euthanasia we are now considering, great suffering is eliminated, and since the patient requests it, there is no question of violating individual rights. That is why, regardless of the difficulties of the Principle of Utility, the utilitarian version of the argument still retains considerable force.

I want now to present a somewhat different version of the argument from mercy, which is inspired by utilitarianism but which avoids the difficulties of the foregoing version by not making the Principle of Utility a premise of the argument. I believe that the following argument is sound and proves that active euthanasia *can* be justified:

1. If an action promotes the best interests of *everyone* concerned and violates *no one's* rights, then that action is morally acceptable.
2. In at least some cases, active euthanasia promotes the best interests of everyone concerned and violates no one's rights.
3. Therefore, in at least some cases, active euthanasia is morally acceptable.

It would have been in everyone's best interests if active euthanasia had been employed in the case of Stewart Alsop's friend Jack. First, and most important, it would have been in Jack's own interests, since it would have provided him with an easier, better death, with-out pain. (Who among us would choose Jack's death, if we had a choice, rather than a quick painless death?) Second, it would have been in the best interests of Jack's wife. Her misery, helplessly watching him suffer, must have been almost equal to his. Third, the hospital staff's best interests would have been served, since if Jack's dying had not been prolonged, they could have turned their atten-tion to other patients whom they could have helped. Fourth, other patients would have benefited, since medical resources would no longer have been used in the sad, pointless maintenance of Jack's physical existence. Finally, if Jack himself requested to be killed, the act would not have violated his rights. Considering all this, how can active euthanasia in this case be wrong? How can it be wrong to do an action that is merciful, that benefits everyone concerned, and that violates no one's rights?

Suggestions for Further Reading

See page 209.

19 *The Immorality of Euthanasia*

Joseph V. Sullivan

Bishop Sullivan, a Roman Catholic priest, was the Ordinary of the Baton Rouge diocese. A leading spokesman for the Catholic view of euthanasia, he is the author of *The Morality of Mercy Killing* (1950).

In this essay I will discuss the moral aspects of mercy killing, whether voluntary or compulsory. The thesis that I will attempt to prove is that it is never lawful for man on his own authority to kill the innocent directly. If the thesis is morally sound, it follows that mercy killing is never permissible. . . .

At the outset it can be admitted that the thesis is not self-

From Joseph V. Sullivan, *The Morality of Mercy Killing* (Westminster, Md: Newman Press, 1950).

evident to all men, at least insofar as it includes mercy killing. Many Christians who condemn suicide and murder believe that euthanasia is consistent with Christian morality. This is evident from the number of ministers who have signed in favor of euthanasia. Furthermore, it must be admitted candidly that without the support of the teaching Church, Revelation, and the general heritage of the West, it is difficult to establish from reason alone that mercy killing, especially voluntary mercy killing, is always under every condition illicit. Though the argument from reason is objectively good, it requires more than reason to present a proof for the thesis that will carry conviction to all. In proving euthanasia illicit, this dissertation will appeal, therefore, not only to reason, but likewise to the great tradition of the West that has been Christian for nearly two thousand years. It will appeal also to the argument of the "wedge principle" and to man's natural desire to live.

Argument from Reason

This argument from reason presupposes belief in a personal God, the immortality of the human soul and the existence of a moral law binding all human beings. To the atheist, of course, this argument would have no appeal. However, since the vast majority of mankind does believe in God and in the other truths mentioned, the argument has a practical validity.

Supreme dominion over life belongs to God alone. God has sovereign dominion over all things, even over the essences of things. According to His providence He has given man a natural dominion over things of the earth inferior to himself to the extent that man may make use of them for his own utility. Man has not full dominion over his life. He has only the use of it; and the natural law obliges man while using a thing that is under the dominion of another not to destroy it. The life of man is solely under the dominion of God. Wherefore, as man may not take his life, neither may another man take it (apart from exceptions given above), since another man would have even less dominion over it. . . .

In a word, it is the belief of Catholics that according to the natural law man does not have direct dominion over human life—either his own life or the life of another man. Yet euthanasia, whether it is voluntary euthanasia or compulsory euthanasia, is the destruction of human life. Destruction is an act proper to the master alone. Hence euthanasia violates God's absolute dominion over human life. The fact that the victim wills to die is an irrelevant consideration. The patient is innocent and hence apart from a divine command and may not be killed directly whether he wills it or not.

An objection might be presented that the common good may sometimes require the killing of an innocent person. If, for example, a diseased man became a grave danger to a community so that unless he were put out of the way many others would die, the state could kill the diseased patient for the common good. It might seem that the state would have the right to cut off a member of its body for the health and safety of the whole body, as a man may cut off a member of his body when it is necessary for the health of the whole body. This is confirmed by the fact that although the state does not have dominion over the life of the citizen it is permitted to kill a citizen in punishment for a crime, because the punishment is useful and vital to the common good of the whole state. Therefore, when it is equally or even more necessary to kill an innocent member for the common good, it seems that it should be permissible.

Some might answer that for the health of the whole body a sick or evil member may be cut off, not a healthy one; thus in like manner a malefactor may be cut off from the state, but not an innocent member. The diseased man is an innocent member of the community and therefore to kill him, to administer compulsory euthanasia to him, is a violation of God's absolute dominion over life.

To such a defense it could be answered—and justly, I believe—that even a healthy member of the natural body of a man may be cut off if it is necessary to save the life of the whole person, as for example when an arm is amputated in order that a person may escape a death trap. It might seem therefore that even a healthy member of society, an innocent member of the community, may be cut off for the sake of the whole. If such is permissible then the original thesis is unsound.

The true response to this objection, therefore, is to be found in the great difference between the members of the natural body of man and the members of the political body. A member of the natural body has no independent existence and no individual rights. The person itself has the right to use the members for they exist for the utility of the person. Wherefore properly they may be cut off when it is necessary for the conservation of the person, for the sake of which they exist. It is a very different relation that exists between the individual human being and the state. The citizens do not exist for the sake of the state, but for their own sake, and to attain their own destiny. A citizen does not serve the utility of the state in the sense that the state has full dominion over him. It is the state that exists for the utility of the citizen. . . .

Hence the state may not cut off or kill an innocent citizen merely for its utility, because this is an encroachment of a fundamental personal right, at least when there is a question of compulsory euthanasia. Even if a sick person were to agree to his own death for the common good and undergo voluntary euthanasia, there would still be committed a grave violation of God's absolute dominion over life. Since man does not have full dominion over his own life, he obviously cannot give up a dominion he does not have.

There is another objection that may be advanced, especially as regards voluntary euthanasia. It might be maintained that life is a gift and as such may be renounced. The answer, however, is that life is not merely a gift. It is indeed a gift, but it has grave obligations, both to God and to one's fellow man, inseparably affixed thereto. Life is given man not only for himself but also for the service of his fellow man and God.

It may further be objected that even though God does have absolute dominion over man's life, yet man does presume the right to mutilate a member of that body when necessary for the good of the whole. And furthermore, it seems, man may even mutilate a part of his body, within certain limits, out of charity for his neighbor. If these two presumptions are permissible it might seem likely that God would allow a man a merciful death out of charity to himself and to those who must care for him. Once a presumption of a minor or a major mutilation is allowed it would appear at least doubtful as to where to draw the line.

This objection is not valid. One can presume reasonably that when he has the administration of a thing belonging to another, a part may be sacrificed when it is necessary to save the whole. Hence it is a reasonable presumption that man may mutilate a part of his body when it is necessary to save the whole body. There is quite a difference between saying this and saying that man may destroy outright what belongs to his master because to retain it causes pain and inconvenience. If a ship is carrying a precious cargo to its owner in a distant port, and it becomes evident to the ship's captain that a part of the cargo must be thrown overboard lest the whole cargo be lost, the captain may presume reasonably that the owner of the cargo would allow him to sacrifice a part of it in order that the whole cargo not be lost. But it would be unreasonable to conclude from this that therefore the captain could destroy the owner's whole cargo because some inconvenience is involved in taking care of it. The line of demarcation seems very evident. It must be remembered that in the two presumptions presented in the objection, it was actually for the prolongation of life that the mutilation was allowed.

Surely, it is illogical to argue that since man is permitted to take certain measures to prolong his life, he may therefore sometimes take measures to destroy it. Man has only the use of his life, and when man uses what belongs to another he has the obligation of taking ordinary care of it. When dealing with a human life, this ordinary care may involve some necessary mutilation for the preservation of that life. Hence man's right to presume a reasonable mutilation of his body not only does not argue against God's supreme dominion over life but rather confirms it. It is because God has the absolute dominion over life that man may even be required to mutilate his body, when this is a part of the ordinary care due what belongs to another.

Another objection that is often advanced by advocates of euthanasia is that to maintain that God would object to killing an incurable sufferer, a useless member of society, one who is a burden to all, is unreasonable. There is no point in forcing certain physically and mentally defective persons to live a miserable existence. To hold the contrary is to manifest a heartless attitude toward the sufferers themselves and to place an unbearable physical, emotional, and financial burden upon the families of many of these unfortunate persons.

The Christian has the only answer to this objection. He knows that no human being is a useless member either to himself or to society or at least need not be, no matter what his physical status may be. If the suffering patient is of sound mind and capable of making an act of divine resignation, then his sufferings become a great means of merit whereby he can gain reward for himself and also win great favors for the souls in Purgatory, perhaps even release them from their suffering. Likewise the sufferer may give good example to his family and friends and teach them how to bear a heavy cross in a Christlike manner.

As regard those that must live in the same house with the incurable sufferer, they have a great opportunity to practice Christian charity. They can learn to see Christ in the sufferer and win the reward promised in the Beatitudes. This opportunity for charity would hold true even when the sufferer is deprived of the use of reason. It may well be that the incurable sufferer in a particular case may be of greater value to society than when he was of some material value to himself and his community.

Argument from Western Tradition

The tradition of the West has been Christian for nearly two thousand years and it is interesting to note that never has this tradition sanctioned the direct killing of the innocent (apart from a divine command). There is no positive approval of direct killing of the innocent in any of the writings of the Fathers. Here there is at least an argument of silence against such a killing. If there had been an opinion in any sense common during those early days of Christianity to the effect that under certain circumstances man may kill the innocent directly, this opinion would have found mention in some of those ancient writings. That such is not the case is in itself an implicit disapproval of direct killing. On the contrary, Christianity from the very beginning opposed self-destruction and homicide; this is positively indicated in the writings of some of the Fathers and Doctors of the Church. St. Augustine affirms this common tradition of the Christian West: "The commandment is, 'Thou shalt not kill man,' therefore neither another nor yourself, for he who kills himself still kills nothing else than man."

The value of this traditional argument toward proving the thesis was noted by St. Augustine himself: "It is not without significance that in no passage of the holy canonical books can there be found either divine precept or permission to take away our life, whether for the sake of entering on the enjoyment of immortality, or for shunning, or ridding ourselves of any evil whatever." . . .

In the Middle Ages one scarcely hears of suicides, and one would be tempted to deny their occurrence during those times were it not for the numerous acts of ecclesiastical and civil legislation condemning and declaring punishable even the very attempt to commit suicide.

The Church had legislated against self-destruction as early as the year 533 at the Council of Orleans. It was determined at that time not to accept the offerings of a man who died at his own hands. Later synods, for instance that of Braga in 563, and Auxere in 576, renewed the penalties against the offenders. In the ninth century the Council of Troyes warns against a free-will death. Even the Catechism of the Council of Trent, published at the command of Pope Pius V, reminds the faithful that murder and suicide are forbidden by Divine Command: "With regard to the person killed, the law extends to all. There is no individual, however humble or lowly his condition, whose life is not shielded by this law." It also forbids suicide: "No man possesses such power over his own life as to be at liberty to put himself to death. Hence we find that the Commandment does not say: *Thou shalt not kill another,* but simply: *Thou shalt not kill.*"

The tradition in the Middle Ages was so strongly set against suicide that not only was Christian burial denied the victim but in addition to this his goods and property were confiscated by the civil authority. Being excluded from the Christian cemetery, the suicide received an ignominious burial on the highway with a stake driven through his body. This severity of civil law was in force throughout the Middle Ages. There was no exception made even for incurable sufferers. And surely there must have been some suicides in this class.

These penalties were gradually mitigated and in the year 824 the English Parliament permitted a suicide's burial in the churchyard, but only between nine and twelve at night.

This past tradition of the Christian West indicates how strongly the people felt against the direct killing of the innocent and especially against suicide.

When the Church laws were codified in 1918 this Western culture was still evidenced, for a definite penalty was placed on suicide. Persons guilty of deliberate suicide are to be denied ecclesiastical burial unless they have before death given some signs of repentance. The same penalty is to be placed on those dying from wounds received in a duel. This is in punishment for exposing their lives and the lives of their adversaries to grave danger. Again, the stand of the Church against the direct killing of unborn infants, the practice of abortion, is another indication of her condemnation of the direct killing of the innocent. The Code states that persons who procure abortion, the mother not excepted, automatically incur excommunication reserved to the Ordinary at the moment the crime takes place. The most *ad rem* decree against a direct killing of the innocent was issued by the Holy Office in 1940 and deals expressly with state eugenic murder, or in other words, compulsory euthanasia.

> *Question:* Is it lawful upon the mandate of authority directly to kill those who, although not having committed any crimes deserving of death, are however, because of the psychic or physical defects, unable to be useful to the nation but, rather, are considered a burden to its vigor and strength? *Answer:* No, because it is contrary to the natural and the divine positive law.

. . . .

The tradition of the West is therefore sternly set against any form of direct killing of the innocent. It is true that the Western tradition does not explicitly condemn merciful euthanasia, because there was no need to do so since no one conceived the idea under a Christian civilization to kill the suffering in order to relieve them of their suffering. But by condemning all forms of direct killing of the innocent the tradition does implicitly condemn euthanasia, for euthanasia, whether voluntary euthanasia or compulsory euthanasia, is direct killing of the innocent. A patient is an innocent person. The fact that the patient is incurably ill, wills euthanasia, and is useless to the community, does not in any way change the fact of the person's innocence. For man to take the life of an innocent person directly, even his own life, for any reason whatsoever, apart from a divine command, has always been against the conscience of the West.

Euthanasia is a reversal from culture to barbarism. Even in most savage tribes there is no record of mercy killing in the strict sense, but a kind of "quasi-euthanasia," as in the abandonment of the aged when in reality little else could be done under primitive living conditions. Only in the most barbaric tribes is there direct killing of the aged and the sick. The advocates of euthanasia must face the fact that they are opposing the traditional Christian teaching on the value of a human life. They must go back beyond two thousand years to a world before Christ, or to some pagan land that has never known Christ, and even then seek a most barbaric tribe to find a practice like to mercy killing.

Argument from the "Wedge Principle"

The "wedge principle" means that an act that would injure humanity if raised to a general line of conduct is wrong even in an individual case. Ordinarily the act even individually is evil, but it can happen in exceptional instances that the act causes no harm but nevertheless on account of the common danger there is a general prohibition. By this principle one may conclude that any course of conduct that works destruction when practiced generally may not be permitted in an individual case. Thus divorce and remarriage might be harmless in some individual case. It may be that the innocent party and her children would be greatly benefited by her second marriage. Perhaps in this particular case there may be many good reasons why a second marriage would be helpful to all concerned, especially the children. Nevertheless, if one exception is allowed to the rule of no marriage after a divorce, other exceptions will soon follow and society will suffer much. (We are concerned with the natural law—not with any exceptions that God Himself may have introduced.)

This principle of the wedge may be applied to euthanasia, both voluntary euthanasia and compulsory euthanasia. Here for the sake of argument it will be presumed that the suffering patient wishes euthanasia and that no evil effects will result to his friends or the common good from the single act of administering the euthanasia to him. Nevertheless, euthanasia must not be administered, for to permit in a single instance the direct killing of an innocent person would be to admit a most dangerous wedge that might eventually put all life in a precarious condition. Once a man is permitted on his own authority to kill an innocent person directly, there is no way of stopping the advancement of that wedge. There exists no longer any rational grounds for saying that the wedge can advance so far and no further. Once the exception has been admitted it is too late; hence the grave reason why no exception may be allowed. That is why euthanasia under any circumstances must be condemned. We are making use of this as a secondary argument; for the primary argument is found in the intrinsic malice of the direct killing of an innocent person. But even one who would not admit this should acknowledge the value of the present argument.

If voluntary euthanasia were legalized, there is good reason to believe that at a later date another bill for compulsory euthanasia would be legalized. Once the respect for human life is so low that an innocent person may be killed directly even at his own request, compulsory euthanasia will necessarily be very near. This could lead easily to killing all incurable charity patients, the aged who are a public care, wounded soldiers, captured enemy soldiers, all deformed children, the mentally afflicted, and so on. Before long the danger would be at the door of every citizen.

Politics also would enter and perhaps political parties would use the law to destroy personae non gratae. This might be done by getting a court order stating that the person in question is an incurable mental case. The possibilities of abusing euthanasia are many. Dishonesty and graft have found their way into nearly every field. There would be many opportunities for these evils to operate under legalized euthanasia to the great danger of society. It is common knowledge that not infrequently a person goes into court to seek the administration of property by having the real owner declared insane. A more effective way of securing property would be open to unscrupulous relatives if euthanasia were legalized.

The most outstanding examples of the extremes to which legalized euthanasia can go are found in the mass eugenic murders within Germany and her conquered territories during the war. Those considered by the state as physically unfit or mentally unfit could be put to death as they were regarded as a grave burden to the common good. Likewise any undesirable citizen could be exterminated, whether man, woman, or child. As a rule the death was an easy death in a gas chamber. Many present-day advocates of euthanasia might accept this procedure as within reason since the unfit and the undesirable are no benefit to society. The point is, however, that all persons unfriendly to the Nazi government were considered by those in power as undesirable citizens. Those who held a philosophy contrary to that of the government might well be considered as mental cases. Hence many thousands were put to death without mercy. It is estimated that thousands of Jews in Austria alone were sent to their death by the government for no reason save that they were non-Aryan and undesirable to the state. Reports indicate that these murders were considered legal by reason of existing compulsory euthanasia legislation. At the time these laws were enacted it was thought that only the incurable mental cases, monstrosities, and the incurables that were a burden to the state would be put to death. However, once the state held this power of life and death over even the innocent members of society, the lives of all the citizens were in danger.

This example of the Nazi government in Germany with regard to euthanasia might be followed by any other government once that government possessed such a power. One might say that the mentality of the American people would never accept such abuse of human life. The point is, however, that once the American people depart so far from Christian tradition as to allow an innocent person to be put to death legally because he is a monstrosity or wills euthanasia, it is difficult to predict how much further this abuse of the power over human life would go.

It is obvious, therefore, that if euthanasia is legalized, even with strict limitation, it would lead to many downright murders and hence by reason of the "wedge principle" may not be allowed in any individual case. . . .

Argument from Man's Desire to Live

Every being has an inclination, or appetite, to fill up the measure of its adequate perfection, and all that is in any way capable of satisfying such inclination is said to be good for that being. All creatures, even the plants and inanimate substances, have a natural tendency or affinity implanted in them that impels them blindly toward what is "suitable to and perfective of their nature, independently of all cognition on their part." So much does every appetite tend toward good that St. Thomas defines good as the object or end of appetite. . . .

St. Thomas uses this argument concerning the natural appetite in man to prove suicide unnatural, for he says: "It is altogether unlawful to kill oneself . . . because everything naturally loves itself, the result being that everything naturally keeps itself in being, and resists corruption so far as it can. Wherefore suicide is contrary to the inclination of nature. . . ."

This inclination in man to prolong his life is verified in practice. It must be remembered that man differs from all other earthly creation in that he possesses an intellect and a will. Though his vegetative and sensuous powers tend necessarily to his continued existence, yet his will is free either to work toward the common goal of a healthy life or to choose self-destruction. The fact that society exists today indicates that man throughout the ages has chosen to live. Man's desire to live is indicated by the great care given human life, from prenatal care to the care given the aged in the social institutions throughout the world. Science has as its greatest goal the prolongation of life. The many health campaigns carried on within the United States, together with the drives to overcome cancer, tuberculosis, and heart disease, are all very indicative of man's desire to live. Even the daily care man gives his physical and mental health testifies to this natural desire to live. War itself is an argument for the value of life, for man's greatest fear in wartime is that either he or some dear friend may be killed. All of these facts make most obvious that universally man loves life and wants to live.

From this universal desire to live we have a strong argument against the direct killing of the innocent, and hence against all forms of euthanasia.

An objection might be raised that all healthy men desire to live but not all incurable sufferers. The very fact that euthanasia is so popular today is an indication that some incurable sufferers desire to die. Therefore the basic principle is false.

The objection is not valid. The incurable sufferer desires in the first place not to die but rather to recover, or at least to be free from pain. Those who seek euthanasia do so because of the great pain. If this pain would cease they would rather live, even though they would not recover. The incurable sufferer's basic desire, like that of all men, is *to live* a healthy life. It is this basic natural desire to which the principle refers. The fact that the incurable patient may wish to end his sufferings, even by euthanasia if necessary, does not argue against his basic natural desire to live, and certainly it does not argue against the universal desire of man to live. It only indicates that man can have a confused sense of values and choose an evil under some aspect of good. Even in this case the incurable sufferer is violating a natural appetite for continued life.

It is likely that many of the present-day advocates of mercy killing are in good faith. They may see that homicide is illicit and that suicide is illicit but they cannot see that euthanasia is necessarily always sinful. They will admit that human life is sacred; they may have respect for the Fifth Commandment, but somehow they feel that voluntary euthanasia is within the limits of morality.

Theologians admit that man may be invincibly ignorant of the more remote conclusions from the natural law. The distance removed from first principles increases this possibility. When man is occupied chiefly with material things he loses a true sense of values and hence his judgments are often incorrect. Likewise man is dependent to a great extent on the culture about him and if this culture is pagan it is likely that he will be in good faith about many violations of the more remote conclusions of the natural law.

This is no argument against the universality of the natural law. All men do participate in the natural law. Monsignor Cooper makes this fact evident.

> The people of the world, however much they may differ as to the details of morality, hold universally, or with practical universality, to at least the following basic precepts. Respect the Supreme Being or the benevolent being or beings who take his place. Do not "blaspheme." Care for your children. Malicious murder or maiming, stealing, deliberate slander or "black" lying, when committed against a friend or unoffending fellow clansman or tribesman, are reprehensible. . . .

The point is that not all are aware of the natural law to the same degree. All have inherent inclinations and at least some power of reason, so we believe that all are cognizant of the natural law at least *in actu primo.* Beyond that it varies with different people. We present here a division of the natural law from the standpoint of those who recognize it:

A. Most Universal Principles: Do good, avoid evil, act according to human nature. (No one with the use of reason can be ignorant of these.)

B. Conclusions Immediately Deduced: The ten Commandments (with the exception of the determination of the Sabbath as the Lord's Day), at least as generally understood under ordinary circumstances. *Per se,* people are not inculpably ignorant of these. *Per accidens,* perhaps some can be ignorant of these for a time.

C. Remote Conclusions: Known in a greater or less measure, depending on education, culture, etc. Of these man can easily be ignorant.

It is our opinion that euthanasia would come under this third division and hence many men, even good Christians, could be inculpably ignorant of the fact that euthanasia is against the natural law and natural ethics.

Suggestions for Further Reading

James Rachels, *The End of Life: Euthanasia and Morality* (Oxford: Oxford University Press, 1986) provides a full treatment of this subject. Marvin Kohl, ed., *Beneficent Euthanasia* (Buffalo, N.Y.: Prometheus Books, 1975) is also recommended; this book contains some good articles defending a variety of views.

Other recommended works are Margaret Pabst Battin, "Euthanasia," in *Health Care Ethics,* edited by Donald VanDeVeer and Tom Regan (Philadelphia: Temple University Press, 1987); A. B. Downing, ed., *Euthanasia and the Right to Death* (Los Angeles: Nash, 1969); Paul Ramsey, *Ethics at the Edges of Life* (New Haven: Yale University Press, 1978); and Joseph Fletcher, *Morals and Medicine* (Princeton, N.J.: Princeton University Press, 1954).

20 Why We Have No Obligations to Animals

Immanuel Kant

For information about Kant, see the comments preceding selection 9. The following selection, from Kant's *Lectures on Ethics,* is his most explicit discussion of the status of nonhuman animals.

Baumgarten speaks of duties towards beings which are beneath us and beings which are above us. But so far as animals are concerned,

From Immanuel Kant, *Lectures on Ethics,* translated by Louis Infield (London: Methuen, 1930). Reprinted by permission.

we have no direct duties. Animals are not self-conscious and are there merely as a means to an end. That end is man. We can ask, "Why do animals exist?" But to ask, "Why does man exist?" is a meaningless question. Our duties towards animals are merely indirect duties towards humanity. Animal nature has analogies to human nature, and by doing our duties to animals in respect of manifestations which correspond to manifestations of human nature, we indirectly do our duty towards humanity. Thus, if a dog has served his master long and faithfully, his service, on the analogy of human service, deserves reward, and when the dog has grown too old to serve, his master ought to keep him until he dies. Such action helps to support us in our duties towards human beings, where they are bounden duties. If then any acts of animals are analogous to human acts and spring from the same principles, we have duties towards the animals because thus we cultivate the corresponding duties towards human beings. If a man shoots his dog because the animal is no longer capable of service, he does not fail in his duty to the dog, for the dog cannot judge, but his act is inhuman and damages in himself that humanity which it is his duty to show towards mankind. If he is not to stifle his human feelings, he must practise kindness towards animals, for he who is cruel to animals becomes hard also in his dealings with men. We can judge the heart of a man by his treatment of animals. Hogarth depicts this in his engravings. He shows how cruelty grows and develops. He shows the child's cruelty to animals, pinching the tail of a dog or a cat; he then depicts the grown man in his cart running over a child; and lastly, the culmination of cruelty in murder. He thus brings home to us in a terrible fashion the rewards of cruelty, and this should be an impressive lesson to children. The more we come in contact with animals and observe their behaviour, the more we love them, for we see how great is their care for their young. It is then difficult for us to be cruel in thought even to a wolf. Leibnitz used a tiny worm for purposes of observation, and then carefully replaced it with its leaf on the tree so that it should not come to harm through any act of his. He would have been sorry—a natural feeling for a humane man—to destroy such a creature for no reason. Tender feelings towards dumb animals develop humane feelings toward mankind. In England butchers and doctors do not sit on a jury because they are accustomed to the sight of death and hardened. Vivisectionists, who use living animals for their experiments, certainly act cruelly, although their aim is praiseworthy, and they can justify their cruelty, since animals must be regarded as man's instruments; but any such cruelty for sport cannot be justified. A master who turns out his ass or his dog because the animal can no longer earn its keep manifests a small mind. The Greeks' ideas in this respect were high-minded, as can be seen from the fable of the ass and the bell of ingratitude. Our duties towards animals, then, are indirect duties towards mankind.

Suggestions for Further Reading

See page 225.

21 The Case for Animal Rights

Tom Regan

Tom Regan, professor of philosophy at North Carolina State University, is the leading defender of animal rights among American philosophers. In addition to *The Case for Animal Rights* (1983), he also wrote *Bloomsbury's Prophet* (1986), a study of the moral philosophy of G. E. Moore.

I regard myself as an advocate of animal rights—as a part of the animal rights movement. That movement, as I conceive it, is committed to a number of goals, including:

From Peter Singer, ed., *In Defense of Animals* (Oxford: Blackwell, 1985). Reprinted by permission of the publisher and the author.

The total abolition of the use of animals in science;

The total dissolution of commercial animal agriculture;

The total elimination of commercial and sport hunting and trapping.

There are, I know, people who profess to believe in animal rights but do not avow these goals. Factory farming, they say, is wrong—it violates animals' rights—but traditional animal agriculture is all right. Toxicity tests of cosmetics on animals violates their rights, but important medical research—cancer research, for example—does not. The clubbing of baby seals is abhorrent, but not the harvesting of adult seals. I used to think I understood this reasoning. Not any more. You don't change unjust institutions by tidying them up.

What's wrong—fundamentally wrong—with the way animals are treated isn't the details that vary from case to case. It's the whole system. The forlornness of the veal calf is pathetic, heart wrenching; the pulsing pain of the chimp with electrodes planted deep in her brain is repulsive; the slow, tortuous death of the raccoon caught in the leg-hold trap is agonizing. But what is wrong isn't the pain, isn't the suffering, isn't the deprivation. These compound what's wrong. Sometimes—often—they make it much, much worse. But they are not the fundamental wrong.

The fundamental wrong is the system that allows us to view animals as *our resources,* here for *us*—to be eaten, or surgically manipulated, or exploited for sport or money. Once we accept this view of animals—as our resources—the rest is as predictable as it is regrettable. Why worry about their loneliness, their pain, their death? Since animals exist for us, to benefit us in one way or another, what harms them really doesn't matter—or matters only if it starts to bother us, makes us feel a trifle uneasy when we eat our veal escalope, for example. So, yes, let us get veal calves out of solitary confinement, give them more space, a little straw, a few companions. But let us keep our veal escalope.

But a little straw, more space and a few companions won't eliminate—won't even touch—the basic wrong that attaches to our viewing and treating these animals as our resources. A veal calf killed to be eaten after living in close confinement is viewed and treated in this way: but so, too, is another who is raised (as they say) 'more humanely'. To right the wrong of our treatment of farm animals requires more than making rearing methods 'more humane'; it requires the total dissolution of commercial animal agriculture.

How we do this, whether we do it or, as in the case of animals in science, whether and how we abolish their use—these are to a large extent political questions. People must change their beliefs before they change their habits. Enough people, especially those elected to public office, must believe in change—must want it—before we will have laws that protect the rights of animals. This process of change is very complicated, very demanding, very exhausting, calling for the efforts of many hands in education, publicity, political organization and activity, down to the licking of envelopes and stamps. As a trained and practising philosopher, the sort of contribution I can make is limited but, I like to think, important. The currency of philosophy is ideas—their meaning and rational foundation—not the nuts and bolts of the legislative process, say, or the mechanics of community organization. That's what I have been exploring over the past ten years or so in my essays and talks and, most recently, in my book, *The Case for Animal Rights*. I believe the major conclusions I reach in the book are true because they are supported by the weight of the best arguments. I believe the idea of animal rights has reason, not just emotion, on its side.

In the space I have at my disposal here I can only sketch, in the barest outline, some of the main features of the book. Its main themes—and we should not be surprised by this—involve asking and answering deep, foundational moral questions about what morality is, how it should be understood and what is the best moral theory, all considered. I hope I can convey something of the shape I think this theory takes. The attempt to do this will be (to use a word a friendly critic once used to describe my work) cerebral, perhaps too cerebral. But this is misleading. My feelings about how animals are sometimes treated run just as deep and just as strong as those of my more volatile compatriots. Philosophers do—to use the jargon of the day—have a right side to their brains. If it's the left side we contribute (or mainly should), that's because what talents we have reside there.

How to proceed? We begin by asking how the moral status of animals has been understood by thinkers who deny that animals have rights. Then we test the mettle of their ideas by seeing how well they stand up under the heat of fair criticism. If we start our thinking in this way, we soon find that some people believe that we have no duties directly to animals, that we owe nothing to them, that we can do nothing that wrongs them. Rather, we can do wrong acts that involve animals, and so we have duties regarding them, though none to them. Such views may be called indirect duty views. By way of illustration: suppose your neighbour kicks your dog. Then your neighbour has done something wrong. But not to your dog. The wrong that has been done is a wrong to you. After all, it is wrong to upset people, and your neighbour's kicking your dog upsets you. So you are the one who is wronged, not your dog. Or again: by kicking your dog your neighbour damages your property. And since it is wrong to damage another person's property, your neighbour has done something wrong—to you, of course, not to your dog. Your neighbour no more wrongs your dog than your car would be wronged if the windshield were smashed. Your neighbour's duties involving your dog are indirect duties to you. More generally, all of our duties regarding animals are indirect duties to one another—to humanity.

How could someone try to justify such a view? Someone might say that your dog doesn't feel anything and so isn't hurt by your neighbour's kick, doesn't care about the pain since none is felt, is as unaware of anything as is your windshield. Someone might say this, but no rational person will, since, among other considerations, such a view will commit anyone who holds it to the position that no human being feels pain either—that human beings also don't care about what happens to them. A second possibility is that though both humans and your dog are hurt when kicked, it is only human pain that matters. But, again, no rational person can believe this. Pain is pain wherever it occurs. If your neighbour's causing you pain is wrong because of the pain that is caused, we cannot rationally ignore or dismiss the moral relevance of the pain that your dog feels.

Philosophers who hold indirect duty views—and many still do—have come to understand that they must avoid the two defects just noted: that is, both the view that animals don't feel anything as well as the idea that only human pain can be morally relevant. Among such thinkers the sort of view now favoured is one or other form of what is called *contractarianism*.

Here, very crudely, is the root idea: morality consists of a set of rules that individuals voluntarily agree to abide by, as we do when we sign a contract (hence the name contractarianism). Those who understand and accept the terms of the contract are covered directly; they have rights created and recognized by, and protected in, the contract. And these contractors can also have protection spelled out for others who, though they lack the ability to understand morality and so cannot sign the contract themselves, are loved or cherished by those who can. Thus young children, for example, are unable to sign contracts and lack rights. But they are protected by the contract none the less because of the sentimental interests of others, most notably their parents. So we have, then, duties involving these children, duties regarding them, but no duties to them. Our duties in their case are indirect duties to other human beings, usually their parents.

As for animals, since they cannot understand contracts, they obviously cannot sign; and since they cannot sign, they have no rights. Like children, however, some animals are the objects of the sentimental interest of others. You, for example, love your dog or cat. So those animals that enough people care about (companion animals, whales, baby seals, the American bald eagle), though they lack rights themselves, will be protected because of the sentimental interests of people. I have, then, according to contractarianism, no duty directly to your dog or any other animal, not even the duty not to cause them pain or suffering; my duty not to hurt them is a duty I have to those people who care about what happens to them. As for other animals, where no or little sentimental interest is present—in the case of farm animals, for example, or laboratory rats—what duties we have grow weaker and weaker, perhaps to vanishing point. The pain and death they endure, though real, are not wrong if no one cares about them.

When it comes to the moral status of animals, contractarianism could be a hard view to refute if it were an adequate theoretical approach to the moral status of human beings. It is not adequate in this latter respect, however, which makes the question of its adequacy in the former case, regarding animals, utterly moot. For consider: morality, according to the (crude) contractarian position before us, consists of rules that people agree to abide by. What people? Well, enough to make a difference—enough, that is, *collectively* to have the power to enforce the rules that are drawn up in the contract. That is very well and good for the signatories but not so good for anyone who is not asked to sign. And there is nothing in contractarianism of the sort we are discussing that guarantees or requires that everyone will have a chance to participate equally in framing the rules of morality. The result is that this approach to ethics could sanction the most blatant forms of social, economic, moral and political injustice, ranging from a repressive caste system to systematic racial or sexual discrimination. Might, according to this theory, does make right. Let those who are the victims of injustice suffer as they will. It matters not so long as no one else—no contractor, or too few of them—cares about it. Such a theory takes one's moral breath away . . . as if, for example, there would be nothing wrong with apartheid in South Africa if few white South Africans were upset by it. A theory with so little to recommend it at the level of the ethics of our treatment of our fellow humans cannot have anything more to recommend it when it comes to the ethics of how we treat our fellow animals.

The version of contractarianism just examined is, as I have noted, a crude variety, and in fairness to those of a contractarian persuasion it must be noted that much more refined, subtle and ingenious varieties are possible. For example, John Rawls, in his *A Theory of Justice,* sets forth a version of contractarianism that forces contractors to ignore the accidental features of being a human being—for example, whether one is white or black, male or female, a genius or of modest intellect. Only by ignoring such features, Rawls believes, can we ensure that the principles of justice that contractors would agree upon are not based on bias or prejudice. Despite the improvement a view such as Rawls's represents over the cruder forms of contractarianism, it remains deficient: it systematically denies that we have direct duties to those human beings who do not have a sense of justice—young children, for instance, and many mentally retarded humans. And yet it seems reasonably certain that, were we to torture a young child or a retarded elder, we would be doing something that wronged him or her, not something that would be wrong if (and only if) other humans with a sense of justice were upset. And since this is true in the case of these humans, we cannot rationally deny the same in the case of animals.

Indirect duty views, then, including the best among them, fail to command our rational assent. Whatever ethical theory we should accept rationally, therefore, it must at least recognize that we have some duties directly to animals, just as we have some duties directly to each other. The next two theories I'll sketch attempt to meet this requirement.

The first I call the cruelty-kindness view. Simply stated, this says that we have a direct duty to be kind to animals and a direct duty not to be cruel to them. Despite the familiar, reassuring ring of these ideas, I do not believe that this view offers an adequate theory. To make this clearer, consider kindness. A kind person acts from a certain kind of motive—compassion or concern, for example. And that is a virtue. But there is no guarantee that a kind act is a right act. If I am a generous racist, for example, I will be inclined to act kindly towards members of my own race, favouring their interests above those of others. My kindness would be real and, so far as it goes, good. But I trust it is too obvious to require argument that my kind acts may not be above moral reproach—may, in fact, be positively wrong because rooted in injustice. So kindness, notwithstanding its status as a virtue to be encouraged, simply will not carry the weight of a theory of right action.

Cruelty fares no better. People or their acts are cruel if they display either a lack of sympathy for or, worse, the presence of enjoyment in another's suffering. Cruelty in all its guises is a bad thing, a tragic human failing. But just as a person's being motivated by kindness does not guarantee that he or she does what is right, so the absence of cruelty does not ensure that he or she avoids doing what is wrong. Many people who perform abortions, for example, are not cruel, sadistic people. But that fact alone does not settle the terribly difficult question of the morality of abortion. The case is no different when we examine the ethics of our treatment of animals. So, yes, let us be for kindness and against cruelty. But let us not suppose that being for the one and against the other answers questions about moral right and wrong.

Some people think that the theory we are looking for is utilitarianism. A utilitarian accepts two moral principles. The first is that of equality: everyone's interests count, and similar interests must be counted as having similar weight or importance. White or black, American or Iranian, human or animal—everyone's pain or frustration matter, and matter just as much as the equivalent pain or frustration of anyone else. The second principle a utilitarian accepts is that of utility: do the act that will bring about the best balance between satisfaction and frustration for everyone affected by the outcome.

As a utilitarian, then, here is how I am to approach the task of deciding what I morally ought to do: I must ask who will be affected if I choose to do one thing rather than another, how much each individual will be affected, and where the best results are most likely to lie—which option, in other words, is most likely to bring about the best results, the best balance between satisfaction and frustration. That option, whatever it may be, is the one I ought to choose. That is where my moral duty lies.

The great appeal of utilitarianism rests with its uncompromising *egalitarianism:* everyone's interests count and count as much as the like interests of everyone else. The kind of odious discrimination that some forms of contractarianism can justify—discrimination based on race or sex, for example—seems disallowed in principle by utilitarianism, as is speciesism, systematic discrimination based on species membership.

The equality we find in utilitarianism, however, is not the sort an advocate of animal or human rights should have in mind. Utilitarianism has no room for the equal moral rights of different individuals because it has no room for their equal inherent value or worth. What has value for the utilitarian is the satisfaction of an individual's interests, not the individual whose interests they are. A universe in which you satisfy your desire for water, food and warmth is, other things being equal, better than a universe in which these desires are frustrated. And the same is true in the case of an animal with similar desires. But neither you nor the animal have any value in your own right. Only your feelings do.

Here is an analogy to help make the philosophical point clearer: a cup contains different liquids, sometimes sweet, sometimes bitter, sometimes a mix of the two. What has value are the liquids: the sweeter the better, the bitterer the worse. The cup, the container, has no value. It is what goes into it, not what they go into, that has value. For the utilitarian you and I are like the cup; we have no value as individuals and thus no equal value. What has value is what goes into us, what we serve as receptacles for; our feelings of satisfaction have positive value, our feelings of frustration negative value.

Serious problems arise for utilitarianism when we remind ourselves that it enjoins us to bring about the best consequences. What does this mean? It doesn't mean the best consequences for me alone, or for my family or friends, or any other person taken individually. No, what we must do is, roughly, as follows: we must add up (somehow!) the separate satisfactions and frustrations of everyone likely to be affected by our choice, the satisfactions in one column, the frustrations in the other. We must total each column for each of the options before us. That is what it means to say the theory is aggregative. And then we must choose that option which is most likely to bring about the best balance of totalled satisfactions over totalled frustrations. Whatever act would lead to this outcome is the one we ought morally to perform—it is where our moral duty lies. And that act quite clearly might not be the same one that would bring about the best results for me personally, or for my family or friends, or for a lab animal. The best aggregated consequences for everyone concerned are not necessarily the best for each individual.

That utilitarianism is an aggregative theory—different individuals' satisfactions or frustrations are added, or summed, or totalled—is the key objection to this theory. My Aunt Bea is old, inactive, a cranky, sour person, though not physically ill. She prefers to go on living. She is also rather rich. I could make a fortune if I could get my hands on her money, money she intends to give me in any event, after she dies, but which she refuses to give me now. In order to avoid a huge tax bite, I plan to donate a handsome sum of my profits to a local children's hospital. Many, many children will benefit from my generosity, and much joy will be brought to their parents, relatives and friends. If I don't get the money rather soon, all these ambitions will come to naught. The once-in-a-lifetime opportunity to make a real killing will be gone. Why, then, not kill my Aunt Bea? Oh, of course I *might* get caught. But I'm no fool and, besides, her doctor can be counted on to co-operate (he has an eye for the same investment and I happen to know a good deal about his shady past). The deed can be done . . . professionally, shall we say. There is *very* little chance of getting caught. And as for my conscience being guilt-ridden, I am a resourceful sort of fellow and will take more than sufficient comfort—as I lie on the beach at Acapulco—in contemplating the joy and health I have brought to so many others.

Suppose Aunt Bea is killed and the rest of the story comes out as told. Would I have done anything wrong? Anything immoral? One would have thought that I had. Not according to utilitarianism. Since what I have done has brought about the best balance between totalled satisfaction and frustration for all those affected by the outcome, my action is not wrong. Indeed, in killing Aunt Bea the physician and I did what duty required.

This same kind of argument can be repeated in all sorts of cases, illustrating, time after time, how the utilitarian's position leads to results that impartial people find morally callous. It *is* wrong to kill my Aunt Bea in the name of bringing about the best results for others. A good end does not justify an evil means. Any adequate moral theory will have to explain why this is so. Utilitarianism fails in this respect and so cannot be the theory we seek.

What to do? Where to begin anew? The place to begin, I think, is with the utilitarian's view of the value of the individual—or, rather, lack of value. In its place, suppose we consider that you and I, for example, do have value as individuals—what we'll call *inherent value*. To say we have such value is to say that we are something more than, something different from, mere receptacles. Moreover, to ensure that we do not pave the way for such injustices as slavery or sexual discrimination, we must believe that all who have inherent value have it equally, regardless of their sex, race, religion, birthplace and so on. Similarly to be discarded as irrelevant are one's talents or skills, intelligence and wealth, personality or pathology, whether one is loved and admired or despised and loathed. The genius and the retarded child, the prince and the pauper, the brain surgeon and the fruit vendor, Mother Teresa and the most unscrupulous used-car salesman—all have inherent value, all possess it equally, and all have an equal right to be treated with respect, to be treated in ways that do not reduce them to the status of things, as if they existed as resources for others. My value as an individual is independent of my usefulness to you. Yours is not dependent on your usefulness to me. For either of us to treat the other in ways that fail to show respect for the other's independent value is to act immorally, to violate the individual's rights.

Some of the rational virtues of this view—what I call the rights view—should be evident. Unlike (crude) contractarianism, for example, the rights view *in principle* denies the moral tolerability of any and all forms of racial, sexual or social discrimination; and unlike utilitarianism, this view *in principle* denies that we can justify good results by using evil means that violate an individual's rights—denies, for example, that it could be moral to kill my Aunt Bea to harvest beneficial consequences for others. That would be to sanction the disrespectful treatment of the individual in the name of the social good, something the rights view will not—categorically will not—ever allow.

The rights view, I believe, is rationally the most satisfactory moral theory. It surpasses all other theories in the degree to which it illuminates and explains the foundation of our duties to one another—the domain of human morality. On this score it has the best reasons, the best arguments, on its side. Of course, if it were possible to show that only human beings are included within its scope, then a person like myself, who believes in animal rights, would be obliged to look elsewhere.

But attempts to limit its scope to humans only can be shown to be rationally defective. Animals, it is true, lack many of the abilities humans possess. They can't read, do higher mathematics, build a bookcase or make *baba ghanoush*. Neither can many human beings, however, and yet we don't (and shouldn't) say that they (these humans) therefore have less inherent value, less of a right to be treated with respect, than do others. It is the *similarities* between those human beings who most clearly, most non-controversially have such value (the people reading this, for example), not our differences, that matter most. And the really crucial, the basic similarity is simply this: we are each of us the experiencing subject of a life, a conscious creature having an individual welfare that has importance to us whatever our usefulness to others. We want and prefer things, believe and feel things, recall and expect things. And all these dimensions of our life, including our pleasure and pain, our enjoyment and suffering, our satisfaction and frustration, our continued existence or our untimely death—all make a difference to the quality of our life as lived, as experienced, by us as individuals. As the same is true of those animals that concern us (the ones that are eaten and trapped, for example), they too must be viewed as the experiencing subjects of a life, with inherent value of their own.

Some there are who resist the idea that animals have inherent value. "Only humans have such value," they profess. How might this narrow view be defended? Shall we say that only humans have the requisite intelligence, or autonomy, or reason? But there are many, many humans who fail to meet these standards and yet are reasonably viewed as having value above and beyond their usefulness to others. Shall we claim that only humans belong to the right species, the species *Homo sapiens*? But this is blatant speciesism. Will it be said, then, that all—and only—humans have immortal souls?

Then our opponents have their work cut out for them. I am myself not ill-disposed to the proposition that there are immortal souls. Personally, I profoundly hope I have one. But I would not want to rest my position on a controversial ethical issue on the even more controversial question about who or what has an immortal soul. That is to dig one's hole deeper, not to climb out. Rationally, it is better to resolve moral issues without making more controversial assumptions than are needed. The question of who has inherent value is such a question, one that is resolved more rationally without the introduction of the idea of immortal souls than by its use.

Well, perhaps some will say that animals have some inherent value, only less than we have. Once again, however, attempts to defend this view can be shown to lack rational justification. What could be the basis of our having more inherent value than animals? Their lack of reason, or autonomy, or intellect? Only if we are willing to make the same judgement in the case of humans who are similarly deficient. But it is not true that such humans—the retarded child, for example, or the mentally deranged—have less inherent value than you or I. Neither, then, can we rationally sustain the view that animals like them in being the experiencing subjects of a life have less inherent value. *All* who have inherent value have it *equally,* whether they be human animals or not.

Inherent value, then, belongs equally to those who are the experiencing subjects of a life. Whether it belongs to others—to rocks and rivers, trees and glaciers, for example—we do not know and may never know. But neither do we need to know, if we are to make the case for animal rights. We do not need to know, for example, how many people are eligible to vote in the next presidential election before we can know whether I am. Similarly, we do not need to know how many individuals have inherent value before we can know that some do. When it comes to the case for animal rights, then, what we need to know is whether the animals that, in our culture, are routinely eaten, hunted and used in our laboratories, for example, are like us in being subjects of a life. And we do know this. We know that many—literally, billions and billions—of these animals are the subjects of a life in the sense explained and so have inherent value if we do. And since, in order to arrive at the best theory of our duties to one another, we must recognize our equal inherent value as individuals, reason—not sentiment, not emotion—reason compels us to recognize the equal inherent value of these animals and, with this, their equal right to be treated with respect.

That, *very* roughly, is the shape and feel of the case for animal rights. Most of the details of the supporting argument are missing. They are to be found in the book to which I alluded earlier. Here, the details go begging, and I must, in closing, limit myself to four final points.

The first is how the theory that underlies the case for animal rights shows that the animal rights movement is a part of, not antagonistic to, the human rights movement. The theory that rationally grounds the rights of animals also grounds the rights of humans. Thus those involved in the animal rights movement are partners in the struggle to secure respect for human rights—the rights of women, for example, or minorities, or workers. The animal rights movement is cut from the same moral cloth as these.

Second, having set out the broad outlines of the rights view, I can now say why its implications for farming and science, among other fields, are both clear and uncompromising. In the case of the use of animals in science, the rights view is categorically abolitionist. Lab animals are not our tasters; we are not their kings. Because these animals are treated routinely, systematically as if their value were reducible to their usefulness to others, they are routinely, systematically treated with a lack of respect, and thus are their rights routinely, systematically violated. This is just as true when they are used in trivial, duplicative, unnecessary or unwise research as it is when they are used in studies that hold out real promise of human benefits. We can't justify harming or killing a human being (my Aunt Bea, for example) just for these sorts of reason. Neither can we do so even in the case of so lowly a creature as a laboratory rat. It is not just refinement or reduction that is called for, not just larger, cleaner cages, not just more generous use of anaesthetic or the elimination of multiple surgery, not just tidying up the system. It is complete replacement. The best we can do when it comes to using animals in science is—not to use them. That is where our duty lies, according to the rights view.

As for commercial animal agriculture, the rights view takes a similar abolitionist position. The fundamental moral wrong here is not that animals are kept in stressful close confinement or in isolation, or that their pain and suffering, their needs and preferences are ignored or discounted. All these *are* wrong, of course, but they are not the fundamental wrong. They are symptoms and effects of the deeper, systematic wrong that allows these animals to be viewed and treated as lacking independent value, as resources for us—as, indeed, a renewable resource. Giving farm animals more space, more natural environments, more companions does not right the fundamental wrong, any more than giving lab animals more anaesthesia or bigger, cleaner cages would right the fundamental wrong in their case. Nothing less than the total dissolution of commercial animal agriculture will do this, just as, for similar reasons I won't develop at length here, morality requires nothing less than the total elimination of hunting and trapping for commercial and sporting ends. The rights view's implications, then, as I have said, are clear and uncompromising.

My last two points are about philosophy, my profession. It is, most obviously, no substitute for political action. The words I have written here and in other places by themselves don't change a thing. It is what we do with the thoughts that the words express—our acts, our deeds—that changes things. All that philosophy can do, and all I have attempted, is to offer a vision of what our deeds should aim at. And the why. But not the how.

Finally, I am reminded of my thoughtful critic, the one I mentioned earlier, who chastised me for being too cerebral. Well, cerebral I have been: indirect duty views, utilitarianism, contractarianism—hardly the stuff deep passions are made of. I am also reminded, however, of the image another friend once set before me—the image of the ballerina as expressive of disciplined passion. Long hours of sweat and toil, of loneliness and practice, of doubt and fatigue: those are the discipline of her craft. But the passion is there too, the fierce drive to excel, to speak through her body, to do it right, to pierce our minds. That is the image of philosophy I would leave with you, not 'too cerebral' but *disciplined passion*. Of the discipline enough has been seen. As for the passion: there are times, and these not infrequent, when tears come to my eyes when I see, or read, or hear of the wretched plight of animals in the hands of humans. Their pain, their suffering, their loneliness, their innocence, their death. Anger. Rage. Pity. Sorrow. Disgust. The whole creation groans under the weight of the evil we humans visit upon these mute, powerless creatures. It *is* our hearts, not just our heads, that call for an end to it all, that demand of us that we overcome, for them, the habits and forces behind their systematic oppression.

All great movements, it is written, go through three stages: ridicule, discussion, adoption. It is the realization of this third stage, adoption, that requires both our passion and our discipline, our hearts and our heads. The fate of animals is in our hands. God grant we are equal to the task.

Suggestions for Further Reading

Peter Singer, *Animal Liberation* (New York: New York Review of Books, 1975) is the book that made the question of animal welfare a topic of serious discussion among contemporary philosophers. It is lively, nontechnical, and easy to read. Also accessible is Singer's "Animals and the Value of Life" in *Matters of Life and Death*, 2nd ed., edited by Tom Regan (New York: Random House, 1985).

Two good anthologies are Tom Regan and Peter Singer, eds., *Animal Rights and Human Obligations* (Englewood Cliffs, N.J.: Prentice-Hall, 1976), which contains essays representing diverse points of view; and Peter Singer, ed., *In Defense of Animals* (New York: Blackwell, 1985), which includes only pro-animal essays.

Tom Regan, *The Case for Animal Rights* (Berkeley: University of California Press, 1983) is the most thorough defense of the view that animals have *rights*, and R. G. Frey, *Rights, Killing, and Suffering: Moral Vegetarianism and Applied Ethics* (Oxford: Blackwell, 1983) is the best presentation of the case on the other side.

---

22 *A Utilitarian View of Punishment*

Jeremy Bentham

Jeremy Bentham (1748–1832) was a philosopher and social reformer who founded a movement in England that sought to reform British law and institutions along utilitarian lines. For more information about him, see the introductory remarks to selection 8 in this book.

As a Utilitarian, Bentham held that the right thing to do is always determined by what would produce the best consequences—the greatest total balance of happiness over unhappiness. In this selection he discusses the implications of this idea for the practice of criminal punishment. Punishment, he points out, always involves an increase in unhappiness for the person who is punished; therefore, it requires some justification. It can be justified, he argues, only if it produces greater happiness in the long run, either for the criminal or for society as a whole.

General View of Cases Unmeet for Punishment

I. *The end of law is, to augment happiness.* The general object which all laws have, or ought to have, in common, is to augment the total happiness of the community; and therefore, in the first place, to exclude, as far as may be, every thing that tends to subtract from that happiness: in other words, to exclude mischief.

II. *But punishment is an evil.* But all punishment is mischief: all punishment in itself is evil. Upon the principle of utility, if it ought at all to be admitted, it ought only to be admitted in as far as it promises to exclude some greater evil.

III. *Therefore ought not to be admitted.* It is plain, therefore, that in the following cases punishment ought not to be inflicted.

1. *Where groundless.* Where it is *groundless:* where there is no mischief for it to prevent; the act not being mischievous upon the whole.
2. *Inefficacious.* Where it must be *inefficacious:* where it cannot act so as to prevent the mischief.
3. *Unprofitable.* Where it is *unprofitable,* or too *expensive:* where the mischief it would produce would be greater than what it prevented.
4. *Or needless.* Where it is *needless:* where the mischief may

From Jeremy Bentham, *Principles of Morals and Legislation* (1789), chs. 13 and 14.

be prevented, or cease of itself, without it: that is, at
a cheaper rate. . . .

Of the Proportion between Punishments and Offences

I. *Recapitulation.* We have seen that the general object of all law is
to prevent mischief; that is to say, when it is worth while; but that,
where there are no other means of doing this than punishment,
there are four cases in which it is *not* worth while.

II. *Four objects of punishment.* When it *is* worth while, there are
four subordinate designs or objects, which, in the course of his
endeavours to compass, as far as may be, that one general object,
a legislator, whose views are governed by the principle of utility,
comes naturally to propose to himself.

III. 1. *1st Object—to prevent all offences.* His first, most extensive,
and most eligible object, is to prevent, in as far as it is possible, and
worth while, all sorts of offences whatsoever; in other words, so to
manage, that no offence whatsoever may be committed.

IV. 2. *2d Object—to prevent the worst.* But if a man must needs
commit an offence of some kind or other, the next object is to
induce him to commit an offence *less* mischievous, *rather* than one
more mischievous: in other words, to choose always the *least* mischievous, of two offences that will either of them suit his purpose.

V. 3. *3d Object—to keep down the mischief.* When a man has resolved upon a particular offence, the next object is to dispose him
to do *no more* mischief than is *necessary* to his purpose: in other
words, to do as little mischief as is consistent with the benefit he has
in view.

VI. 4. *4th Object—to act at the least expense.* The last object is,
whatever the mischief be, which it is proposed to prevent, to prevent
it at as *cheap* a rate as possible.

VII. *Rules of proportion between punishments and offences.* Subservient to these four objects, or purposes, must be the rules or canons
by which the proportion of punishments to offences is to be governed.

VIII. Rule 1. *Outweigh the profit of the offence.* The first object, it
has been seen, is to prevent, in as far as it is worth while, all sorts
of offences; therefore,

*The value of the punishment must not be less in any case than what is
sufficient to outweigh that of the profit of the offence.*

If it be, the offence (unless some other considerations, independent of the punishment, should intervene and operate efficaciously in the character of tutelary motives) will be sure to be committed notwithstanding: the whole lot of punishment will be thrown away: it will be altogether *inefficacious.*

IX. *The propriety of taking the strength of the temptation for a ground of abatement, no objection to this rule.* The above rule has been often objected to, on account of its seeming harshness: but this can only have happened for want of its being properly understood. The strength of the temptation, ceteris paribus, is as the profit of the offence: the quantum of the punishment must rise with the profit of the offence: ceteris paribus, it must therefore rise with the strength of the temptation. This there is no disputing. True it is, that the stronger the temptation, the less conclusive is the indication which the act of delinquency affords of the depravity of the offender's disposition. So far then as the absence of any aggravation, arising from extraordinary depravity of disposition, may operate, or at the utmost, so far as the presence of a ground of extenuation, resulting from the innocence or beneficence of the offender's disposition, can operate, the strength of the temptation may operate in abatement of the demand for punishment. But it can never operate so far as to indicate the propriety of making the punishment ineffectual, which it is sure to be when brought below the level of the apparent profit of the offence.

The partial benevolence which should prevail for the reduction of it below this level, would counteract as well those purposes which such a motive would actually have in view, as those more extensive purposes which benevolence ought to have in view: it would be cruelty not only to the public, but to the very persons in whose behalf it pleads: in its effects, I mean, however opposite in its intention. Cruelty to the public, that is cruelty to the innocent, by suffering them, for want of an adequate protection, to lie exposed to the mischief of the offence: cruelty even to the offender himself, by punishing him to no purpose, and without the chance of compassing that beneficial end, by which alone the introduction of the evil of punishment is to be justified.

X. Rule 2. *Venture more against a great offence than a small one.* But whether a given offence shall be prevented in a given degree by a given quantity of punishment, is never any thing better than a chance; for the purchasing of which, whatever punishment is employed, is so much expended in advance. However, for the sake of giving it the better chance of outweighing the profit of the offence,

The greater the mischief of the offence, the greater is the expense, which it may be worth while to be at, in the way of punishment.

XI. Rule 3. *Cause the least of two offences to be preferred.* The next object is, to induce a man to choose always the least mischievous of two offences; therefore

Where two offences come in competition, the punishment for the greater offence must be sufficient to induce a man to prefer the less.

XII. Rule 4. *Punish for each particle of the mischief.* When a man has resolved upon a particular offence, the next object is, to induce him to do no more mischief than what is necessary for his purpose: therefore

The punishment should be adjusted in such manner to each particular offence, that for every part of the mischief there may be a motive to restrain the offender from giving birth to it.

XIII. Rule 5. *Punish in no degree without special reason.* The last object is, whatever msichief is guarded against, to guard against it all as cheap a rate as possible: therefore

The punishment ought in no case to be more than what is necessary to bring it into conformity with the rules here given.

XIV. Rule 6. *Attend to circumstances influencing sensibility.* It is further to be observed, that owing to the different manners and degrees in which persons under different circumstances are affected by the same exciting cause, a punishment which is the same in name will not always either really produce, or even so much as appear to others to produce, in two different persons the same degree of pain: therefore

That the quantity actually inflicted on each individual offender may correspond to the quantity intended for similar offenders in general, the several circumstances influencing sensibility ought always to be taken into account.

XV. *Comparative view of the above rules.* Of the above rules of proportion, the four first, we may perceive, serve to mark out the limits on the side of diminution; the limits *below* which a punishment ought not to be *diminished:* the fifth, the limits on the side of increase; the limits *above* which it ought not to be *increased.* The five first are calculated to serve as guides to the legislator: the sixth is calculated, in some measure, indeed, for the same purpose; but principally for guiding the judge in his endeavours to conform, on both sides, to the intentions of the legislator.

xvi. *Into the account of the value of a punishment must be taken its deficiency in point of certainty and proximity.* Let us look back a little. The first rule, in order to render it more conveniently applicable to practice, may need perhaps to be a little more particularly unfolded. It is to be observed, then, that for the sake of accuracy, it was necessary, instead of the word *quantity* to make use of the less perspicuous term *value.* For the word *quantity* will not properly include the circumstances either of certainty or proximity: circumstances which, in estimating the value of a lot of pain or pleasure, must always be taken into the account. Now, on the one hand, a lot of punishment is a lot of pain; on the other hand, the profit of an offence is a lot of pleasure, or what is equivalent to it. But the profit of the offence *is* commonly more *certain* than the punishment, or, what comes to the same thing, *appears* so at least to the offender. It is at any rate commonly more *immediate.* It follows, therefore, that, in order to maintain its superiority over the profit of the offence, the punishment must have its value made up in some other way, in proportion to that whereby it falls short in the two points of *certainty* and *proximity.* Now there is no other way in which it can receive any addition to its *value,* but by receiving an addition in point of *magnitude.* Wherever then the value of the punishment falls short, either in point of *certainty,* or of *proximity,* of that of the profit of the offence, it must receive a proportionable addition in point of *magnitude.*

xvii. *Also, into the account of the mischief, and profit of the offence, the mischief and profit of other offences of the same habit.* Yet farther. To make sure of giving the value of the punishment the superiority over that of the offence, it may be necessary, in some cases, to take into the account the profit not only of the *individual* offence to which the punishment is to be annexed, but also of such *other* offences of the *same sort* as the offender is likely to have already committed without detection. This random mode of calculation, severe as it is, it will be impossible to avoid having recourse to, in certain cases: in such, to wit, in which the profit is pecuniary, the chance of detection very small, and the obnoxious act of such a nature as indicates a habit: for example, in the case of frauds against the coin. If it be *not* recurred to, the practice of committing the offence will be sure to be, upon the balance of the account, a gainful practice. That being the case, the legislator will be absolutely sure of *not* being able to suppress it, and the whole punishment that is bestowed upon it will be thrown away. In a word (to keep to the same expressions we set out with) that whole quantity of punishment will be *inefficacious.*

XVIII. Rule 7. *Want of certainty must be made up in magnitude.* These things being considered, the three following rules may be laid down by way of supplement and explanation to Rule 1.

To enable the value of the punishment to outweigh that of the profit of the offence, it must be increased, in point of magnitude, in proportion as it falls short in point of certainty.

XIX. Rule 8. *(So also want of proximity.)* Punishment must be further increased in point of magnitude, in proportion as it falls short in point of proximity.

XX. Rule 9. *(For acts indicative of a habit punish as for the habit.) Where the act is conclusively indicative of a habit, such an increase must be given to the punishment as may enable it to outweigh the profit not only of the individual offence, but of such other like offences as are likely to have been committed with impunity by the same offender.*

XXI. *The remaining rules are of less importance.* There may be a few other circumstances or considerations which may influence, in some small degree, the demand for punishment: but as the propriety of these is either not so demonstrable, or not so constant, or the application of them not so determinate, as that of the foregoing, it may be doubted whether they be worth putting on a level with the others.

XXII. Rule 10. *(For the sake of quality, increase in quantity.) When a punishment, which in point of quality is particularly well calculated to answer its intention, cannot exist in less than a certain quantity, it may sometimes be of use, for the sake of employing it, to stretch a little beyond that quantity which, on other accounts, would be strictly necessary.*

XXIII. Rule 11. *(Particularly for a moral lesson.) In particular, this may sometimes be the case, where the punishment proposed is of such a nature as to be particularly well calculated to answer the purpose of a moral lesson.*

XXIV. Rule 12. *Attend to circumstances which may render punishment unprofitable.* The tendency of the above considerations is to dictate an augmentation in the punishment: the following rule operates in the way of diminution. There are certain cases (it has been seen) in which, by the influence of accidental circumstances, punishment may be rendered unprofitable in the whole: in the same cases it may chance to be rendered unprofitable as to a part only. Accordingly,

In adjusting the quantum of punishment, the circumstances, by which all punishment may be rendered unprofitable, ought to be attended to.

XXV. Rule 13. *For simplicity's sake, small disproportions may be neglected.* It is to be observed, that the more various and minute any set of provisions are, the greater the chance is that any given article in them will not be borne in mind: without which, no benefit can ensue from it. Distinctions, which are more complex than what the conceptions of those whose conduct it is designed to influence can take in, will even be worse than useless. The whole system will present a confused appearance: and thus the effect, not only of the proportions established by the articles in question, but of whatever is connected with them, will be destroyed. To draw a precise line of direction in such case seems impossible. However, by way of memento, it may be of some use to subjoin the following rule.

Among provisions designed to perfect the proportion between punishments and offences, if any occur, which, by their own particular good effects, would not make up for the harm they would do by adding to the intricacy of the Code, they should be omitted.

XXVI. *Auxiliary force of the physical, moral, and religious sanction, not here allowed for—why.* It may be remembered, that the political sanction, being that to which the sort of punishment belongs, which in this chapter is all along in view, is but one of four sanctions, which may all of them contribute their share towards producing the same effects. It may be expected, therefore, that in adjusting the quantity of political punishment, allowance should be made for the assistance it may meet with from those other controlling powers. True it is, that from each of these several sources a very powerful assistance may sometimes be derived. But the case is, that (setting aside the moral sanction, in the case where the force of it is expressly adopted into and modified by the political) the force of those other powers is never determinate enough to be depended upon. It can never be reduced, like political punishment, into exact lots, nor meted out in number, quantity, and value. The legislator is therefore obliged to provide the full complement of punishment, as if he were sure of not receiving any assistance whatever from any of those quarters. If he does, so much the better: but lest he should not, it is necessary he should, at all events, make that provision which depends upon himself.

Suggestions for Further Reading

See page 236.

23 *A Retributivist View of Punishment*

Immanuel Kant

For information about Kant, see the introduction to selection 9. In the following selection Kant discusses the application of his theory to the question of criminal punishment. In Kant's view, punishment is justified not by reference to any good results that might be achieved, but simply as "paying back" the criminal for a wicked deed.

The right of administering punishment, is the right of the sovereign as the supreme power to inflict pain upon a subject on account of a crime committed by him. The head of the state cannot therefore be punished: but his supremacy may be withdrawn from him. Any transgression of the public law which makes him who commits it incapable of being a citizen, constitutes a *crime*, either simply as a private crime *(crimen)*, or also as a *public* crime *(crimen publicum)*. Private crimes are dealt with by a civil court; public crimes by a criminal court.—Embezzlement or peculation of money or goods entrusted in trade, fraud in purchase or sale, if done before the eyes of the party who suffers, are private crimes. On the other hand, coining false money or forging bills of exchange, theft, robbery, etc., are public crimes, because the commonwealth, and not merely some particular individual, is endangered thereby. Such crimes may be divided into those of a *base* character *(indolis abjectae)* and those of a *violent* character *(indolis violentiae)*.

Judicial or juridical punishment *(poena forensis)* is to be distinguished from natural punishment *(poena naturalis)*, in which crime as vice punishes itself, and does not as such come within the cogni-

From Immanuel Kant, *The Philosophy of Law*, Part II, translated by W. Hastie (1887).

zance of the legislator. Juridical punishment can never be administered merely as a means for promoting another good, either with regard to the criminal himself or to civil society, but must in all cases be imposed only because the individual on whom it is inflicted *has committed a crime.* For one man ought never to be dealt with merely as a means subservient to the purpose of another, nor be mixed up with the subjects of real right. Against such treatment his inborn personality has a right to protect him, even although he may be condemned to lose his civil personality. He must first be found guilty and *punishable,* before there can be any thought of drawing from his punishment any benefit for himself or his fellow-citizens. The penal law is a categorical imperative; and woe to him who creeps through the serpent-windings of utilitarianism to discover some advantage that may discharge him from the justice of punishment, or even from the due measure of it, according to the pharisaic maxim: 'It is better that *one* man should die than that the whole people should perish.' For if justice and righteousness perish, human life would no longer have any value in the world.—What, then, is to be said of such a proposal as to keep a criminal alive who has been condemned to death, on his being given to understand that if he agreed to certain dangerous experiments being performed upon him, he would be allowed to survive if he came happily through them? It is argued that physicians might thus obtain new information that would be of value to the commonweal. But a court of justice would repudiate with scorn any proposal of this kind if made to it by the medical faculty; for justice would cease to be justice, if it were bartered away for any consideration whatever.

But what is the mode and measure of punishment which public justice takes as its principle and standard? It is just the principle of equality, by which the pointer of the scale of justice is made to incline no more to the one side than the other. It may be rendered by saying that the undeserved evil which any one commits on another, is to be regarded as perpetrated on himself. Hence it may be said: 'If you slander another, you slander yourself; if you steal from another, you steal from yourself; if you strike another, you strike yourself; if you kill another, you kill yourself.' This is the right of retaliation *(jus talionis);* and properly understood, it is the only principle which in regulating a public court, as distinguished from mere private judgment, can definitely assign both the quality and the quantity of a just penalty. All other standards are wavering and uncertain; and on account of other considerations involved in them, they contain no principle conformable to the sentence of pure and strict justice. It may appear, however, that difference of social status would not admit the application of the principle of retaliation, which is that of 'like with like.' But although the application may not in all cases be possible according to the letter, yet as regards the effect it may always be attained in practice, by due regard being given to the disposition and sentiment of the parties in the higher social sphere. Thus a pecuniary penalty on account of a verbal injury, may have no direct proportion to the injustice of slander; for one who is wealthy may be able to indulge himself in this offence for his own gratification. Yet the attack committed on the honour of the party aggrieved may have its equivalent in the pain inflicted upon the pride of the aggressor, especially if he is condemned by the judgment of the court, not only to retract and apologize, but to submit to some meaner ordeal, as kissing the hand of the injured person. In like manner, if a man of the highest rank has violently assaulted an innocent citizen of the lower orders, he may be condemned not only to apologize but to undergo a solitary and painful imprisonment, whereby, in addition to the discomfort endured, the vanity of the offender would be painfully affected, and the very shame of his position would constitute an adequate retaliation after the principle of like with like. But how then would we render the statement: 'If you *steal* from another, you steal from yourself'? In this way, that whoever steals anything makes the property of all insecure; he therefore robs himself of all security in property, according to the right of retaliation. Such a one has nothing, and can acquire nothing, but he has the will to live; and this is only possible by others supporting him. But as the state should not do this gratuitously, he must for this purpose yield his powers to the state to be used in penal labour; and thus he falls for a time, or it may be for life, into a condition of slavery.—But whoever has committed murder, must *die*. There is, in this case, no juridical substitute or surrogate, that can be given or taken for the satisfaction of justice. There is no *likeness* or proportion between life, however painful, and death; and therefore there is no equality between the crime of murder and the retaliation of it but what is judicially accomplished by the execution of the criminal. His death, however, must be kept free from all maltreatment that would make the humanity suffering in his person loathsome or abominable. Even if a civil society resolved to dissolve itself with the consent of all its members—as might be supposed in the case of a people inhabiting an island resolving to separate and emselves throughout the whole world—the last murderer lying in the prison ought to be executed before the resolution was carried out. This ought to be done in order that every one may realize the desert of his deeds, and that bloodguiltiness may not remain upon the people; for otherwise they might all be regarded as participators in the murder as a public violation of justice.

The equalization of punishment with crime, is therefore only possible by the cognition of the judge extending even to the penalty of death, according to the right of retaliation.

Suggestions for Further Reading

The philosophical debate about the nature and justification of punishment is chronicled in two useful anthologies: Gertrude Ezorsky, ed., *Philosophical Perspectives on Punishment* (Albany: State University of New York Press, 1972); and H. B. Acton, ed., *The Philosophy of Punishment* (London: Macmillan, 1969).

On capital punishment, see Hugo A. Bedau, *The Death Penalty in America* (Garden City, N.Y.: Anchor, 1964), and "Capital Punishment," in *Matters of Life and Death,* 2nd ed., edited by Tom Regan (New York: Random House, 1985).

On the idea of rehabilitation, see the splendid work prepared by the American Friends Service Committee, *Struggle for Justice* (New York: Hill and Wang, 1971).

---

24 *Letter from the Birmingham City Jail*

Martin Luther King, Jr.

Born in 1929, Martin Luther King, Jr., followed in his father's footsteps and became a Baptist minister. In 1956, while he was pastor of the Dexter Avenue Baptist Church in Mont-

gomery, Alabama, he led a boycott of that city's segregated
public buses, and then went on to become the leading
spokesman for the American civil rights movement. He was
awarded the Nobel Peace Prize in 1964. Dr. King was assassinated in 1968.

In 1963, while incarcerated in an Alabama jail, he read
a statement that had been issued by some of his fellow clergymen. The statement sympathized with the goals of his movement but questioned the wisdom of his tactics. King
advocated—and practiced—nonviolent civil disobedience,
whereas these critics argued that the law ought to be obeyed
even by those who worked within it to bring about change.
Using a pen smuggled in to him by his lawyers and some
tattered scraps of paper that were lying about, King wrote an
"open letter" replying to them. The "Letter from the Birmingham City Jail" was printed in many liberal magazines
and newspapers until almost a million copies were in circula-
tion. It became the single most famous document of the
movement.

My dear Fellow Clergymen,

While confined here in the Birmingham City Jail, I came across your
recent statement calling our present activities "unwise and untimely." Seldom, if ever, do I pause to answer criticism of my work
and ideas. If I sought to answer all of the criticisms that cross my
desk, my secretaries would be engaged in little else in the course of
the day, and I would have no time for constructive work. But since
I feel that you are men of genuine goodwill and your criticisms are
sincerely set forth, I would like to answer your statement in what I
hope will be patient and reasonable terms.

I think I should give the reason for my being in Birmingham,
since you have been influenced by the argument of "outsiders coming in." I have the honor of serving as president of the Southern
Christian Leadership Conference, an organization operating in
every Southern state, with headquarters in Atlanta, Georgia. We
have some eighty-five affiliate organizations all across the South—
one being the Alabama Christian Movement for Human Rights.
Whenever necessary and possible we share staff, educational and
financial resources with our affiliates. Several months ago our local

affiliate here in Birmingham invited us to be on call to engage in a nonviolent direct action program if such were deemed necessary. We readily consented and when the hour came we lived up to our promises. So I am here, along with several members of my staff, because we were invited here. I am here because I have basic organizational ties here.

Beyond this, I am in Birmingham because injustice is here. Just as the eighth century prophets left their little villages and carried their "thus saith the Lord" far beyond the boundaries of their home towns; and just as the Apostle Paul left his little village of Tarsus and carried the gospel of Jesus Christ to practically every hamlet and city of the Graeco-Roman world, I too am compelled to carry the gospel of freedom beyond my particular home town. Like Paul, I must constantly respond to the Macedonian call for aid.

Moreover, I am cognizant of the interrelatedness of all communities and states. I cannot sit idly by in Atlanta and not be concerned about what happens in Birmingham. Injustice anywhere is a threat to justice everywhere. We are caught in an inescapable network of mutuality, tied in a single garment of destiny. Whatever affects one directly affects all indirectly. Never again can we afford to live with the narrow, provincial "outside agitator" idea. Anyone who lives inside the United States can never be considered an outsider anywhere in this country.

You deplore the demonstrations that are presently taking place in Birmingham. But I am sorry that your statement did not express a similar concern for the conditions that brought the demonstrations into being. I am sure that each of you would want to go beyond the superficial social analyst who looks merely at effects, and does not grapple with underlying causes. I would not hesitate to say that it is unfortunate that so-called demonstrations are taking place in Birmingham at this time, but I would say in more emphatic terms that it is even more unfortunate that the white power structure of this city left the Negro community with no other alternative.

In any nonviolent campaign there are four basic steps: 1) Collection of the facts to determine whether injustices are alive, 2) Negotiation, 3) Self-purification and 4) Direct Action. We have gone through all of these steps in Birmingham. There can be no gainsaying of the fact that racial injustice engulfs this community.

Birmingham is probably the most thoroughly segregated city in the United States. Its ugly record of police brutality is known in every section of this country. Its injust treatment of Negroes in the courts is a notorious reality. There have been more unsolved bombings of Negro homes and churches in Birmingham than any city in this nation. These are the hard, brutal and unbelievable facts. On the basis of these conditions Negro leaders sought to negotiate with the city fathers. But the political leaders consistently refused to engage in good faith negotiation.

Then came the opportunity last September to talk with some of the leaders of the economic community. In these negotiating sessions certain promises were made by the merchants—such as the promise to remove the humiliating racial signs from the stores. On the basis of these promises Rev. Shuttlesworth and the leaders of the Alabama Christian Movement for Human Rights agreed to call a moratorium on any type of demonstrations. As the weeks and months unfolded we realized that we were the victims of a broken promise. The signs remained. Like so many experiences of the past we were confronted with blasted hopes, and the dark shadow of a deep disappointment settled upon us. So we had no alternative except that of preparing for direct action, whereby we would present our very bodies as a means of laying our case before the conscience of the local and national community. We were not unmindful of the difficulties involved. So we decided to go through a process of self-purification. We started having workshops on non-violence and repeatedly asked ourselves the questions, "Are you able to accept blows without retaliating?" "Are you able to endure the ordeals of jail?" We decided to set our direct action program around the Easter season, realizing that with the exception of Christmas, this was the largest shopping period of the year. Knowing that a strong economic withdrawal program would be the by-product of direct action, we felt that this was the best time to bring pressure on the merchants for the needed changes. Then it occurred to us that the March election was ahead and so we speedily decided to postpone action until after election day. When we discovered that Mr. Connor was in the run-off, we decided again to postpone action so that the demonstrations could not be used to cloud the issues. At this time we agreed to begin our nonviolent witness the day after the run-off.

This reveals that we did not move irresponsibly into direct action. We too wanted to see Mr. Connor defeated; so we went through postponement after postponement to aid in this commuter this we felt that direct action could be delayed no

You may well ask, "Why direct action? Why sit-ins, marches, etc.? Isn't negotiation a better path?" You are exactly right in your call for negotiation. Indeed, this is the purpose of direct action. Nonviolent direct action seeks to create such a crisis and establish such creative tension that a community that has constantly refused to negotiate is forced to confront the issue. It seeks so to dramatize the issue that it can no longer be ignored. I just referred to the creation of tension as a part of the work of the nonviolent resister. This may sound rather shocking. But I must confess that I am not afraid of the word tension. I have earnestly worked and preached against violent tension, but there is a type of constructive nonviolent tension that is necessary for growth. Just as Socrates felt that it was necessary to create a tension in the mind so that individuals could rise from the bondage of myths and half-truths to the unfettered realm of creative analysis and objective appraisal, we must see the need of having nonviolent gadflies to create the kind of tension in society that will help men to rise from the dark depths of prejudice and racism to the majestic heights of understanding and brotherhood. So the purpose of the direct action is to create a situation so crisis-packed that it will inevitably open the door to negotiation. We, therefore, concur with you in your call for negotiation. Too long has our beloved Southland been bogged down in the tragic attempt to live in monologue rather than dialogue.

One of the basic points in your statement is that our acts are untimely. Some have asked, "Why didn't you give the new administration time to act?" The only answer that I can give to this inquiry is that the new administration must be prodded about as much as the outgoing one before it acts. We will be sadly mistaken if we feel that the election of Mr. Boutwell will bring the millennium to Birmingham. While Mr. Boutwell is much more articulate and gentle than Mr. Connor, they are both segregationists, dedicated to the task of maintaining the status quo. The hope I see in Mr. Boutwell is that he will be reasonable enough to see the futility of massive resistance to desegregation. But he will not see this without pressure from the devotees of civil rights. My friends, I must say to you that we have not made a single gain in civil rights without determined legal and nonviolent pressure. History is the long and tragic story of the fact that privileged groups seldom give up their privileges voluntarily. Individuals may see the moral light and voluntarily give up their unjust posture; but as Reinhold Niebuhr has reminded us, groups are more immoral than individuals.

We know through painful experience that freedom is never voluntarily given by the oppressor; it must be demanded by the oppressed. Frankly, I have never yet engaged in a direct action movement that was "well timed," according to the timetable of those who have not suffered unduly from the disease of segregation. For years now I have heard the word "Wait!" It rings in the ear of every Negro with a piercing familiarity. This "Wait" has almost always meant "Never." It has been a tranquilizing thalidomide, relieving the emotional stress for a moment, only to give birth to an ill-formed infant of frustration. We must come to see with the distinguished jurist of yesterday that "justice too long delayed is justice denied." We have waited for more than three hundred and forty years for our constitutional and God-given rights. The nations of Asia and Africa are moving with jet-like speed toward the goal of political independence, and we still creep at horse and buggy pace toward the gaining of a cup of coffee at a lunch counter. I guess it is easy for those who have never felt the stinging darts of segregation to say, "Wait." But when you have seen vicious mobs lynch your mothers and fathers at will and drown your sisters and brothers at whim; when you have seen hate-filled policemen curse, kick, brutalize and even kill your black brothers and sisters with impunity; when you see the vast majority of your twenty million Negro brothers smothering in an air-tight cage of poverty in the midst of an affluent society; when you suddenly find your tongue twisted and your speech stammering as you seek to explain to your six-year-old daughter why she can't go to the public amusement park that has just been advertised on television, and see tears welling up in her little eyes when she is told that Funtown is closed to colored children, and see the depressing clouds of inferiority begin to form in her little mental sky, and see her begin to distort her little personality by unconsciously developing a bitterness toward white people; when you have to concoct an answer for a five-year-old son asking in agonizing pathos: "Daddy, why do white people treat colored people so mean?"; when you take a cross country drive and find it necessary to sleep night after night in the uncomfortable corners of your automobile because no motel will accept you; when you are humiliated day in and day out by nagging signs reading "white" and "colored"; when your first name becomes "nigger" and your middle name becomes "boy" (however old you are) and your last name becomes "John," and when your wife and mother are never given the respected title "Mrs."; when you are harried by day and haunted at night by the fact that you are a Negro, living constantly at tip-toe stance never quite knowing what to expect next, and plagued with inner fears and outer resentments; when you are forever fighting a degenerating sense of "nobodiness"; then you will understand why we find it difficult to wait. There comes a time when the cup of endurance runs over, and men are no longer willing to be plunged into an abyss of injustice where they experience the blackness of corroding despair. I hope, sirs, you can understand our legitimate and unavoidable impatience.

You express a great deal of anxiety over our willingness to break laws. This is certainly a legitimate concern. Since we so diligently urge people to obey the Supreme Court's decision of 1954 outlawing segregation in the public schools, it is rather strange and paradoxical to find us consciously breaking laws. One may well ask, "How can you advocate breaking some laws and obeying others?" The answer is found in the fact that there are two types of laws: There are *just* and there are *unjust* laws. I would agree with Saint Augustine that "An unjust law is no law at all."

Now what is the difference between the two? How does one determine when a law is just or unjust? A just law is a man-made code that squares with the moral law or the law of God. An unjust law is a code that is out of harmony with the moral law. To put it in the terms of Saint Thomas Aquinas, an unjust law is a human law that is not rooted in eternal and natural law. Any law that uplifts human personality is just. Any law that degrades human personality is unjust. All segregation statutes are unjust because segregation distorts the soul and damages the personality. It gives the segregator a false sense of superiority, and the segregated a false sense of inferiority. To use the words of Martin Buber, the great Jewish philosopher, segregation substitutes an "I-it" relation ship for the "I-thou" relationship, and ends up relegating persons to the status of things. So segregation is not only politically, economically and sociologically unsound, but it is morally wrong and sinful. Paul Tillich has said that sin is separation. Isn't segregation an existential expression of man's tragic separation, an expression of his awful estrangement, his terrible sinfulness? So I can urge men to disobey segregation ordinances because they are morally wrong.

Let us turn to a more concrete example of just and unjust laws. An unjust law is a code that a majority inflicts on a minority that is not binding on itself. This is difference made legal. On the other hand a just law is a code that a majority compels a minority to follow that it is willing to follow itself. This is sameness made legal.

Let me give another explanation. An unjust law is a code inflicted upon a minority which that minority had no part in enacting or creating because they did not have the unhampered right to vote. Who can say that the legislature of Alabama which set up the segregation laws was democratically elected? Throughout the state of Alabama all types of conniving methods are used to prevent Negroes from becoming registered voters and there are some counties without a single Negro registered to vote despite the fact that the Negro constitutes a majority of the population. Can any law set up in such a state be considered democratically structured?

These are just a few examples of unjust and just laws. There are some instances when a law is just on its face and unjust in its application. For instance, I was arrested Friday on a charge of parading without a permit. Now there is nothing wrong with an ordinance which requires a permit for a parade, but when the ordinance is used to preserve segregation and to deny citizens the First Amendment privilege of peaceful assembly and peaceful protest, then it becomes unjust.

I hope you can see the distinction I am trying to point out. In no sense do I advocate evading or defying the law as the rabid segregationist would do. This would lead to anarchy. One who breaks an unjust law must do it *openly, lovingly* (not hatefully as the white mothers did in New Orleans when they were seen on television screaming "nigger, nigger, nigger"), and with a willingness to accept the penalty. I submit that an individual who breaks a law that conscience tells him is unjust, and willingly accepts the penalty by staying in jail to arouse the conscience of the community over its injustice, is in reality expressing the very highest respect for law.

Of course, there is nothing new about this kind of civil disobedience. It was seen sublimely in the refusal of Shadrach, Meshach and Abednego to obey the laws of Nebuchadnezzar because a higher moral law was involved. It was practiced superbly by the early

Christians who were willing to face hungry lions and the excruciating pain of chopping blocks, before submitting to certain unjust laws of the Roman empire. To a degree academic freedom is a reality today because Socrates practiced civil disobedience.

We can never forget that everything Hitler did in Germany was "legal" and everything the Hungarian freedom fighters did in Hungary was "illegal." It was "illegal" to aid and comfort a Jew in Hitler's Germany. But I am sure that if I had lived in Germany during that time I would have aided and comforted my Jewish brothers even though it was illegal. If I lived in a Communist country today where certain principles dear to the Christian faith are suppressed, I believe I would openly advocate disobeying these anti-religious laws. I must make two honest confessions to you, my Christian and Jewish brothers. First, I must confess that over the last few years I have been gravely disappointed with the white moderate. I have almost reached the regrettable conclusion that the Negro's great stumbling block in the stride toward freedom is not the White Citizen's Council-er or the Ku Klux Klanner, but the white moderate who is more devoted to "order" than to justice; who prefers a negative peace which is the absence of tension to a positive peace which is the presence of justice; who constantly says, "I agree with you in the goal you seek, but I can't agree with your methods of direct action"; who paternalistically feels that he can set the timetable for another man's freedom; who lives by the myth of time and who constantly advises the Negro to wait until a "more convenient season." Shallow understanding from people of goodwill is more frustrating than absolute misunderstanding from people of ill will. Lukewarm acceptance is much more bewildering than outright rejection.

I had hoped that the white moderate would understand that law and order exist for the purpose of establishing justice, and that when they fail to do this they become dangerously structured dams that block the flow of social progress. I had hoped that the white moderate would understand that the present tension of the South is merely a necessary phase of the transition from an obnoxious negative peace, where the Negro passively accepted his unjust plight, to a substance-filled positive peace, where all men will respect the dignity and worth of human personality. Actually, we who engage in nonviolent direct action are not the creators of tension. We merely bring to the surface the hidden tension that is already alive. We bring it out in the open where it can be seen and dealt with. Like a boil that can never be cured as long as it is covered up but must be opened with all its pus-flowing ugliness to the natural medicines of air and light, injustice must likewise be exposed, with all of the tension its exposing creates, to the light of human conscience and the air of national opinion before it can be cured.

In your statement you asserted that our actions, even though peaceful, must be condemned because they precipitate violence. But can this assertion be logically made? Isn't this like condemning the robbed man because his possession of money precipitated the evil act of robbery? Isn't this like condemning Socrates because his unswerving commitment to truth and his philosophical delvings precipitated the misguided popular mind to make him drink the hemlock? Isn't this like condemning Jesus because His unique God-Consciousness and never-ceasing devotion to His will precipitated the evil act of crucifixion? We must come to see, as federal courts have consistently affirmed, that it is immoral to urge an individual to withdraw his efforts to gain his basic constitutional rights because the quest precipitates violence. Society must protect the robbed and punish the robber.

I had also hoped that the white moderate would reject the myth of time. I received a letter this morning from a white brother in Texas which said: "All Christians know that the colored people will receive equal rights eventually, but it is possible that you are in too great of a religious hurry. It has taken Christianity almost 2000 years to accomplish what it has. The teachings of Christ take time to come to earth." All that is said here grows out of a tragic misconception of time. It is the strangely irrational notion that there is something in the very flow of time that will inevitably cure all ills. Actually time is neutral. It can be used either destructively or constructively. I am coming to feel that the people of ill will have used time much more effectively than the people of goodwill. We will have to repent in this generation not merely for the vitriolic words and actions of the bad people, but for the appalling silence of the good people. We must come to see that human progress never rolls in on wheels of inevitability. It comes through the tireless efforts and persistent work of men willing to be co-workers with God, and without this hard work time itself becomes an ally of the forces of social stagnation. We must use time creatively, and forever realize that the time is always ripe to do right. Now is the time to make real the promise of democracy, and transform our pending national elegy into a creative psalm of brotherhood. Now is the time to lift our national policy from the quicksand of racial injustice to the solid rock of human dignity.

You spoke of our activity in Birmingham as extreme. At first I was rather disappointed that fellow clergymen would see my non-violent efforts as those of the extremist. I started thinking about the fact that I stand in the middle of two opposing forces in the Negro community. One is a force of complacency made up of Negroes who, as a result of long years of oppression, have been so completely drained of self-respect and a sense of "somebodiness" that they have adjusted to segregation, and, of a few Negroes in the middle class who, because of a degree of academic and economic security, and because at points they profit by segregation, have unconsciously become insensitive to the problems of the masses. The other force is one of bitterness and hatred, and comes perilously close to advocating violence. It is expressed in the various black nationalist groups that are springing up over the nation, the largest and best known being Elijah Muhammad's Muslim movement. This movement is nourished by the contemporary frustration over the continued existence of racial discrimination. It is made up of people who have lost faith in America, who have absolutely repudiated Christianity, and who have concluded that the white man is an incurable "devil." I have tried to stand between these two forces, saying that we need not follow the "do-nothingism" of the complacent or the hatred and despair of the black nationalist. There is the more excellent way of love and nonviolent protest. I'm grateful to God that, through the Negro church, the dimension of nonviolence entered our struggle. If this philosophy had not emerged, I am convinced that by now many streets of the South would be flowing with floods of blood. And I am further convinced that if our white brothers dismiss as "rabble rousers" and "outside agitators" those of us who are working through the channels of nonviolent direct action and refuse to support our nonviolent efforts, millions of Negroes, out of frustration and despair, will seek solace and security in black nationalist ideologies, a development that will lead inevitably to a frightening racial nightmare.

Oppressed people cannot remain oppressed forever. The urge for freedom will eventually come. This is what happened to the American Negro. Something within has reminded him of his birthright of freedom; something without has reminded him that he can gain it. Consciously and unconsciously, he has been swept in by what the Germans call the *Zeitgeist,* and with his black brothers of Africa, and his brown and yellow brothers of Asia, South America and the Caribbean, he is moving with a sense of cosmic urgency toward the promised land of racial justice. Recognizing this vital urge that has engulfed the Negro community, one should readily understand public demonstrations. The Negro has many pent-up resentments and latent frustrations. He has to get them out. So let him march sometime; let him have his prayer pilgrimages to the city hall; understand why he must have sit-ins and freedom rides. If his repressed emotions do not come out in these nonviolent ways, they will come out in ominous expressions of violence. This is not a threat; it is a fact of history. So I have not said to my people "get rid of your discontent." But I have tried to say that this normal and healthy discontent can be channelized through the creative outlet of nonviolent direct action. Now this approach is being dismissed as extremist. I must admit that I was initially disappointed in being so categorized.

But as I continued to think about the matter I gradually gained a bit of satisfaction from being considered an extremist. Was not Jesus an extremist in love—"Love your enemies, bless them that curse you, pray for them that despitefully use you." Was not Amos an extremist for justice—"Let justice roll down like waters and righteousness like a mighty stream." Was not Paul an extremist for the gospel of Jesus Christ—"I bear in my body the marks of the Lord Jesus." Was not Martin Luther an extremist—"Here I stand; I can do none other so help me God." Was not John Bunyan an extremist—"I will stay in jail to the end of my days before I make a butchery of my conscience." Was not Abraham Lincoln an extremist—"This nation cannot survive half slave and half free." Was not Thomas Jefferson an extremist—"We hold these truths to be self-evident, that all men are created equal." So the question is not whether we will be extremist but what kind of extremist will we be. Will we be extremists for hate or will we be extremists for love? Will we be extremists for the preservation of injustice—or will we be extremists for the cause of justice? In that dramatic scene on Calvary's hill, three men were crucified. We must not forget that all three were crucified for the same crime—the crime of extremism. Two were extremists for immorality, and thusly fell below their environment. The other, Jesus Christ, was an extremist for love, truth and goodness, and thereby rose above his environment. So, after all, maybe the South, the nation and the world are in dire need of creative extremists.

I had hoped that the white moderate would see this. Maybe I was too optimistic. Maybe I expected too much. I guess I should have realized that few members of a race that has oppressed another race can understand or appreciate the deep groans and passionate yearnings of those that have been oppressed and still fewer have the vision to see that injustice must be rooted out by strong, persistent and determined action. I am thankful, however, that some of our white brothers have grasped the meaning of this social revolution and committed themselves to it. They are still all too small in quantity, but they are big in quality. Some like Ralph McGill, Lillian Smith, Harry Golden and James Dabbs have written about our struggle in eloquent, prophetic and understanding terms. Others have marched with us down nameless streets of the South. They have languished in filthy roach-infested jails, suffering the abuse and brutality of angry policemen who see them as "dirty nigger lovers." They, unlike so many of their moderate brothers and sisters, have recognized the urgency of the moment and sensed the need for powerful "action" antidotes to combat the disease of segregation.

Let me rush on to mention my other disappointment. I have been so greatly disappointed with the white church and its leadership. Of course, there are some notable exceptions. I am not unmindful of the fact that each of you has taken some significant stands on this issue. I commend you, Rev. Stallings, for your Christian stand on this past Sunday, in welcoming Negroes to your worship service on a non-segregated basis. I commend the Catholic leaders of this state for integrating Springhill College several years ago.

But despite these notable exceptions I must honestly reiterate that I have been disappointed with the church. I do not say that as one of the negative critics who can always find something wrong with the church. I say it as a minister of the gospel, who loves the church; who was nurtured in its bosom; who has been sustained by its spiritual blessings and who will remain true to it as long as the cord of life shall lengthen.

I had the strange feeling when I was suddenly catapulted into the leadership of the bus protest in Montgomery several years ago that we would have the support of the white church. I felt that the white ministers, priests and rabbis of the South would be some of our strongest allies. Instead, some have been outright opponents, refusing to understand the freedom movement and misrepresenting its leaders; all too many others have been more cautious than courageous and have remained silent behind the anesthetizing security of the stained-glass windows.

In spite of my shattered dreams of the past, I came to Birmingham with the hope that the white religious leadership of this community would see the justice of our cause, and with deep moral concern, serve as the channel through which our just grievances would get to the power structure. I had hoped that each of you would understand. But again I have been disappointed. I have heard numerous religious leaders of the South call upon their worshippers to comply with a desegregation decision because it is the *law*, but I have longed to hear white ministers say, "Follow this decree because integration is morally *right* and the Negro is your brother." In the midst of blatant injustices inflicted upon the Negro, I have watched white churches stand on the sideline and merely mouth pious irrelevancies and sanctimonious trivialities. In the midst of a mighty struggle to rid our nation of racial and economic injustice, I have heard so many ministers say, "Those are social issues with which the gospel has no real concern," and I have watched so many churches commit themselves to a completely other-worldly religion which made a strange distinction between body and soul, the sacred and the secular.

So here we are moving toward the exit of the twentieth century with a religious community largely adjusted to the status quo, standing as a tail-light behind other community agencies rather than a headlight leading men to higher levels of justice.

I have traveled the length and breadth of Alabama, Mississippi and all the other southern states. On sweltering summer days and crisp autumn mornings I have looked at her beautiful churches with their lofty spires pointing heavenward. I have beheld the impressive outlay of her massive religious education buildings. Over and over again I have found myself asking: "What kind of people worship here? Who is their God? Where were their voices when the lips of Governor Barnett dripped with words of interposition and nullification? Where were they when Governor Wallace gave the clarion call for defiance and hatred? Where were their voices of support when tired, bruised and weary Negro men and women decided to rise from the dark dungeons of complacency to the bright hills of creative protest?"

Yes, these questions are still in my mind. In deep disappointment, I have swept over the laxity of the church. But be assured that my tears have been tears of love. There can be no deep disappointment where there is not deep love. Yes, I love the church; I love her sacred walls. How could I do otherwise? I am in the rather unique position of being the son, the grandson and the great-grandson of preachers. Yes, I see the church as the body of Christ. But, oh! How we have blemished and scarred that body through social neglect and fear of being nonconformists.

There was a time when the church was very powerful. It was during that period when the early Christians rejoiced when they were deemed worthy to suffer for what they believed. In those days the church was not merely a thermometer that recorded the ideas and principles of popular opinion; it was a thermostat that transformed the mores of society. Wherever the early Christians entered a town the power structure got disturbed and immediately sought to convict them for being "disturbers of the peace" and "outside agitators." But they went on with the conviction that they were "a colony of heaven," and had to obey God rather than man. They were small in number but big in commitment. They were too God-intoxicated to be "astronomically intimidated." They brought an end to such ancient evils as infanticide and gladiatorial contest.

Things are different now. The contemporary church is often a weak, ineffectual voice with an uncertain sound. It is so often the arch supporter of the status quo. Far from being disturbed by the presence of the church, the power structure of the average community is consoled by the church's silent and often vocal sanction of things as they are.

But the judgment of God is upon the church as never before. If the church of today does not recapture the sacrificial spirit of the early church, it will lose its authentic ring, forfeit the loyalty of millions, and be dismissed as an irrelevant social club with no meaning for the twentieth century. I am meeting young people every day whose disappointment with the church has risen to outright disgust.

Maybe again, I have been too optimistic. Is organized religion too inextricably bound to the status quo to save our nation and the world? Maybe I must turn my faith to the inner spiritual church, the church within the church, as the true *ecclesia* and the hope of the world. But again I am thankful to God that some noble souls from the ranks of organized religion have broken loose from the paralyzing chains of conformity and joined us as active partners in the struggle for freedom. They have left their secure congregations and walked the streets of Albany, Georgia, with us. They have gone through the highways of the South on tortuous rides for freedom. Yes, they have gone to jail with us. Some have been kicked out of their churches, and lost support of their bishops and fellow ministers. But they have gone with the faith that right defeated is stronger than evil triumphant. These men have been the leaven in the lump of the race. Their witness has been the spiritual salt that has preserved the true meaning of the Gospel in these troubled times. They have carved a tunnel of hope through the dark mountain of disappointment.

I hope the church as a whole will meet the challenge of this decisive hour. But even if the church does not come to the aid of justice, I have no despair about the future. I have no fear about the outcome of our struggle in Birmingham, even if our motives are presently misunderstood. We will reach the goal of freedom in Birmingham and all over the nation, because the goal of America is freedom. Abused and scorned though we may be, our destiny is tied up with the destiny of America. Before the pilgrims landed at Plymouth we were here. Before the pen of Jefferson etched across the pages of history the majestic words of the Declaration of Independence, we were here. For more than two centuries our foreparents labored in this country without wages; they made cotton king; and they built the homes of their masters in the midst of brutal injustice and shameful humiliation—and yet out of a bottomless vitality they continued to thrive and develop. If the inexpressible cruelties of slavery could not stop us, the opposition we now face will surely fail. We will win our freedom because the sacred heritage of our nation and the eternal will of God are embodied in our echoing demands.

I must close now. But before closing I am impelled to mention one other point in your statement that troubled me profoundly. You warmly commended the Birmingham police force for keeping "order" and "preventing violence." I don't believe you would have so warmly commended the police force if you had seen its angry violent dogs literally biting six unarmed, nonviolent Negroes. I don't believe you would so quickly commend the policemen if you would observe their ugly and inhuman treatment of Negroes here in the city jail; if you would watch them push and curse old Negro women and young Negro girls; if you would see them slap and kick old Negro men and young boys; if you will observe them, as they did on two occasions, refuse to give us food because we wanted to sing our grace together. I'm sorry that I can't join you in your praise for the police department.

It is true that they have been rather disciplined in their public handling of the demonstrators. In this sense they have been rather publicly "nonviolent." But for what purpose? To preserve the evil system of segregation. Over the last few years I have consistently preached that nonviolence demands that the means we use must be as pure as the ends we seek. So I have tried to make it clear that it is wrong to use immoral means to attain moral ends. But now I must affirm that it is just as wrong, or even more so, to use moral means to preserve immoral ends. Maybe Mr. Connor and his policemen have been rather publicly nonviolent, as Chief Pritchett was in Albany, Georgia, but they have used the moral means of nonviolence to maintain the immoral end of flagrant racial injustice. T. S. Eliot has said that there is no greater treason than to do the right deed for the wrong reason.

I wish you had commended the Negro sit-inners and demonstrators of Birmingham for their sublime courage, their willingness to suffer and their amazing discipline in the midst of the most inhuman provocation. One day the South will recognize its real heroes. They will be the James Merediths, courageously and with a majestic sense of purpose facing jeering and hostile mobs and the agonizing loneliness that characterizes the life of the pioneer. They will be old, oppressed, battered Negro women, symbolized in a seventy-two year old woman of Montgomery, Alabama, who rose up with a sense of dignity and with her people decided not to ride the segregated buses, and responded to one who inquired about her tiredness with ungrammatical profundity: "My feet is tired, but my soul is rested." They will be the young high school and college students, young ministers of the Gospel and a host of their elders courageously and nonviolently sitting-in at lunch counters and willingly going to jail for conscience's sake. One day the South will know that when these disinherited children of God sat down at lunch counters they were in reality standing up for the best in the American dream and the most sacred values in our Judeo-Christian heritage, and thusly, carrying our whole nation back to those great wells of democracy which were dug deep by the founding fathers in the formulation of the Constitution and the Declaration of Independence.

Never before have I written a letter this long (or should I say a book?). I'm afraid that it is much too long to take your precious time. I can assure you that it would have been much shorter if I had been writing from a comfortable desk, but what else is there to do when you are alone for days in the dull monotony of a narrow jail cell other than write long letters, think strange thoughts, and pray long prayers?

If I have said anything in this letter that is an overstatement of the truth and is indicative of an unreasonable impatience, I beg you to forgive me. If I have said anything in this letter that is an understatement of the truth and is indicative of my having a patience that makes me patient with anything less than brotherhood, I beg God to forgive me.

I hope this letter finds you strong in the faith. I also hope that circumstances will soon make it possible for me to meet each of you, not as an integrationist or a civil-rights leader, but as a fellow clergyman and a Christian brother. Let us all hope that the dark clouds of racial prejudice will soon pass away and the deep fog of misunderstanding will be lifted from our fear-drenched communities and in some not too distant tomorrow the radiant stars of love and brotherhood will shine over our great nation with all of their scintillating beauty.

Yours for the cause of Peace and Brotherhood,
Martin Luther King, Jr.

Suggestions for Further Reading

See page 270.

25 *The Justification of Civil Disobedience*

John Rawls

In 1971 John Rawls, a professor of philosophy at Harvard, published a book called *A Theory of Justice.* Rawls's leading ideas were already well known, because he had presented them in a series of influential articles during the preceding two decades. The book, which had been eagerly awaited, became an instant classic. It was widely hailed as one of the most important philosophical works of the century. It has since been the subject of intense study, not only by philosophers, but by theoretical economists, legal scholars, and political scientists as well.

There are two reasons (aside from its intrinsic merits) why Rawls's book created such a sensation. First, it was a radical departure from much of the moral philosophy that had been written in the twentieth century. As philosophy had developed in the English-speaking countries during the first half of this century, ethics had become a technical subject dealing mainly with abstract questions about the meaning of moral language—what does it *mean,* for example, to say that something is good, or that an action ought to be done? These were considered to be purely theoretical questions of logical analysis that had no implications at all for practical matters of right and wrong. Indeed, as often as not, philosophers deliberately avoided substantive questions about how we ought to live, considering them to be outside the province of philosophy and best left to "priests, politicians, and marriage counselors."

Rawls's book signaled the end of this period in moral philosophy. Rawls took it as the business of moral theory to establish the most fundamental principles that ought to govern a morally decent society. He did not have much to say about the "meaning" or the "logic" of moral language. Instead, he attempted to discover and explain the actual principles that determine whether societies are just.

The second reason Rawls's book was received so enthusiastically is that it represented the revival of a tradition in moral philosophy that was almost dead—the social contract tradition. Beginning in the nineteenth century, the triumph of Utilitarian theory had been so complete that little was heard of other alternatives. Many philosophers were unhappy with Utilitarianism, and argued against it, but they had nothing impressive to offer in its place. Now Rawls offered an attractive alternative. He had worked out, in great detail, a contemporary version of the contract theory.

Rawls's key idea was that the principles of justice are principles that rational, self-interested people would choose to govern the society in which they are going to live, *provided that* they did not know, at the time they chose the principles, exactly what their own place in society would be. What does this mean?

Suppose you are a white man, and your friends are mostly white men. In addition, let us say that you are a doctor, and that your friends are doctors, lawyers, business executives, and the like. Now suppose you are asked to choose the principles that will govern life in your society. You might very well prefer principles that favor the interests of "successful" white males; you would have little reason to be concerned with blacks, women, or working-class people.

But now suppose you have to choose the principles that will govern your society, and *you do not know* whether you will be male or female, black or white, talented or clumsy, rich or poor, and so on. You are placed behind a "veil of ignorance" with respect to particular facts about yourself. Rawls calls this "the original position." In this position, you will be motivated to choose principles that are fair to everybody because if you choose principles that favor some people over others, you might discover when the veil of ignorance is lifted that you have been unfair to yourself! The principles of justice, then, are the principles that rational people would choose in the original position.

In 1966, three years after Martin Luther King, Jr.'s "Letter from the Birmingham City Jail," Rawls lectured to the American Political Science Association, explaining how a contractarian philosopher would view civil disobedience. The text of that lecture follows.

I. Introduction

I should like to discuss briefly, and in an informal way, the grounds of civil disobedience in a constitutional democracy. Thus, I shall limit my remarks to the conditions under which we may, by civil disobedience, properly oppose legally established democratic authority; I am not concerned with the situation under other kinds of government nor, except incidentally, with other forms of resistance. My thought is that in a reasonably just (though of course not perfectly just) democratic regime, civil disobedience, when it is justified, is normally to be understood as a political action which addresses the sense of justice of the majority in order to urge reconsideration of the measures protested and to warn that in the firm opinion of the dissenters the conditions of social cooperation are not being honored. This characterization of civil disobedience is intended to apply to dissent on fundamental questions of internal policy, a limitation which I shall follow to simplify our question.

II. The Social Contract Doctrine

It is obvious that the justification of civil disobedience depends upon the theory of political obligation in general, and so we may appropriately begin with a few comments on this question. The two chief virtues of social institutions are justice and efficiency, where by the efficiency of institutions I understand their effectiveness for certain social conditions and ends the fulfillment of which is to everyone's advantage. We should comply with and do our part in just and efficient social arrangements for at least two reasons: first of all, we have a natural duty not to oppose the establishment of just and efficient institutions (when they do not yet exist) and to uphold and comply with them (when they do exist); and second, assuming that we have knowingly accepted the benefits of these institutions and plan to continue to do so, and that we have encouraged and expect others to do their part, we also have an obligation to do our share when, as the arrangement requires, it comes our turn. Thus, we often have both a natural duty as well as an obligation to support

From Hugo Adam Bedau, ed., *Civil Disobedience: Theory and Practice* (New York: Pegasus, 1969). © 1968 by John Rawls. Reprinted by permission of the author.

just and efficient institutions, the obligation arising from our voluntary acts while the duty does not.

Now all this is perhaps obvious enough, but it does not take us very far. Any more particular conclusions depend upon the conception of justice which is the basis of a theory of political obligation. I believe that the appropriate conception, at least for an account of political obligation in a constitutional democracy, is that of the social contract theory from which so much of our political thought derives. If we are careful to interpret it in a suitably general way, I hold that this doctrine provides a satisfactory basis for political theory, indeed even for ethical theory itself, but this is beyond our present concern. The interpretation I suggest is the following: that the principles to which social arrangements must conform, and in particular the principles of justice, are those which free and rational men would agree to in an original position of equal liberty; and similarly, the principles which govern men's relations to institutions and define their natural duties and obligations are the principles to which they would consent when so situated. It should be noted straightway that in this interpretation of the contract theory the principles of justice are understood as the outcome of a hypothetical agreement. They are principles which would be agreed to if the situation of the original position were to arise. There is no mention of an actual agreement nor need such an agreement ever be made. Social arrangements are just or unjust according to whether they accord with the principles for assigning and securing fundamental rights and liberties which would be chosen in the original position. This position is, to be sure, the analytic analogue of the traditional notion of the state of nature, but it must not be mistaken for a historical occasion. Rather it is a hypothetical situation which embodies the basic ideas of the contract doctrine; the description of this situation enables us to work out which principles would be adopted. I must now say something about these matters.

The contract doctrine has always supposed that the persons in the original position have equal powers and rights, that is, that they are symmetrically situated with respect to any arrangements for reaching agreement, and that coalitions and the like are excluded. But it is an essential element (which has not been sufficiently observed although it is implicit in Kant's version of the theory) that there are very strong restrictions on what the contracting parties are presumed to know. In particular, I interpret the theory to hold that the parties do not know their position in society, past, present, or future; nor do they know which institutions exist. Again, they do not know their own place in the distribution of natural talents and abilities, whether they are intelligent or strong, man or woman, and so on. Finally, they do not know their own particular interests and preferences or the system of ends which they wish to advance: they do not know their conception of the good. In all these respects the parties are confronted with a veil of ignorance which prevents any one from being able to take advantage of his good fortune or particular interests or from being disadvantaged by them. What the parties do know (or assume) is that Hume's circumstances of justice obtain: namely, that the bounty of nature is not so generous as to render cooperative schemes superfluous nor so harsh as to make them impossible. Moreover, they assume that the extent of their altruism is limited and that, in general, they do not take an interest in one another's interests. Thus, given the special features of the original position, each man tries to do the best he can for himself by insisting on principles calculated to protect and advance his system of ends whatever it turns out to be.

I believe that as a consequence of the peculiar nature of the original position there would be an agreement on the following two principles for assigning rights and duties and for regulating distributive shares as these are determined by the fundamental institutions of society: first, each person is to have an equal right to the most extensive liberty compatible with a like liberty for all; second, social and economic inequalities (as defined by the institutional structure or fostered by it) are to be arranged so that they are both to everyone's advantage and attached to positions and offices open to all. In view of the content of these two principles and their application to the main institutions of society, and therefore to the social system as a whole, we may regard them as the two principles of justice. Basic social arrangements are just insofar as they conform to these principles, and we can, if we like, discuss questions of justice directly by reference to them. But a deeper understanding of the justification of civil disobedience requires, I think, an account of the derivation of these principles provided by the doctrine of the social contract. Part of our task is to show why this is so.

III. The Grounds of Compliance with an Unjust Law

If we assume that in the original position men would agree both to the principle of doing their part when they have accepted and plan to continue to accept the benefits of just institutions (the principle of fairness), and also to the principle of not preventing the establishment of just institutions and of upholding and complying with them when they do exist, then the contract doctrine easily accounts for our having to conform to just institutions. But how does it account for the fact that we are normally required to comply with unjust laws as well? The injustice of a law is not a sufficient ground for not complying with it any more than the legal validity of legislation is always sufficient to require obedience to it. Sometimes one hears these extremes asserted, but I think that we need not take them seriously.

   An answer to our question can be given by elaborating the social contract theory in the following way. I interpret it to hold that one is to envisage a series of agreements as follows: first, men are to agree upon the principles of justice in the original position. Then they are to move to a constitutional convention in which they choose a constitution that satisfies the principles of justice already chosen. Finally they assume the role of a legislative body and guided by the principles of justice enact laws subject to the constraints and procedures of the just constitution. The decisions reached in any stage are binding in all subsequent stages. Now whereas in the original position the contracting parties have no knowledge of their society or of their own position in it, in both a constitutional convention and a legislature, they do know certain general facts about their institutions, for example, the statistics regarding employment and output required for fiscal and economic policy. But no one knows particular facts about his own social class or his place in the distribution of natural assets. On each occasion the contracting parties have the knowledge required to make their agreement rational from the appropriate point of view, but not so much as to make them prejudiced. They are unable to tailor principles and legislation to take advantage of their social or natural position; a veil of ignorance prevents their knowing what this position is. With this series of agreements in mind, we can characterize just laws and policies as those which would be enacted were this whole process correctly carried out.

In choosing a constitution the aim is to find among the just constitutions the one which is most likely, given the general facts about the society in question, to lead to just and effective legislation. The principles of justice provide a criterion for the laws desired; the problem is to find a set of political procedures that will give this outcome. I shall assume that, at least under the normal conditions of a modern state, the best constitution is some form of democratic regime affirming equal political liberty and using some sort of majority (or other plurality) rule. Thus it follows that on the contract theory a constitutional democracy of some sort is required by the principles of justice. At the same time it is essential to observe that the constitutional process is always a case of what we may call imperfect procedural justice: that is, there is no feasible political procedure which guarantees that the enacted legislation is just even though we have (let us suppose) a standard for just legislation. In simple cases, such as games of fair division, there are procedures which always lead to the right outcome (assume that equal shares is fair and let the man who cuts the cake take the last piece). These situations are those of perfect procedural justice. In other cases it does not matter what the outcome is as long as the fair procedure is followed: fairness of the process is transferred to the result (fair gambling is an instance of this). These situations are those of pure procedural justice. The constitutional process, like a criminal trial, resembles neither of these; the result matters and we have a standard for it. The difficulty is that we cannot frame a procedure which guarantees that only just and effective legislation is enacted. Thus even under a just constitution unjust laws may be passed and unjust policies enforced. Some form of the majority principle is necessary but the majority may be mistaken, more or less willfully, in what it legislates. In agreeing to a democratic constitution (as an instance of imperfect procedural justice) one accepts at the same time the principle of majority rule. Assuming that the constitution is just and that we have accepted and plan to continue to accept its benefits, we then have both an obligation and a natural duty (and in any case the duty) to comply with what the majority enacts even though it may be unjust. In this way we become bound to follow unjust laws, not always, of course, but provided the injustice does not exceed certain limits. We recognize that we must run the risk of suffering from the defects of one another's sense of justice; this burden we are prepared to carry as long as it is more or less evenly distributed or does not weigh too heavily. Justice binds us to a just constitution and to the unjust laws which may be enacted under it in precisely the same way that it binds us to any other social arrangement. Once we take the sequence of stages into account, there is nothing unusual in our being required to comply with unjust laws.

It should be observed that the majority principle has a secondary place as a rule of procedure which is perhaps the most efficient one under usual circumstances for working a democratic constitution. The basis for it rests essentially upon the principles of justice and therefore we may, when conditions allow, appeal to these principles against unjust legislation. The justice of the constitution does not insure the justice of laws enacted under it; and while we often have both an obligation and a duty to comply with what the majority legislates (as long as it does not exceed certain limits), there is, of course, no corresponding obligation or duty to regard what the majority enacts as itself just. The right to make law does not guarantee that the decision is rightly made; and while the citizen submits in his conduct to the judgment of democratic authority, he does not submit his judgment to it. And if in his judgment the enactments of the majority exceed certain bounds of injustice, the citizen may consider civil disobedience. For we are not required to accept the majority's acts unconditionally and to acquiesce in the denial of our and others' liberties; rather we submit our conduct to democratic authority to the extent necessary to share the burden of working a constitutional regime, distorted as it must inevitably be by men's lack of wisdom and the defects of their sense of justice.

IV. The Place of Civil Disobedience in a Constitutional Democracy

We are now in a position to say a few things about civil disobedience. I shall understand it to be a public, nonviolent, and conscientious act contrary to law usually done with the intent to bring about a change in the policies or laws of the government. Civil disobedience is a political act in the sense that it is an act justified by moral principles which define a conception of civil society and the public good. It rests, then, on political conviction as opposed to a search for self or group interest; and in the case of a constitutional democracy, we may assume that this conviction involves the conception of justice (say that expressed by the contract doctrine) which underlies the constitution itself. That is, in a viable democratic regime there is a common conception of justice by reference to which its citizens regulate their political affairs and interpret the constitution. Civil disobedience is a public act which the dissenter believes to be justified by this conception of justice and for this reason it may be understood as addressing the sense of justice of the majority in order to urge reconsideration of the measures protested and to warn that, in the sincere opinion of the dissenters, the conditions of social cooperation are not being honored. For the principles of justice express precisely such conditions, and their persistent and deliberate violation in regard to basic liberties over any extended period of time cuts the ties of community and invites either submission or forceful resistance. By engaging in civil disobedience a minority leads the majority to consider whether it wants to have its acts taken in this way, or whether, in view of the common sense of justice, it wishes to acknowledge the claims of the minority.

Civil disobedience is also civil in another sense. Not only is it the outcome of a sincere conviction based on principles which regulate civic life, but it is public and nonviolent, that is, it is done in a situation where arrest and punishment are expected and accepted without resistance. In this way it manifests a respect for legal procedures. Civil disobedience expresses disobedience to law within the limits of fidelity to law, and this feature of it helps to establish in the eyes of the majority that it is indeed conscientious and sincere, that it really is meant to address their sense of justice. Being completely open about one's acts and being willing to accept the legal consequences of one's conduct is a bond given to make good one's sincerity, for that one's deeds are conscientious is not easy to demonstrate to another or even before oneself. No doubt it is possible to imagine a legal system in which conscientious belief that the law is unjust is accepted as a defense for noncompliance, and men of great honesty who are confident in one another might make such a system work. But as things are such a scheme would be unstable; we must pay a price in order to establish that we believe our actions have a moral basis in the convictions of the community.

The nonviolent nature of civil disobedience refers to the fact that it is intended to address the sense of justice of the majority and as such it is a form of speech, an expression of conviction. To engage in violent acts likely to injure and to hurt is incompatible with civil disobedience as a mode of address. Indeed, an interference with the basic rights of others tends to obscure the civilly disobedient quality of one's act. Civil disobedience is nonviolent in the further sense that the legal penalty for one's action is accepted and that resistance is not (at least for the moment) contemplated. Nonviolence in this sense is to be distinguished from nonviolence as a religious or pacifist principle. While those engaging in civil disobedience have often held some such principle, there is no necessary connection between it and civil disobedience. For on the interpretation suggested, civil disobedience in a democratic society is best understood as an appeal to the principles of justice, the fundamental conditions of willing social cooperation among free men, which in the view of the community as a whole are expressed in the constitution and guide its interpretation. Being an appeal to the moral basis of public life, civil disobedience is a political and not primarily a religious act. It addresses itself to the common principles of justice which men can require one another to follow and not to the aspirations of love which they cannot. Moreover by taking part in civilly disobedient acts one does not foreswear indefinitely the idea of forceful resistance; for if the appeal against injustice is repeatedly denied, then the majority has declared its intention to invite submission or resistance and the latter may conceivably be justified even in a democratic regime. We are not required to acquiesce in the crushing of fundamental liberties by democratic majorities which have shown themselves blind to the principles of justice upon which justification of the constitution depends.

V. The Justification of Civil Disobedience

So far we have said nothing about the justification of civil disobedience, that is, the conditions under which civil disobedience may be engaged in consistent with the principles of justice that support a democratic regime. Our task is to see how the characterization of civil disobedience as addressed to the sense of justice of the majority (or to the citizens as a body) determines when such action is justified.

First of all, we may suppose that the normal political appeals to the majority have already been made in good faith and have been rejected, and that the standard means of redress have been tried. Thus, for example, existing political parties are indifferent to the claims of the minority and attempts to repeal the laws protested met with further repression since legal institutions are in the control of the majority. While civil disobedience should be recognized, I think, as a form of political action within the limits of fidelity to the rule of law, at the same time it is a rather desperate act just within these limits, and therefore it should, in general, be undertaken as a last resort when standard democratic processes have failed. In this sense it is not a normal political action. When it is justified there has been a serious breakdown; not only is there grave injustice in the law but a refusal more or less deliberate to correct it.

Second, since civil disobedience is a political act addressed to the sense of justice of the majority, it should usually be limited to substantial and clear violations of justice and preferably to those which, if rectified, will establish a basis for doing away with remaining injustices. For this reason there is a presumption in favor of restricting civil disobedience to violations of the first principle of justice, the principle of equal liberty, and to barriers which contravene the second principle, the principle of open offices which protects equality of opportunity. It is not, of course, always easy to tell whether these principles are satisfied. But if we think of them as guaranteeing the fundamental equal political and civil liberties (including freedom of conscience and liberty of thought) and equality of opportunity, then it is often relatively clear whether their principles are being honored. After all, the equal liberties are defined by the visible structure of social institutions; they are to be incorporated into the recognized practice, if not the letter, of social arrangements. When minorities are denied the right to vote or to hold certain political offices, when certain religious groups are repressed and others denied equality of opportunity in the economy, this is often obvious and there is no doubt that justice is not being given. However, the first part of the second principle which requires that inequalities be to everyone's advantage is a much more imprecise and controversial matter. Not only is there a problem of assigning it a determinate and precise sense, but even if we do so and agree on what it should be, there is often a wide variety of reasonable opinion as to whether the principle is satisfied. The reason for this is that the principle applies primarily to fundamental economic and social policies. The choice of these depends upon theoretical and speculative beliefs as well as upon a wealth of concrete information, and all of this mixed with judgment and plain hunch, not to mention

in actual cases prejudice and self-interest. Thus unless tl
taxation are clearly designed to attack a basic equal libe
should not be protested by civil disobedience; the appeal to justice
is not sufficiently clear and its resolution is best left to the political
process. But violations of the equal liberties that define the common
status of citizenship are another matter. The deliberate denial of
these more or less over any extended period of time in the face of
normal political protest is, in general, an appropriate object of civil
disobedience. We may think of the social system as divided roughly
into two parts, one which incorporates the fundamental equal liberties (including equality of opportunity) and another which embodies social and economic policies properly aimed at promoting
the advantage of everyone. As a rule civil disobedience is best limited to the former where the appeal to justice is not only more
definite and precise, but where, if it is effective, it tends to correct
the injustices in the latter.

Third, civil disobedience should be restricted to those cases
where the dissenter is willing to affirm that everyone else similarly
subjected to the same degree of injustice has the right to protest in
a similar way. That is, we must be prepared to authorize others to
dissent in similar situations and in the same way, and to accept the
consequences of their doing so. Thus, we may hold, for example,
that the widespread disposition to disobey civilly clear violations of
fundamental liberties more or less deliberate over an extended
period of time would raise the degree of justice throughout society
and would insure men's self-esteem as well as their respect for one
another. Indeed, I believe this to be true, though certainly it is partly
a matter of conjecture. As the contract doctrine emphasizes, since
the principles of justice are principles which we would agree to in
an original position of equality when we do not know our social
position and the like, the refusal to grant justice is either the denial
of the other as an equal (as one in regard to whom we are prepared
to constrain our actions by principles which we would consent to)
or the manifestation of a willingness to take advantage of natural
contingencies and social fortune at his expense. In either case,
injustice invites submission or resistance; but submission arouses
the contempt of the oppressor and confirms him in his intention. If
straightway, after a decent period of time to make reasonable political appeals in the normal way, men were in general to dissent by civil
disobedience from infractions of the fundamental equal liberties,

these liberties would, I believe, be more rather than less secure. Legitimate civil disobedience properly exercised is a stabilizing device in a constitutional regime, tending to make it more firmly just.

Sometimes, however, there may be a complication in connection with this third condition. It is possible, although perhaps unlikely, that there are so many persons or groups with a sound case for resorting to civil disobedience (as judged by the foregoing criteria) that disorder would follow if they all did so. There might be serious injury to the just constitution. Or again, a group might be so large that some extra precaution is necessary in the extent to which its members organize and engage in civil disobedience. Theoretically the case is one in which a number of persons or groups are equally entitled to and all want to resort to civil disobedience, yet if they all do this, grave consequences for everyone may result. The question, then, is who among them may exercise their right, and it falls under the general problem of fairness. I cannot discuss the complexities of the matter here. Often a lottery or a rationing system can be set up to handle the case; but unfortunately the circumstances of civil disobedience rule out this solution. It suffices to note that a problem of fairness may arise and that those who contemplate civil disobedience should take it into account. They may have to reach an understanding as to who can exercise their right in the immediate situation and to recognize the need for special constraint.

The final condition, of a different nature, is the following. We have been considering when one has a right to engage in civil disobedience, and our conclusion is that one has this right should three conditions hold: when one is subject to injustice more or less deliberate over an extended period of time in the face of normal political protests; where the injustice is a clear violation of the liberties of equal citizenship; and provided that the general disposition to protest similarly in similar cases would have acceptable consequences. These conditions are not, I think, exhaustive but they seem to cover the more obvious points; yet even when they are satisfied and one has the right to engage in civil disobedience, there is still the different question of whether one should exercise this right, that is, whether by doing so one is likely to further one's ends. Having established one's right to protest one is then free to consider these tactical questions. We may be acting within our rights but still foolishly if our action only serves to provoke the harsh retaliation of the majority; and it is likely to do so if the majority lacks a sense of justice, or if the action is poorly timed or not well designed to make the appeal to the sense of justice effective. It is easy to think of instances of this sort, and in each case these practical questions have to be faced. From the standpoint of the theory of political obligation we can only say that the exercise of the right should be rational and reasonably designed to advance the protester's aims, and that weighing tactical questions presupposes that one has already established one's right, since tactical advantages in themselves do not support it.

VI. Conclusion: Several Objections Considered

In a reasonably affluent democratic society justice becomes the first virtue of institutions. Social arrangements irrespective of their efficiency must be reformed if they are significantly unjust. No increase in efficiency in the form of greater advantages for many justifies the loss of liberty of a few. That we believe this is shown by the fact that in a democracy the fundamental liberties of citizenship are not understood as the outcome of political bargaining nor are they subject to the calculus of social interests. Rather these liberties are fixed points which serve to limit political transactions and which determine the scope of calculations of social advantage. It is this fundamental place of the equal liberties which makes their systematic violation over any extended period of time a proper object of civil disobedience. For to deny men these rights is to infringe the conditions of social cooperation among free and rational persons, a fact which is evident to the citizens of a constitutional regime since it follows from the principles of justice which underlie their institutions. The justification of civil disobedience rests on the priority of justice and the equal liberties which it guarantees.

It is natural to object to this view of civil disobedience that it relies too heavily upon the existence of a sense of justice. Some may hold that the feeling for justice is not a vital political force, and that what moves men are various other interests, the desire for wealth, power, prestige, and so on. Now this is a large question the answer to which is highly conjectural and each tends to have his own opinion. But there are two remarks which may clarify what I have said: first, I have assumed that there is in a constitutional regime a common sense of justice the principles of which are recognized to support the constitution and to guide its interpretation. In any given situation particular men may be tempted to violate these principles, but the collective force in their behalf is usually effective since they are seen as the necessary terms of cooperation among free men; and presumably the citizens of a democracy (or sufficiently many of them) want to see justice done. Where these assumptions fail, the justifying conditions for civil disobedience (the first three) are not affected, but the rationality of engaging in it certainly is. In this case, unless the costs of repressing civil dissent injures the economic self-interest (or whatever) of the majority, protest may simply make the position of the minority worse. No doubt as a tactical matter civil disobedience is more effective when its appeal coincides with other interests, but a constitutional regime is not viable in the long run without an attachment to the principles of justice of the sort which we have assumed.

Then, further, there may be a misapprehension about the manner in which a sense of justice manifests itself. There is a tendency to think that it is shown by professions of the relevant principles together with actions of an altruistic nature requiring a considerable degree of self-sacrifice. But these conditions are obviously too strong, for the majority's sense of justice may show itself simply in its being unable to undertake the measures required to suppress the minority and to punish as the law requires the various acts of civil disobedience. The sense of justice undermines the will to uphold unjust institutions, and so a majority despite its superior power may give way. It is unprepared to force the minority to be subject to injustice. Thus, although the majority's action is reluctant and grudging, the role of the sense of justice is nevertheless essential, for without it the majority would have been willing to enforce the law and to defend its position. Once we see the sense of justice as working in this negative way to make established injustices indefensible, then it is recognized as a central element of democratic politics.

Finally, it may be objected against this account that it does not settle the question of who is to say when the situation is such as to justify civil disobedience. And because it does not answer this question, it invites anarchy by encouraging every man to decide the matter for himself. Now the reply to this is that each man must indeed settle this question for himself, although he may, of course, decide wrongly. This is true on any theory of political duty and obligation, at least on any theory compatible with the principles of a democratic constitution. The citizen is responsible for what he does. If we usually think that we should comply with the law, this is because our political principles normally lead to this conclusion. There is a presumption in favor of compliance in the absence of good reasons to the contrary. But because each man is responsible and must decide for himself as best he can whether the circumstances justify civil disobedience, it does not follow that he may decide as he pleases. It is not by looking to our personal interests or to political allegiances narrowly construed, that we should make up our mind. The citizen must decide on the basis of the principles of justice that underlie and guide the interpretation of the constitution and in the light of his sincere conviction as to how these principles should be applied in the circumstances. If he concludes that conditions obtain which justify civil disobedience and conducts himself accordingly, he has acted conscientiously and perhaps mistakenly, but not in any case at his convenience.

In a democratic society each man must act as he thinks the principles of political right require him to. We are to follow our understanding of these principles, and we cannot do otherwise. There can be no morally binding legal interpretation of these principles, not even by a supreme court or legislature. Nor is there any infallible procedure for determining what or who is right. In our system the Supreme Court, Congress, and the President often put forward rival interpretations of the Constitution. Although the Court has the final say in settling any particular case, it is not immune from powerful political influence that may change its reading of the law of the land. The Court presents its point of view by reason and argument; its conception of the Constitution must, if it is to endure, persuade men of its soundness. The final court of appeal is not the Court, or Congress, or the President, but the electorate as a whole. The civilly disobedient appeal in effect to this body. There is no danger of anarchy as long as there is a sufficient working agreement in men's conceptions of political justice and what it requires. That men can achieve such an understanding when the essential political liberties are maintained is the assumption implicit in democratic institutions. There is no way to avoid entirely the risk of divisive strife. But if legitimate civil disobedience seems to threaten civil peace, the responsibility falls not so much on those est as upon those whose abuse of authority and power justifies such opposition.

Suggestions for Further Reading

Hugo Adam Bedau, ed., *Civil Disobedience: Theory and Practice* (New York: Pegasus Books, 1969) is a good collection of essays.

Also recommended are Michael Walzer, *Obligations* (Cambridge, Mass.: Harvard University Press, 1970); Peter Singer, *Democracy and Disobedience* (Oxford: Oxford University Press, 1973); and Carl Cohen, *Civil Disobedience* (New York: Columbia University Press, 1971).

For some bibliographical suggestions about John Rawls, see Suggestions for Further Reading at the conclusion of selection 10.

Index

Hardin, Garrett, 184
Herodotus, 4–5
History (Herodotus), 4
Hobbes, Thomas, 30, 102–3
Hogarth, William, 210
homosexuality
    and Christianity, 10–12, 154–55,
        163n.14, 164
    control over, 158–60
    as criminal act, 160
    culturally different views of,
        158, 171–72
    and discrimination, 151–53, 160
    and immorality, 153–55
    and mental illness, 149
    and Natural Law Theory, 71
    pervasiveness of, 147–48
    social acceptability for, 160–62
    and stereotypes, 148–51
    as unnatural, 155–58, 164–73
Hooker, Evelyn, 149
Hume, David, 6–7, 57–58, 258
hunting, and animal rights, 212

immorality
    defined by Sumner, 56
    of homosexuality, 153–55
imprisonment, 20
incest, 155
infanticide, 35–36, 133–46
ingratitude, Hume's writing on,
        60–61
intracranial hemorrhage, 139, 140,
        141, 142

Judaism, and morality, 8
Julius Caesar, 73
justice. *See also* punishment
    and altruism, 76
    and natural law, 69
    and Retributivism, 21, 28
    and social rules, 106
    in Utilitarianism, 21

Kant, Immanuel, 22–28, 91–92,
        209, 233
killing, 16, 132n.1. *See also*
    abortion; capital

punishment; euthanasia;
    infanticide; murder; suicide
King, Martin Luther, Jr., 30,
        236–37
Kinsey, Alfred, 147
Koop, Dr. C. Everett, 137, 144, 146
Kuhse, Helga, 134–35

Lectures on Ethics (Kant), 209
Leiser, Burton M., 164
lesbianism. *See* homosexuality
Leo XIII (pope), 68
Leviathan (Hobbes, 1651), 102
liberty, and society, 107, 108
Liberty, Justice, and Morals (Leiser,
        1986), 164
lifeboat ethics, 186–87
Locke, John, 30, 111
logic. *See* argumentation,
        philosophical; reason
Lorber, Dr. John, 145

McGill, Ralph, 248
malnutrition
    and Ethical Egoism, 14
    prevalence of, 175
mankind. *See also* society
    causes of quarrels among, 104–5
    and desire to live, 206–8
    divine control over, 197–98, 199
    equality among, 103–4
    and need for social rules, 29,
        105–7
    superiority of, 26
masturbation, 169, 171, 172
materialism, 102
mental retardation, 32, 135, 142
mercy killing. *See* euthanasia
Meredith, James, 252
Meshach, 243
Metaphysics of Morals (Kant, 1797),
        28
Milk, Harvey, 152
Mill, Harriet Taylor, 80
Mill, James, 80
Mill, John Stuart, 15, 19, 20,
        79–80
Mohr, Richard D., 147

About the Author

James Rachels is University Professor of Philosophy at the University of Alabama at Birmingham. He is the author of *The End of Life: Euthanasia and Morality* and articles on such subjects as the right to privacy, reverse discrimination, and the treatment of nonhuman animals. He has also written on chess and the movies.